I0791870

LUMINALIBRIA

THE SECRET ORIGINS OF HUMANITY: THE GREAT COMPENDIUM OF THE MOST FASCINATING THEORIES

From Daniken to Hancock: The Investigations of Many Famous Researchers Who Have Rewritten Human History

FRANCESCA FERRARI

LUMINALIBRIA

DEDICATION

To you, explorer of the vast universe of ideas and tireless seeker of hidden truths, I dedicate this book. May each chapter serve as an open window to unknown worlds and ancient wisdom, illuminating your path with new perspectives and profound reflections. In weaving together the threads of the past and present, I hope to offer you the tools to build bridges towards possible and unexplored futures.

This work is the result of years of research and passion, a journey we have embarked on together, step by step, page by page. Each discovery reflects the relentless desire to understand more, to push beyond the limits of the known, and to look with fresh eyes at what has long been overlooked or forgotten.

I invite you to take an active part in this journey of discovery, not only as a reader but as part of a global community of thinkers and dreamers who, like us, believe in the transformative power of knowledge.

With deep gratitude and the sincere wish that the pages of this book may inspire you to seek, to question, and to dream without bounds.

With affection and hope for the journey that lies ahead,

Francesca Ferrari

TABLE OF CONTENTS

INTRODUCTION

The beating heart of our history is shrouded in mysteries yet to be unveiled, echoes of a past as enigmatic as it is fundamental to understanding our current identity. In these pages, we celebrate the intellectual daring of thinkers and researchers who, with critical and innovative spirit, have questioned established narratives, prompting us to reconsider everything we thought we knew about the origins of humanity. These visionaries have paved new roads in the interpretation of our history, suggesting that the reality we know might be just a fraction of a broader and more complex truth.

Among these bold explorers of the past, we find prominent figures like **Erich von Däniken,** known for his groundbreaking theories on ancient astronauts. Von Däniken has proposed that the gods of ancient earthly civilizations may not have been mythological deities but rather extraterrestrial visitors equipped with advanced technologies. His theories, supported by bold interpretations of historical artifacts and ancient texts, have sparked renewed interest in archaeology and have opened the debate on possible prehistoric interactions between humans and alien civilizations. In this book, we will delve deeply into his engaging theses.

Graham Hancock, another pillar of these investigations, has explored the lost civilizations of the world with an approach that challenges traditional historical chronologies. Hancock has examined the possible connections between these ancient civilizations and a corpus of knowledge and technologies surprisingly advanced for their time. Through his thorough studies, Hancock has suggested that there may have been moments in human history when technological and spiritual knowledge was much more advanced than generally recognized, hypothesizing that this knowledge may have been lost due to global catastrophes or periods of cultural regression.

These authors have not only expanded the boundaries of our historical and archaeological knowledge but have also challenged our perception of the past, proposing a worldview where the history of humanity is much more interconnected and intriguing than traditionally narrated. Their theories, while sometimes controversial and debated, have undoubtedly enriched scientific and cultural debate, shedding light on the possibility that human history is much richer and more varied than we could have imagined.

Michael Tellinger has revolutionized the field of archaeology with his meticulous investigations into the ancient mining sites of southern Africa. His research suggests that these mining operations, of surprising size and complexity, may not have been the result of human ingenuity of the time but rather the result of interventions by extraterrestrial civilizations. Tellinger proposes that these space visitors may have used Earth as a sort of base for their mining activities, seeking valuable resources perhaps rare in their home worlds. Tellinger's hypothesis is based on detailed analysis of tools, extraction techniques, and geological artifacts found at these sites, which seem advanced beyond the technological capability of the local populations at that time.

In parallel, **Billy Carson** has explored new interpretations of ancient myths and archaeological artifacts, presenting a view of human history that extends far beyond the boundaries accepted by traditional historiography. Carson has examined a series of artifacts and ancient texts, finding in them clues to a possible presence and interaction with non-terrestrial civilizations. His theories suggest that many of the myths we consider purely symbolic may have been, in fact, attempts by our ancestors to document encounters with these advanced entities. This approach has opened new perspectives on the interpretation of myths and has suggested that our understanding of the past may be radically incomplete without considering these possible extraterrestrial contacts.

Together, the research of Tellinger and Carson is pushing the boundaries of conventional history, inviting us to consider the possibility that Earth may have had visitors long before modern science has ever speculated. These theories not only challenge our current archaeological and historical knowledge but also open fascinating discussions about the origins of humanity and the interactions between different civilizations in antiquity. Their research is crucial for understanding not only human history but also the potential impact of extraterrestrial civilizations on our cultural and technological evolution.

Drunvalo Melchizedek, another interesting author we will examine in the book, has offered a synthesis of ancient wisdom, and his esoteric knowledge provides a unique lens through which to examine and reinterpret historical and archaeological phenomena that modern science still struggles to fully explain. Connecting the spiritual traditions of many cultures, scholars like Drunvalo Melchizedek have sought to decipher the messages and symbols left by past civilizations, proposing that these elements can be understood as testimonies of a deeper and more universal understanding of reality, often expressed through spiritual concepts. This approach not only enriches our understanding of historical contexts but also opens up possibilities for interpretation that transcend temporal and cultural barriers, tying together human experience in surprisingly coherent and revealing ways.

Greg Braden, for his part, has explored how ancient prophecies, often described in mystical or spiritual terms, may be correlated with modern scientific phenomena, such as climate change and Earth's geomagnetic alterations. His work emphasizes an interconnectedness between ancient cycles of knowledge and modern scientific discoveries, suggesting that ancient civilizations may have had insights into the natural cycles of the planet that we are only beginning to understand scientifically. This bridge between mystical past and scientific present invites deeper reflection on the common roots of human knowledge and the possible lost wisdom of ancient cultures.

Mathias de Stefano introduces an additional layer of complexity with his narrative that combines memories of past lives and ancestral knowledge to provide explanations for historical events from a spiritual perspective. Through his approach, he proposes that individuals can access memories spanning different existences, using this information to shed light on obscure aspects of our history. His vision suggests that, through spiritual understanding, we can access a level of awareness that transcends individual lives and contributes to a more holistic and integrated understanding of human history.

Finally, **Tim Tactical** explores how advanced ancient civilizations may have used sophisticated strategies to influence geopolitical and environmental events, suggesting that these manipulation techniques may have been passed down through generations of knowledge custodians. His study proposes the idea that these secret knowledges, kept by wise elites, may have played a crucial role in shaping the directions of entire civilizations. His research not only opens new perspectives on power and control mechanisms in antiquity but also on how these dynamics may echo in modern geopolitical contexts, offering valuable lessons and warnings for the present.

Through their work, we have begun to see clues of advanced civilizations whose existence far predates the accepted historical chronologies and of technologies so sophisticated as to seem almost out of place in their respective times. With each theory explored, this book aims to stimulate critical and open dialogue, enriching our understanding of the hidden origins of humanity and inspiring a new generation to seek answers where previously only questions were dared. Welcome to a journey of discovery, reflection, and endless wonder.

The evidence of advanced civilizations, whose existence far predates the traditionally accepted historical chronologies, poses an intriguing challenge for scholars and history enthusiasts. Evidence of sophisticated technologies, which seem almost out of place for the periods to which they are attributed, raises fundamental questions about the linearity and accuracy of our historical understanding. Enigmatic artifacts, architecturally complex structures, and undecipherable writings suggest that ancient civilizations may have reached levels of knowledge and technological ability surprisingly advanced. These relics, often ignored or downplayed in conventional historical narratives, could indicate the presence of an alternative history of humanity, rich in discoveries and innovations lost over time.

With each theory explored in these pages, this book aims to stimulate critical and open dialogue, enriching our understanding of the hidden origins of humanity. Each chapter invites deep and critical reflection, challenging established perceptions and promoting fearless intellectual inquiry. The goal is to inspire a new generation of thinkers and researchers to seek answers where previously only questions were dared, to boldly question the limits of our knowledge, and to explore possible connections between the remote past and modern technologies.

Welcome to this journey of discovery, reflection, and endless wonder, a journey that winds through the pages of this book. Here, the reader is invited to immerse themselves in an exploration that transcends temporal and geographical boundaries, to consider the boldest theories and to evaluate evidence with a critical and inquisitive eye. This exploration is more than just reading; it is a transformative experience that can change our perception of history and our place in the world. Each discovery and each theory represents not only an addition to our knowledge but a challenge to expand our thinking and to consider new possibilities for the future of humanity.

BEYOND EARTH: THE REVOLUTIONARY VISIONS OF ERICH VON DÄNIKEN

CHARIOTS OF THE GODS: ANCIENT ASTRONAUTS AND THE REWRITING OF HUMAN ORIGINS

Erich von Däniken recounts that, during his years in a Jesuit-run college, he developed a profound knowledge of the Bible through the translation of texts from Greek to Latin and from Latin to German. This rigorous approach allowed him to notice inconsistencies in the biblical narrative that cast doubt on the divine nature of the God described in the Bible. In particular, von Däniken was struck by the fact that this God needed a vehicle to move around and that, contrary to what one would expect from a supreme being, he made several errors. These questions prompted von Däniken to investigate beyond the boundaries of religious tradition, exploring ancient legends and myths from a new perspective. His research led him to the revolutionary theory that many stories of gods and miracles might have been actually misinterpreted encounters with extraterrestrial visitors. This suggestive and provocative view proposes that aliens played a direct role in human evolution, influencing not only our biology but also the development of our ancient societies. According to von Däniken, millions of years ago, an advanced extraterrestrial civilization deliberately spread DNA in well-selected areas of the Milky Way, thus predetermining the sites where life would have the greatest likelihood of developing in ways compatible with their existence. These "cosmic seeders" then intervened more directly, genetically altering a primitive ancestor of modern man. Von Däniken describes how these genetic manipulations were performed with surgical precision, inserting altered DNA into a cell that was then implanted into the uterus of a female of the same species. This process not only accelerated human evolution but also created a clear biological distinction that would give rise to Homo sapiens sapiens. The idea that our evolution may be the result of extraterrestrial intervention not only rewrites our history but also opens up new horizons of thought about our place in the universe. Von Däniken has used this hypothesis to challenge the existing academic and religious paradigm, inviting all of us to reconsider not only our own origins but also the potential future interactions with other cosmic civilizations. His narrative is not simply an exploration of the roots of humanity; it is an invitation to expand our perception, to look beyond the stars, and to question our true cosmic heritage. According to his interpretations, humans were created in the image of the gods, supporting the idea that we are direct descendants of these extraterrestrial entities. Von Däniken argues that these cosmic beings deeply understand us because of a familial bond we share with them. Despite having the ability and opportunity to destroy us many times over the millennia, they chose not to, thus highlighting a genetic kinship. In his interpretation of the Adam and Eve narrative, he introduces the concept of an artificial mutation within the genealogy of our primitive ancestor. This artificial mutation, a direct intervention of the gods, is seen as an extension of the theory of evolution, which goes beyond the evolutionary line that led to primates like chimpanzees, to include a human branch emerging from this genetic modification. Before leaving our planet, these entities, whom von Däniken identifies with the gods described in the biblical paradise, imparted to humans the freedom to rule over everything, with the sole exception of sexual relations with unmutated members of their species, as such unions would have led to the birth of anomalous creatures. This story is connected to the flood myth, described not only in the Bible but also in the Book of Enoch, and is interpreted by von Däniken as an event deliberately caused by the gods to eliminate hybrids, known in many myths around the world as the so-called "giants." The Book of Enoch further details how some of the so-called "heavenly guardians" rebelled, desiring to establish sexual contacts with humans, despite being forbidden. This rebellion led to the creation of various creatures and giants, according to von Däniken, a clear testimony of extraterrestrial interventions in our evolution. Another remarkable fact recalls when Moses ascended the sacred mountain and, according to von Däniken, was ordered to build the Ark of the Covenant following precise measurements and using specific materials, in order to replicate an original object shown to him earlier, suggesting advanced technology possessed by extraterrestrial visitors. Upon Moses' return, the ark, possibly integrated with an advanced machine, was able to produce manna, providing sustenance to the hungry people. All these interpretations by von Däniken certainly offer an alternative and revolutionary view of human and biblical history, proposing that our existence and technological capabilities may have roots in extraterrestrial interventions, significantly extending traditional narratives and inviting deep reflection on our place in the universe and our cosmic heritage.

According to his interpretation, the manna was simply earthly sustenance, created by the Ark of the Covenant, an extremely dangerous object that, as he said, produced radioactivity. In biblical accounts, especially in the second book of Kings, there is a description of an episode where the Ark, during transport, seemed to be about to fall from the cart and then a priest named Uzzah touched it and died immediately, as if he had been struck by an electric shock. Also in the book of Samuel, it is narrated that anyone who approached the Ark too closely would die immediately, and detailed physical symptoms associated with death can be read, such as pallor of the skin, falling nails, and blindness. Von Däniken interprets these events as indicative that the Ark could be a plutonium reactor, arguing that such reactors are only used today in satellites stationed outside Earth, to provide them with energy for decades, given their dangerousness and the high radioactivity of plutonium. This theory suggests that the advanced technology contained in the Ark was of extraterrestrial origin and not fully understood by the humans of the time. Once returned to the Israelites, the Ark caused the death of 72 people, including children, simply because they were too close to the object.

Solomon, who according to von Däniken possessed flying machines as described in the Kebra Nagast, a text of the kings of Ethiopia, built a temple with a separate room to keep the Ark safe. The narrative then becomes complicated with the story of Menelik, son of Solomon and the Queen of Sheba, who, despite his father's prohibition, replaced the Ark with a copy and fled with the original to Ethiopia using one of these flying machines. The original Ark, once in Ethiopia, was placed in a hole in the ground for fear of its destructive powers and is still, according to tradition, under the cathedral of the Holy Virgin Mary in Axum, Ethiopia. This interpretation by von Däniken not only rewrites the understanding of biblical objects like the Ark of the Covenant but also opens up speculation about the possible extraterrestrial origins of ancient technology and the role of aliens in human history. It proposes a link between biblical descriptions of powerful and dangerous devices and modern advanced technologies, arguing that humanity has been in contact with cosmic visitors who have left traces of their superior technology. Von Däniken often discusses the challenge of finding concrete evidence of the existence of extraterrestrials, using the Ark of the Covenant as an example. If even a piece of it had survived, it could then be considered definitive proof. However, von Däniken observes that religious issues often prevent in-depth scientific investigations into such objects, suggesting that "the time is not yet ripe" for such revelations, and that a change in the "spirit of the time" is necessary to allow such studies. According to his interpretation of the sacred texts, God, in his view, would certainly not need a vehicle to move around, being omnipresent and pure spirit. However, in the biblical narrative, the prophet Ezekiel describes an unusual story that occurs when Jerusalem was under Babylonian rule. Ezekiel, being a high-ranking priest, was among those deported to Babylon. While working as a slave, Ezekiel describes hearing a loud noise from the sky and seeing an object descending, emitting a noise that he compared to the roar of a waterfall or the noise of war chariots. Initially, thinking it was a divine manifestation, Ezekiel knelt down to pray, but then realized it was not God. In the biblical account, he describes in detail what he saw, including the movement of the wings of the object, which emitted a deafening noise, and the "wheels," which amazed him for their ability to move in all directions without having to steer, a technology that did not exist at that time. And speaking of this theory of his about the technological objects described in the Bible, von Daniken also talks about an episode where, about thirty years ago, he gave a secret speech at NASA headquarters in Huntsville, United States. After the speech, during a dinner, Joseph Blumrich, then head of the construction department at NASA, approached von Däniken to discuss his claims about Ezekiel. Initially skeptical, Blumrich then decided to read Ezekiel for himself and ended up writing a book entitled "The Spaceship of Ezekiel," in which he concluded that what Ezekiel had described could only be interpreted as an extraterrestrial spacecraft, specifically a type of spacecraft similar to modern shuttles, used to travel from a larger mothership. These reflections by von Däniken raise deep questions about the possible technological interpretation of ancient religious texts, suggesting that what has been transmitted as miraculous or divine could instead have been the result of advanced technologies not understood by the populations of the time.

Erich von Däniken further analyzes Ezekiel's vision, who also claims to have seen God seated on a flying chariot. However, von Däniken, consistent with his interpretation, argues that in his view, God certainly wouldn't need a flying chariot, as his spiritual qualities include omnipresence. Continuing in the book of Ezekiel, the prophet describes how the "splendor of the highest" arrived a second time, and this time "the hand of the highest" placed him on the throne, which von Däniken interprets as the co-pilot seat of a spacecraft. Ezekiel recounts that when the spacecraft began to move, he felt pressure on his chest, a clear reference to gravity during takeoff. Not knowing the destination of the journey, he describes being taken to a "very, very high" mountain and seeing beneath him something resembling a city with a temple at its center. Von Däniken emphasizes the term "temple," explaining that for our ancestors, a temple was a place where the gods dwelled, not simply a religious building as we understand it today. The prophet then describes how the flying object slowly stopped above the temple and how the noise of its wings was louder than he had ever heard before, amplified by the echo of the temple walls. When the spacecraft stopped, Ezekiel descended, and a luminous being appeared to him, reproaching him for his inability to truly see and listen. He was then given a measuring instrument to evaluate the dimensions of the entire structure, which initially led him not to connect the episode to God's will but to understand it simply as something technologically advanced.

Another interesting episode reported by our scholar connects to a contemporary story, that of a German engineer, Hans Herbert Beier, who, by carefully reading Ezekiel's measurements, decided to verify if they could correspond to a real building. His calculations revealed that the described building resembled a stadium or a soccer field. This led von Däniken to connect Beier with NASA engineer Joseph Blumrich, who had already reconstructed the spacecraft described by Ezekiel. Together, they discovered that the dimensions of the "temple" perfectly matched the base of an extraterrestrial spacecraft, suggesting that the temple was actually a base station for the landing and maintenance of spacecraft. Von Däniken then emphasizes how, despite subsequent translations often interpreting Ezekiel's descriptions as future events, the original Semitic language of the text described the events in present terms, indicating that the temple was a concrete reality in Ezekiel's time, not a future vision. This interpretation reinforces the idea that Ezekiel could have had real contact with advanced technologies, masked as deities in traditional narratives, and that these experiences were then sacralized in religious texts. Ezekiel's detailed descriptions of his experiences and the objects he observed would become part of humanity's sacred texts. Extraterrestrials, understanding the enduring nature of religious texts translated into multiple languages, would have anticipated that these narratives would survive through the centuries, despite human conflicts and wars. Von Däniken suggests that in the future, when humanity would develop the ability to fly and understand more advanced technologies, it would reread ancient texts like Ezekiel's and recognize in them not divine manifestations but evidence of advanced technology. Ezekiel's narrative, interpreted as the description of an extraterrestrial spacecraft rather than a divine chariot, would thus become a reference point for reinterpreting other "temples" mentioned in ancient texts as extraterrestrial bases.

As for the location of the "temple" mentioned by Ezekiel, Daniken hypothesizes that it could be located in elevated places, similar to the "very, very high" mountain described. He cites the site of Chavín de Huántar in Peru, situated at 3,800 meters in the Andes, a place that archaeological historiography struggles to fully comprehend. Chavín de Huántar does not easily fit into the typical cultural development of Andean civilizations, suggesting a possible anomalous or external origin. The peculiarities of Chavín de Huántar, such as the wall heads with unusual appearances, some depicted with helmets, and engravings of winged beings that archaeologists have described as "winged genies," could correspond to the "winged beings" described by Ezekiel. This correspondence could indicate that Chavín de Huántar was one of the extraterrestrial bases on Earth, necessary for supply operations similar to those of base camps used by climbers in the Himalayas. Von Däniken concludes that the discovery of winged figures and other unusual representations in ancient temples like Chavín de Huántar could not only confirm the presence of extraterrestrial beings but also help reconnect biblical descriptions to real historical events interpreted through the lens of advanced space technologies. These connections, once recognized, could redefine our understanding of human history and our place in the universe.

27

CROP CIRCLES AND EXTRATERRESTRIAL SIGNS

Erich von Däniken has also addressed the fascinating subject of crop circles. Over the past three decades, we have witnessed a phenomenon that has sparked great interest and debate: crop circles. Originally, these were simple circles, but over time they have evolved into increasingly large and complex formations, prompting society to seek plausible explanations. In an attempt to understand this phenomenon, various theories have been proposed. Initially, some argued that they were the work of human pranks, with people admitting to creating them and demonstrating how they were capable of doing so. However, while pranks have played a role in some cases, the sudden appearance of gigantic and intricate figures, often completed in minutes, suggests deeper reasons. These huge and complex formations in the crops seem to convey a message, a form of communication that goes beyond mere pranks. Some suggest that we may be facing signs from extraterrestrial entities who, knowing our tendency to seek rational explanations, use these designs to establish gradual contact, without causing a devastating impact on our social and religious structures. The phenomenon of crop circles, along with numerous reports of UFO sightings by thousands of people worldwide, urges us to reconsider our perception of reality and history. In the past, ancient civilizations like those who created the enigmatic Nazca lines in Peru, visible only from above, left similar signs, suggesting that interaction with non-terrestrial entities could be a recurring theme in human history. These ancient geoglyphs, also discovered in remote locations such as Saudi Arabia, Australia, the United States, and Mexico, reinforce the idea that such phenomena are not exclusive to the present but part of a broader dialogue between humanity and possible extraterrestrial civilizations. During numerous visits to the Nazca Lines, Erich von Däniken recounts having personally taken over 5,000 photographs of these enigmatic drawings, never shown on television. The grandeur and complexity of these figures have continued to evoke awe and questions. To this day, the scientific community has put forward various theories about the origin and meaning of these geoglyphs: some interpret them as an astronomical calendar, others attribute them to religious cults dedicated to weather gods, mountain gods, or agriculture. However, none of these explanations seems entirely satisfactory; the proposed theories often do not align with the reality of Nazca's climate and terrain, too arid to support any form of traditional agriculture. Other explanations suggest that the lines may have been used as landing strips for hot air balloons or as processional routes for religious ceremonies, but these theories do not explain the need for such extensive and intricate lines. Some scholars have even hypothesized that they may represent a prehistoric map or cultural atlas, but these interpretations have never found concrete confirmation. What is certain is that the size and precision of the lines imply that they can be fully appreciated only from above, suggesting that the ancient creators intended to communicate or signal something to observers who could only see them from the sky. This leads to speculation that they may have had a function or meaning related to flight or perhaps to visitors arriving from above. Von Däniken did not limit himself to photographic documentation but also conducted field research with scientific teams. They measured the electrical resistance of the soil in the Nazca lines, discovering that, unlike the surrounding areas where sand acts as an insulator, the lines have much lower resistance, suggesting the presence of underlying materials or structures that influence such measurements. These results are supported by anomalies in the detected magnetic fields, which are exceptionally high right under the lines. These findings raise further questions about the true nature and origin of the Nazca lines. The fact that they are so rigorously protected that any attempt at excavation or more invasive exploration is severely limited by Peruvian authorities makes a real on-site investigation impossible. Nonetheless, evidence suggests that there may be something more than simple drawings in the ground beneath the Nazca lines. Von Däniken theorizes that Nazca could have been a point of reference or a base for ancient civilizations or perhaps for extraterrestrial visitors. Perhaps the lines served as signals or maps for high-level aerial navigation, long before modern humanity began exploring the sky. This hypothesis remains a matter of speculation until further evidence is available or until more in-depth investigations can be conducted at this enigmatic archaeological site. It could be that an automatic space probe, landing, scattered sand and stones, finally coming to rest on the Nazca plain. A native might have observed this event, interpreting it as a divine sign from the sky. The probe, making measurements such as magnetic field or the presence of elements like gold or uranium, would have left a minimal trace, a simple groove created by the dispersed material. This sign, perceived by natives as a divine intervention, may have given rise to a religious cult, prompting the local population to create additional lines and figures in the ground. The Nazca lines, varying greatly in size and shape, from small trenches up to 23 kilometers long to actual runways that seem designed for the landing of large aircraft, have, according to Erich von Däniken, been inspired by these initial events. He suggests that extraterrestrials may have found something of value in that area, perhaps a particular material or resource, and that the operations to extract it may have included sharp cuts on the mountains, leaving debris and significantly altering the landscape. Von Däniken theorizes that the machines used by extraterrestrials for landing may have required a particular magnetic field, and that the zigzagging lines beneath the runways may have been created to stabilize or guide these machines during landing or takeoff operations. These advanced technologies, in his view, differ significantly from the simpler figures created by natives, which include representations of fish, spiders, monkeys, and birds, made by removing superficial brown stones to reveal a brighter underlying layer.

In conclusion, the Nazca lines represent, to Daniken, a fusion of high technology, presumably extraterrestrial, necessary for specific operations, and the more rudimentary practices of the natives, who continued to create figures and lines in an attempt to communicate or honor these visiting "deities." This mix of influences suggests that, while extraterrestrials may have left the region after obtaining what they were seeking, their cultural and technological impact remained, inspiring successive generations to keep the tradition of geoglyphs alive. When one is on the Nazca plains, on foot, the terrain does not present any apparent differences to the naked eye. It is only when standing directly above the lines that one can see how they sink into the ground by about four or five centimeters. At a distance of two meters, the distinction completely disappears, blending in with the brown sand of the surrounding desert. According to Erich von Däniken, the ancient inhabitants of Nazca would have created these huge geoglyphs to communicate with deities whom they claimed came from the sky. After completing their works on Earth, these entities promised to return after thousands of years and then disappeared, leaving behind generations of natives who passed down tales of the "sky gods." Driven by the desire to keep communication alive, priests and local leaders decided to create signals in the ground, visible only from above, to signify their presence and devotion in anticipation of the gods' return. The Nazca lines, therefore, are not isolated in terms of culture or aerial technology. As we have already seen. Von Däniken refers to the "Kebra Nagast," an ancient Ethiopian text, which recounts how King Solomon possessed flying machines and detailed maps of the Earth, suggesting that he might have visited Nazca. Hindu mythology also speaks of the Maruts, twins who traveled the world on flying machines. These narratives support the idea that historical and mythological figures may have interacted with these lines, inspiring the natives to

32

create ground signals to communicate with these flying entities. Additionally, von Däniken describes a particular geometric figure in Nazca, composed of a large circle with smaller circles and surrounding triangles, which he has photographed hundreds of times but is never shown to tourists. This geometric complexity surpasses the capabilities attributed to ancient Nazca and remains an unsolved mystery. The relationship between ancient Nazca and these alleged aerial visits creates a fascinating narrative that invites us to consider the lines not only as art or ceremonial but as part of an ancient signaling system or map intended for beings from the sky. Von Däniken suggests that these figures may have been created to communicate with these entities, offering food and hospitality in exchange for knowledge and protection, solidifying a cultural and spiritual bond that they hoped could be renewed with the return of their "gods."

A few years ago, in England, a drawing similar to what Erich von Däniken describes as a mandala emerged, a design reminiscent of the formations found in Nazca, despite the distance of about 20,000 miles between the two locations. Similarly, in the desert of Jordan, gigantic figures have been discovered, visible only from above, with hundreds of designs including rings, circles, and triangles. This global phenomenon suggests that, in prehistoric times, populations from various parts of the world made drawings to communicate with the gods, visible only from the sky. These ancient practices reflect a tradition in which humans built structures in honor of the gods to ensure that future generations would remember their presence. Contrary to antiquity, the contemporary context does not see cultures building giant works to worship celestial deities, highlighting a significant shift in religious and cultural practices. A notable example of this ancestral tradition comes from the Dogon people in Africa, who claim to have been visited by beings from the Sirius star system. The Dogon received names from the gods, which, however, have no understandable meaning for us today, leaving a mystery about their origins and destinations. Von Däniken suggests that, thousands of years ago, extraterrestrials directly influenced human evolution, creating the first humans, as symbolized by biblical figures such as Adam and Eve. These beings, according to the narrative, were the first to speak and name things, thus establishing the foundation of human communication. Von Däniken's idea is that the first human language was that of the extraterrestrials, a concept supported by the biblical account of the Tower of Babel, which describes how, originally, all humanity spoke a single language before dispersing and developing different dialects. These theories by von Däniken offer a fascinating perspective on the interaction between humans and extraterrestrial entities, proposing that the signs and languages left by the ancients are not only cultural legacies but also testimonies of historical contact with civilizations beyond Earth. Erich von Däniken lived in a small village in the Swiss Alps, a country known for its wealth of different dialects; in Switzerland alone, there are 23, as every society develops its own language. He reflects on how, if extraterrestrials wanted to communicate with us using their technology, they could send an unequivocal signal visible to all, like a huge inscription projected onto the moon with a laser during full or new moon phases. However, von Däniken argues that the most crucial information does not reside in the skies but within our own genetic code. Von Däniken proposes the idea that humanity is not only the result of natural evolutionary processes but has been influenced by artificial mutations induced by extraterrestrials. According to him, these genetic modifications are the key to understanding our true origin and the abilities we possess. He argues that denying hypotheses of extraterrestrial visits in the past is nonsensical, as multiple clues seem to point in this direction. The definitive answer, he asserts, lies in our genes and the information we pass down from generation to generation, which, once deciphered, may reveal the true extent of extraterrestrial influence on our species.

BEYOND CHEOPS: THE HIDDEN
HISTORY OF THE GREAT PYRAMID

According to archaeological tradition, the Great Pyramid was built by the pharaoh known as Khufu, commonly referred to as Cheops. However, there are no direct inscriptions, sculptures, or Cheops's mummy that unequivocally confirm this attribution. About 2,000 years ago, historians like Theodorus of Sicily, Strabo, Plutarch, and Herodotus visited Egypt and encountered the Great Pyramid, speaking with local priests about the identity of the builder. The answer given to these esteemed ancient historians was that the pyramid had been erected before the Great Flood, thus leaving a veil of mystery over its origin. During his extended stay in Egypt around 450 B.C., Herodotus wrote two books in which he clearly distinguished between what he could personally verify and what was told to him. In his writings, he reports being told that a tyrant named Khufu, known to the Greeks as Cheops, had built the pyramid. This assertion became the foundation for modern archaeologists to attribute the pyramid to Cheops, despite other historians of the time, like Theodorus of Sicily, challenging this version, instead indicating a pharaoh named Saurid, a figure that coincides with Enoch according to Jewish traditions. The writings of ancient Arab authors, such as Al-Masudi and Ibrahim Abdul Al-Makrizi, argue that it was not Cheops but Saurid, identifiable with Enoch, who built the Great Pyramid, long before the Great Flood. This narrative raises serious questions about the actual chronology of events and the technological evolution required for such an imposing structure.

The Great Pyramid, composed of about two and a half million stone blocks, requires advanced technological knowledge and meticulous planning. This raises doubts about whether Cheops, whose father Sneferu and grandfather came directly from the Stone Age, could have had the technological skills necessary for such construction. If instead, as von Daniken suggests, we accept that the builder was Enoch, instructed by extraterrestrials in construction techniques and other advanced knowledge, the historical and technological picture becomes more coherent. Our ancestors gradually learned to use increasingly sophisticated tools and techniques, but the internal complexity of the Great Pyramid, with its kilometers of precisely designed corridors and chambers, suggests an engineering knowledge far beyond that available in Cheops's time. Therefore, the hypothesis that Enoch, educated by extraterrestrials before the Great Flood, may have been the true architect of the Great Pyramid, offers a plausible explanation that connects ancient technical knowledge to advanced external influences.

Ibrahim Abdul Al-Makrissi, an Arab historian, argued that inside and beneath the Great Pyramid are thousands of books written by Enoch for the future of humanity. Thanks to modern technologies, more chambers have been discovered inside the pyramid than previously known. However, access to these chambers remains extremely limited due to the narrow size of the corridors leading to them, only about 14 centimeters wide, making entry without the aid of advanced technologies currently used to explore these spaces impossible.

Within the Great Pyramid of Giza, three main chambers have been identified: the King's Chamber at the top, the Queen's Chamber positioned lower down, and a third called the "unfinished chamber," carved into the rock beneath the structure. In the Queen's Chamber, there are two openings in the north and south walls. About 25 years ago, a German engineer named Rudolf Gantenbrink, using a small robot he designed, obtained permission from the Department of Archaeology to explore one of these passages. Archaeologists believed the passage was only eight meters long and ended there, symbolically created so the pharaoh's soul could ascend to the stars. Contrary to expectations, Gantenbrink's robot surpassed the expected eight-meter length, continuing to ascend and discovering various types of stone along the way, such as granite, alabaster, and sandstone. Along the passage, the robot encountered doors that seemed to block the passage but continued to advance until it reached, 62 meters away, a small door with two metal latches, one of which was broken and lying on the ground. The robot was equipped with a laser that was used to explore what lay behind the door, confirming the presence of additional spaces. These discoveries, made about 25 years ago, were disseminated through the press and some television broadcasts. Years later, the National Geographic Society built a new robot with a drill with which they drilled the small door during an international television broadcast, promising to show the world what lay behind it. However, despite expectations, the images transmitted revealed that there was nothing behind the door, disappointing the global audience. The mystery of the Great Pyramid continues to be a topic of fervent discussion and speculation, fueled by new technologies and research that gradually reveal more secrets of this ancient wonder. The National Geographic Society of the United States also went to Egypt, where they built a new robot equipped with a drill. With this tool, they drilled a hole in what appeared to be a small door. During an international television broadcast, they announced that they would insert a camera through the hole to show the world what was hidden behind the door. Unfortunately, this turned out to be another illusion; the photographs taken before the broadcast had already demonstrated that there was nothing behind the door; it was empty. Otherwise, they would never have shown such images to the global public. Nevertheless, the first door had a hole, and the laser detected that there was another wall behind it, about 22 centimeters thick. After eighteen years, a wealthy businessman from Singapore proposed to the Department of Antiquities to destroy this second wall using sound waves, but the proposal was rejected. Eventually, he was allowed to drill an extremely small hole, sufficient only for the insertion of an endoscope. With this instrument, hundreds of photographs were taken which, once assembled by the computer, revealed the existence of another chamber. This discovery underscores the advanced level of planning and engineering design required to build the Great Pyramid, a level of complexity that does not seem congruent with Cheops's era, dated around 2500 B.C., a period just beyond the Stone Age. If instead it was Enoch, who lived before the Great Flood and was instructed by extraterrestrials, who built the pyramid, then the technological capabilities required would be consistent with such advanced engineering. Enoch, described as the seventh patriarch before the Flood and known to have been instructed by extraterrestrials, may indeed have had the skills required for such an imposing work, as suggested in his texts, where he claims to have learned everything about construction and engineering. Rebuilding the pyramid today would be an enormously costly endeavor, given the precision with which two and a half million stone blocks were assembled, together with the complexity of the internal chambers, such as the King's Chamber, the Queen's Chamber, and other underground structures. This level of complexity significantly exceeds the capabilities of a pharaoh like Cheops and suggests that, while the physical labor was performed by humans, the planning and engineering may have had extraterrestrial origins.

The Great Pyramid is considered one of the wonders of the world. When historians arrived in Egypt about 2,000 years ago, the Great Pyramid was already there, standing as a gigantic monument to humanity. Faced with this majestic construction, numerous questions arose: Who built it? Why? And for what exact purpose? Daniken suggests that it was built for the gods, not as a tomb, since no burial has ever been found inside, least of all that of Cheops. Therefore, it is likely that it was erected as a legacy for the future of humanity. Daniken's theory presupposes that within the Great Pyramid, books recounting very remote times, preceding the Great Flood, dated by some to 5,000 or 6,000 years ago, could be discovered. Directly below the Great Pyramid, as we have seen, is a chamber known from time immemorial as the "Unfinished Chamber." This chamber, accessible through a shaft 119 meters long and only about a meter high, forces those who descend into it to proceed almost on their knees. Inside the Unfinished Chamber, there are no inscriptions or workings, only raw rock, and no one understands its purpose, making it a mystery. Herodotus, the Greek historian who visited Egypt around 450 B.C., mentioned the existence of an underground lake beneath the pyramid, containing a sarcophagus with the remains or gifts of the god Osiris, also identified with the constellation of Orion. Despite initial skepticism, modern archaeologists have indeed discovered this underground lake. During an exploration, one first enters a small room with stairs leading to another shaft, wide enough for two stairs. Descending further, one reaches a chamber carved into the rock containing seven niches, but only two of these contain sarcophagi, one made of black basalt and the other of granite, unusual materials for the area, indicating the importance of the place. Descending even further, through a second shaft narrower than the first, one finally reaches a small lake or stream of crystal-clear water, where indeed rests a sarcophagus. Despite measurements and photographs confirming Herodotus's claims, archaeologists remain uncertain about the contents of the sarcophagus, maintaining a veil of mystery over what may have been deposited centuries ago in that remote place beneath the Great Pyramid. For centuries, the archaeological community

41

has argued that it was impossible to directly link the Great Pyramid to dates as remote as 11,240 years ago, which far exceed the commonly accepted chronology of Egyptian civilization, dated around 3000 B.C. However, Herodotus's narrative placing the events in a much earlier era has found new supporters in modern times. According to this view, the Great Pyramid would not only be an ancient construction but a relic of a much more advanced civilization, built before the Great Flood using advanced technologies transmitted by Enoch, who in turn learned them from extraterrestrials. The planning and engineering of such an extraordinary work would therefore have been the result of non-terrestrial knowledge. This perspective suggests that the Great Pyramid was intended as a kind of treasure trove or archive to preserve knowledge for future generations, especially those post-Flood. Enoch, described as the seventh patriarch before the flood, would have imparted this advanced knowledge, including construction and engineering methods. Before leaving Earth, Enoch would have entrusted his son Methuselah with about 300 books, with the task of preserving them for the future. The Great Pyramid, therefore, may conceal within it a library, the contents of which could revolutionize our understanding of the past. The theory that the three pyramids of Giza are connected to Orion's belt, proposed by the historian Robert Bauval, and that gods like Osiris (associated with Orion) and Isis (associated with Sirius) are depictions of extraterrestrial visitors, offers an astronomically and mythologically coherent explanation of these celestial connections. Such theories suggest that the pyramids, besides being monuments or tombs, served as catalysts for human teaching, transmitting advanced knowledge in astronomy and mathematics, considered gifts of the gods, who were actually visitors from other worlds. Future exploration of the Great Pyramid could therefore reveal not only archaeological artifacts but actual ancient texts that would confirm this extraordinary interstellar legacy, radically changing our interpretation of ancient history.

CELESTIAL CODES: EXTRATERRESTRIAL HERITAGE AND THE REVELATIONS OF ENOCH

In the biblical text, we find Ezekiel, who was taken into space. In apocryphal texts, we find Abraham, who had a similar experience. In the Book of Enoch, it is narrated how Enoch found himself among the "guardians of the sky" and learned their language. Erich von Däniken offers these four examples to illustrate how analogous situations also occur in the ancient scriptures of India. One of the young men mentioned in the Indian sacred texts, named Arjuna, who later became a king, was taken by extraterrestrials into space, just like Ezekiel and Enoch. During his time in space, Arjuna not only learned the language of the extraterrestrials but also witnessed a conflict among them. Some extraterrestrials disagreed on whether to help humans or exploit Earth's natural resources, such as gold. This division led to a space war, during which Arjuna saw lightning bolts emanating from one of the flying machines, destroying two of the floating cities in space, while only one of these cities survived. Upon his return to Earth, Arjuna shared his experiences with his people, and later these accounts were transcribed in the Vedic scriptures, precisely in the fifth book of the Mahabharata. The Mahabharata is a vast collection of texts, considered the greatest mythology of the ancient world in India. In these texts, Arjuna describes how he was taken into space, also mentioning the pilot of the spacecraft, Matali, and recounting seeing a gigantic city composed of hundreds of modules, or vaguely specified "bulls," nested within each other, forming three large cities in orbit around Earth. This account by Arjuna reflects a similar theme to that described by Enoch: both narrate destructions and rebellions. Enoch speaks of mutiny and destruction, while Arjuna, from India, tells of destruction and mutiny caused not by humans, but by the extraterrestrials themselves in a celestial war. Von Däniken suggests that the term "heaven" is a mistaken translation and should be replaced with "space," as the wars described would have taken place in this context. Furthermore, he proposes revising the traditional conception of angels, commonly depicted with wings and halos, describing them not as benevolent spirits but as beings that physically interacted with humans, including having sex and waging wars. According to von Däniken, changing just a dozen words in the sacred texts would profoundly alter their meaning, indicating that "angels" could be interpreted as "extraterrestrials," and "archangels" as leaders of these extraterrestrial groups. In our time, we are witnessing a resurgence in the understanding of ancient texts thanks to modern translations that utilize current knowledge. A significant example is the work of Professor Dr. Dileep Kumar Kanjilal, who translated descriptions of flying machines in ancient India, demonstrating that these are not mere fantasies but scientifically verifiable realities. Dr. Hermann Burgard, an expert in Sumerology, has also undertaken the translation of the Temple Wall of Enchiridwana, high priestess and daughter of the Sumerian king Sargon I, around 2300 B.C. His works unequivocally clarify that Enchiridwana's writings describe extraterrestrial beings, not deities or natural phenomena like storms or earthquakes. This new era of translations reveals that past errors were not due to bad intentions or stupidity, but rather to a lack of current knowledge. Just fifty years ago, concepts like space flight or genetics were nonexistent or in their infancy. Today, however, we possess the technologies and scientific knowledge that could definitively confirm the existence of extraterrestrial life. We can send shuttles into space to search for extraterrestrial objects or time capsules, which could be, as Daniken asserts, in orbit around Earth. The change in the "spirit of the times" is essential. With our modern knowledge, we can reconsider and reinterpret ancient accounts in a new light, finding deeper and more meaningful answers regarding our origins and our future. Von Däniken suggests that we are part of a larger cosmic family and that we need not fear these extraterrestrial connections.

The concept of "virgin births," for example, existed long before Christianity. A noteworthy case in this context is that of Noah. About fifty years ago, one of the Dead Sea Scrolls was discovered, known as the Scroll of Lamech. Lamech, a wealthy shepherd, returned home after months of absence to find his wife, Batenosh, had just given birth to a child. Lamech suspected that the child was not his, given his long absence and the physical differences of the child compared to his other children. However, Batenosh swore she had not been touched by anyone. Confused, Lamech turned to his father, Methuselah, and then to the child's grandfather, Enoch, who had traveled into space and learned the language of extraterrestrials. This story suggests a possible extraterrestrial explanation for the child's birth, further linking ancient accounts with extraterrestrial interactions. In conclusion, the modern approach to rereading ancient texts through the prism of current science opens new perspectives on the interaction between humans and extraterrestrial civilizations, suggesting that our history may be much more intertwined with the cosmos than previously imagined. According to Enoch's account, he instructed his son Methuselah to speak to Lamech, his son, to convince him to accept the child as his own, teach him the language, and ensure him the best education possible. This was because, according to the sky guardians, massive destruction on Earth through a universal flood was imminent. The child, who would later be called Noah, was destined to become the father of the future human generation. From this account, it is evident that Noah was born through a process of artificial insemination, suggesting that his mother, Batenosh, was artificially impregnated. Consequently, all modern humans, being descendants of Noah, would carry within them extraterrestrial genes. This theory, unthinkable just a century ago, finds greater acceptance today thanks to the evolution of our ability to understand and accept hypotheses involving advanced science. The idea that the Flood was an event orchestrated by extraterrestrials, with Noah's Ark functioning as a kind of biological container, suggests that inside it were preserved the seeds of various plants and the species of various animals, including humans, to ensure the survival of terrestrial life. This concept finds a modern parallel in the global "Seed Vault" in Norway, where the seeds of numerous plant species are preserved in ice to safeguard them from potential future catastrophes. Noah's story finds correspondences in other ancient texts, such as the Epic of Gilgamesh, a Sumerian tale preceding the biblical version. In the Sumerian epic, the flood survivor is not Noah but Utnapishtim, and unlike Noah, who saved pairs of every animal species, Utnapishtim took with him artisans and workers of all kinds. This detail emphasizes the importance not only of physical survival but also of preserving knowledge and human skills through generations. This narrative demonstrates how ancient legends can be interpreted in a new light thanks to scientific and technological advances, suggesting a deep and ancient connection between humanity and extraterrestrial civilizations, capable of directly influencing the course of human history.

In the Bible, there are only two sentences concerning Enoch. He is described as the seventh patriarch before the Great Flood and as the first human to leave our planet on a chariot of fire. Enoch preceded the prophet Elijah and was recognized as such in several translations identifying him as the seventh patriarch. In-depth knowledge about Enoch mainly derives from the "Book of Enoch," discovered about 170 years ago by a British man who spent thirty years in a convent in Abyssinia. There he learned Enoch's language and discovered the book in the old convent library. The "Book of Enoch" is written in the first person, as a direct testimony of events, which is crucial for its authenticity. In the book, Enoch recounts that one evening, as his village was preparing to sleep, a noise from the sky drew everyone out of their houses. The villagers saw an object descending from the sky and two beings in shimmering garments approaching. While everyone fled in fear, Enoch, then twelve years old, remained to witness the scene. Despite the fear, when the beings approached, he fell to the ground. One of the strangers helped him up, demonstrating they had no hostile intentions. These beings, who spoke his language, reassured him not to be afraid. They did not call him by name, indicating they were not omniscient like deities; they simply recognized him as a human being. They then offered him to follow them to learn important knowledge for his society. Enoch accepted, showing great courage. During the preparation for the journey, one of the extraterrestrials commented on Enoch's unpleasant smell, ordering him to remove his clothes and plunge into a nearby river to cleanse himself. Once clean, he was given a fragrant cream to spread all over his body. The visitors from the sky then provided him with garments similar to theirs, and one of them had to explain how to wear pants. Clothed in their attire, Enoch felt like one of them. Similarly to what is narrated about Abraham, Enoch had the opportunity to fly above the Earth. During the journey, he observed giant crystals and doors that opened automatically inside the flying vehicle. He was led through a garden with unknown plants and vegetables and then into a large round hall with a throne at the center, where the "highest," as he calls it, welcomed him by rising from the throne, advancing toward him, and shaking his hand in welcome. This account, rich in details about Enoch's encounters with extraterrestrials, emphasizes his unique experience and the profound implications of these interactions for human understanding of the cosmos. What I am explaining

49

now is actually part of the Book of Enoch, but not in the form I just told it. Why this difference? Our scholars of 150 or 160 years ago had no notion of flight and the like, so they had to interpret the texts in terms of the knowledge of their time. Reading the text, they believed that angels had taken a human to heaven. In the original version of Enoch, it is written that two angels descended. I said that two extraterrestrials intervened. In the Book of Enoch, it is written that Enoch emitted a bad smell, and the strangers immersed him in water. In the original version, it is narrated that he was baptized, which is absurd considering that baptism did not exist before the great flood. Enoch received a cream that, according to von Daniken, was a disinfectant. In the religious version, it is described as the anointing of the high priest. Then he was given shimmering clothes, which von Daniken interprets as spacesuits, while the religious translation claims he was dressed as a high priest. The translations were completely wrong. Enoch, arriving in this garden with plants of different odors and colors, is described in the religious version as if he were walking through paradise or the heavenly garden. But according to von Daniken, it was simply a plantation, because in an extraterrestrial spacecraft, you have to grow your own food. Arriving in the grand hall with the throne at the center, the religious version states that Enoch was in the highest of heavens, in front of the throne of the Almighty God, which is absurd, because a true Almighty God, even if he had a throne, would not rise to shake hands with a human welcoming him to heaven. All these mistranslations do not derive from stupidity but from the temporal limitations of the time.

About a thousand years ago, there were thousands of scrolls and written texts of all kinds. The so-called Fathers of the Church, gathered, could not understand many of these writings. So, some texts were accepted, and others, incomprehensible, were rejected. Often, the rejected texts were incomplete. From a part of these texts, the Bible was composed, and from the other part, the texts considered apocryphal, including the Book of Enoch, were categorized as apocryphal texts. Thus, the Book of Enoch became part of the apocryphal texts, separated from the canonical Bible due to its incompleteness and the difficulty of interpretation by the Fathers of the Church.

The Vatican is often seen as a custodian of ancient secrets, including knowledge about entities that many identify as deities. Erich von Däniken suggests that, in reality, these deities could be interpreted as extraterrestrial beings, a notion he believes is also known to the most erudite members of the Catholic clergy, especially the Jesuits. The latter, known for their rigorous academic path and extensive education, would have the ability and skills to understand and interpret ancient texts that could reveal hidden truths about extraterrestrials. Von Däniken, who spent six years in a Jesuit-led Catholic institute, had the opportunity to appreciate the intellectual depth of these educators, many of whom hold more than one doctorate. Despite their vast erudition, he argues that there is reluctance to disclose this information to the general public. The reason for this hesitation, according to von Däniken, is related to the "spiritual time," or spirit of the times, which is not yet mature to welcome and accept the truth about extraterrestrials without undermining the foundations of current religious and social beliefs. Von Däniken criticizes the resistance to change by religious institutions and other conservative societies, which, in his view, hinder progress to maintain control and power. The evolution of our understanding of topics such as space travel and genetics, he argues, has already changed the spirit of the times, making us ready for challenges and revelations that our ancestors could not even imagine. Despite his advanced age, von Däniken remains optimistic about future generations, prophesying that within the next ten years, there will be an official encounter with extraterrestrials. This event, he predicts, will completely revolutionize our understanding of the past and our religious beliefs, leading to an inevitable collapse of many accepted dogmas. In his visionary scenario, contact with extraterrestrials will not only confirm theories he has long advocated but also pave the way for new understandings of who we are and where we come from, solidifying the idea of humanity as part of a much larger cosmic family.

UNIVERSAL DELUGE: GLOBAL MYTHOLOGIES AND ANCIENT ASTRONOMY

Legends and myths from our history have always fascinated humanity, but as we are beginning to understand, there is another narrative, another unwritten chapter that transcends conventional understandings, and which we must acknowledge if we are to approach the truth about our origins. In the times of prehistory, our ancestors, beings of stone, gazed up at the sky with reverence and wonder. The small, distant lights in the nighttime firmament were for them an enigma shrouded in mystery; lights of different shapes and colors dancing across the celestial vault without apparent explanation. This mystery marked the dawn of astronomy, as humanity began to ponder the celestial dynamics without yet possessing the tools to fully comprehend them. Over the years, these stargazers noticed that the celestial movements followed an annual cycle, repeating with precision. This discovery was astonishing and fueled the early natural religions, with cults devoted to the moon and the sun, luminous and powerful deities, yet still inscrutable in their cosmic essences. Thunder and lightning remained unfathomable phenomena, signs of a power surpassing human understanding. In this context of wonder and veneration, it is said that one day the heavens opened, and beings from other worlds descended from the cosmos. These extraterrestrial visitors were not merely passive observers but presented themselves as the first teachers of humanity, imparting lessons on the structure of the universe and astronomical connectivity.

One of the oldest monuments linked to this stellar heritage is Newgrange in Ireland, an ancient dolmen that stands as a silent witness to a distant age. Despite much research, the true purpose of this structure remains shrouded in mystery. Artificially constructed by Neolithic peoples, Newgrange features a precise opening in its passageway that, only during the summer solstice, on June 21st, channels sunlight directly down the corridor, illuminating a strategically placed stone at the rear of the structure. This phenomenon transforms the dolmen into a burst of light, almost as if traversed by laser beams. The reason for this precise astronomical alignment remains an open question, as do the identity of its builders and the depth of their celestial knowledge. A similar enigma surrounds Stonehenge, another ancient monument whose origins and functions continue to stimulate theories and debates. The structure consists of several stone circles, and surprisingly, the distances between these circles correspond to the distances between the planets of our solar system. Official archaeology has dated the first construction of Stonehenge to around 2800 BC, with subsequent additions made in different phases. However, more recent research suggests that the site could be much older. Theories about Stonehenge are numerous, but one suggests that the arrangement of the stone circles is not random: each circle would represent a planet, from Mercury to Jupiter, with a large gap between Mars and Jupiter that would reflect the asteroid belt, a knowledge that presumably requires advanced technologies to acquire.

These monuments, testimonies to ancient astronomical mastery, raise fundamental questions: who were these ancient builders? Where did they draw such precise knowledge of the universe from? The answer may lie not only in the earth beneath our feet but in the stars above us.

In our solar system, the Sun occupies the central position, followed by the planets Mercury, Venus, Earth, and Mars, up to Jupiter. Between Mars and Jupiter lies a notable gap represented by the asteroid belt. This astronomical pattern finds a surprising parallel in the arrangement of the circles at Stonehenge, where rings corresponding to the planets up to Mars are observed, followed by a large void symbolizing the asteroid belt, and finally, distanced from the others, a massive stone representing Jupiter, the giant of the solar system. The precise and detailed knowledge of the order of the planets and the asteroid belt suggests that the builders of Stonehenge, Stone Age men, would have had to be instructed by mentors endowed with an advanced understanding of astronomy, a knowledge impossible without the use of powerful telescopes, which obviously were not available at that time. Far from Europe, similar examples of advanced astronomical knowledge are found in Colombia, in the jungle-hidden city called Buritaca 200 (Teyuna). This city consists of several pyramidal terraces on which wooden and straw structures are built, oriented according to precise astronomical alignments. For example, in the "house of man" and the "house of woman" of Buritaca, particular pillars align during the spring equinox in such a way that the shadows interact symbolically, suggesting the time for sowing. The Kogi, the indigenous inhabitants of this region, believe that their astronomical knowledge was imparted by "celestial teachers," who also warned of the impending universal flood, advising the construction of an ark to survive. This theme of the flood and the construction of an ark is found in many cultures, including the biblical narrative of Noah. The construction of an ark is a technological endeavor that requires time and advance planning; it is not an instantaneous miracle. This suggests that the "teachers" foresaw catastrophic events such as a shift in the Earth's magnetic poles. These predictions and the subsequent transmission of technological and survival knowledge indicate that such teachers may not be deities or angels but extraterrestrial beings with access to technologies and information far surpassing those of humans at the time.

In summary, the astonishing planning capabilities and advanced knowledge of astronomical and geological events demonstrate that humanity may have had contact with extraterrestrial visitors, who left an indelible mark on our ancient civilizations, guiding the construction of complex structures and the survival of global cataclysms. In ancient Sumeria, there exists a list of kings known as the "King's List," preserved today at the British Museum in London. This document lists the oldest rulers, predating the Great Flood, followed by a new descent of the gods from the sky to humans, once the waters receded. This narrative finds a parallel in the traditions of the Kogi in Colombia, considered technically primitive, who possessed detailed knowledge of the flood and built an ark in anticipation of such an event. Similarly, Kogi mythology recounts that after the waters receded, the gods returned to Earth. This recurring pattern manifests in numerous mythologies and ancient legends. Distinct civilizations such as the Maya and the Greeks, with Plato mentioning a great flood, share similar accounts despite the absence of direct contacts, suggesting a globally shared flood event. In all these stories, the deities warn humans in advance, allowing them to prepare and build life-saving vessels, and then return to visit the post-flood Earth. Even in Europe, specifically in French Brittany, astronomically arranged dolmens and megaliths are found, which were initially thought to be only tombs. However, aerial surveys have revealed that these stones are not randomly arranged but form precise geometric configurations, such as Pythagorean triangles, demonstrating sophisticated planning and precise intention behind their arrangement. These ancient builders, guided by their celestial "teachers," were tasked with erecting monuments in honor of the gods, following precise instructions on the positioning of the stones. Although humans did the "dirty work," they did not understand that the end result of these constructions would be geometrically significant, like the Pythagorean triangles, which would only later be recognized and measured by descendants.

The extraterrestrials who imparted this knowledge were aware that such monuments would survive for millennia, leaving future generations to measure them and ponder their meaning. This intentional legacy was designed to stimulate questions and research, laying the groundwork for a deeper understanding of human capabilities and knowledge in relation to the cosmos, underscoring a deliberate connection between ancient astronomical knowledge and the guidance of advanced entities from space. Nowadays, after asking the questions, it is not clear from which solar system these extraterrestrials originated, nor is the technology they use to traverse these vast distances known. It is not known what color they were or what they were exactly like. However, some answers have been found: the planet was visited by beings from space. This is now demonstrable through numerous ancient sacred texts and many concrete facts. The extraterrestrial teachers must have been particularly sensitive and chose to educate some humans they deemed more intelligent, who then became leaders, imparting lessons in astronomy and mathematics, essential for the development of such knowledge. Some time ago, Daniken visited a site in Indonesia called Gunung Padang, located in the jungle where practically no one had ever been before. Archaeology suggests that this site is 23,000 years old and consists of tens of thousands of blocks of volcanic stone, known as basalt, extremely hard. It is a mystery who transported these blocks to such a remote location.

Another site of great antiquity is Göbekli Tepe, located in modern-day Turkey, dating back to at least 11,000 BC. There are no clear explanations as to why stone structures were erected at Göbekli Tepe. Von Daniken hypothesizes a connection with the proximity of this site to the place where the patriarch Abraham lived, about 10 kilometers away. Abraham, in apocryphal texts attributed to him, recounts hearing a noise coming from the sky while sitting outside his tent. Non-human beings descended from the sky and offered him to leave the planet to see it from above. Abraham accepted and, without understanding how it worked, found himself in a huge place that continuously rotated around itself in orbit around our planet. Abraham recounts feeling drawn downward, toward the Earth, suggesting that he was not on Earth at that time. He also described how the place he was in kept turning over, allowing him to see the Earth above himself and the stars below. This indicates that he was in a mothership, which, by rotating itself, generated centrifugal force to create artificial gravity. However, this concept was beyond Abraham's understanding, who interpreted the experience as a stay in heaven when he was actually in space. These erroneous interpretations of ancient texts, where "heaven" actually means "space," demonstrate how much our understanding of past events has been influenced by the cultural and technological limitations of previous epochs. Thus, the importance of reviewing these ancient accounts in light of modern knowledge is highlighted, recognizing the potential contact between humanity and extraterrestrial civilizations.

Many ancestors of humanity were taken into the skies. Daniken recounts that during his childhood in Switzerland, he was taught that paradise is the place of absolute happiness, where, if one lives an honorable life, one is united with God after death. However, as an adult, learning Greek and Latin, Daniken discovered that the heavens of sacred texts were actually the scene of battles. Even in the Judeo-Christian tradition, an archangel named Lucifer challenged God, leading to a war in heaven, which contradicts the idea of paradise as a place of pure happiness. This discovery led Daniken to reinterpret the concept of "heaven" as "space," suggesting that many of human mythologies, which include celestial wars, should be seen in this new context. Not only in the Judeo-Christian tradition are these battles found, but also in Greek mythology, where the god Zeus fought against Cronos before settling in our solar system. Returning to Göbekli Tepe, located about 10 kilometers from where Abraham experienced his celestial experiences, Daniken hypothesizes that this site may have been created in honor of the beings who took Abraham into space. This is just one of the many speculations Daniken proposes, reflecting on how ancient sites might have been influenced by extraterrestrial encounters and considering Göbekli Tepe as a potential site of veneration or commemoration of such events. Today it is known that even the three pyramids are astronomically oriented, representing the belt of the Orion constellation. The ancient Egyptian deity Osiris, according to modern theories, is identified with the constellation Orion, also highlighted in the written form of the hieroglyphs. Daniken argues that although the ancient structures were built by humans, it was extraterrestrials who guided them, teaching them the knowledge necessary to realize them. However, the hardest work was done by humans. Extraterrestrials, foreseeing that these stone monuments would survive for millennia, knew that future human generations would ask the same questions that we ask today: how

60

was it possible to build such structures? Why did our ancestors make such a massive effort, moving huge stones for astronomical purposes? And what purpose did they serve? These questions are essential because they push for answers. Daniken claims that the presence of extraterrestrial teachers is the most plausible explanation behind the construction of these imposing structures. His career is not limited to the study of stone structures but also encompasses world mythology, cultural relationships, and ancient sacred texts. Bringing together all this knowledge, he concludes that there is no doubt: our planet, and particularly Stone Age civilizations, received visits from beings from outer space, who were astronomy teachers for our ancestors. For these visitors, the ancients built these gigantic stone structures, leaving a legacy of mysteries and questions that still stimulate research and human curiosity today.

ANCIENT HYBRIDS: TRACES OF EXTRATERRESTRIAL GENETIC ENGINEERING IN HISTORY

Hybrid creatures were once considered a reality, not just mythology. According to Erich von Däniken, these hybrids actually existed. A well-known example of such creatures is the Sphinx of Giza, a hybrid with the head of a human, often thought to be that of a pharaoh, and the body of a lion. While traditionally interpreted as symbolizing intelligence with the head and strength with the body, Däniken argues that these hybrid creatures were real, not just symbolic. During his travels in Egypt, the Greek historian Herodotus, around 450 B.C., visited Thebes, modern-day Luxor. Here, a priest showed him 241 statues, each representing a long history of 11,340 years in which, according to the priest, the gods "from the firmament" were present on Earth. This historical period would thus extend for about 14,000 years, adding the 2,500 years since Herodotus made his observations. Herodotus also mentions hybrid creatures in his writings, a common theme also found in other ancient historians like Theodore Siculus and Strabo. Even Manetho, an Egyptian writer, wrote about hybrid creatures, but many of his works have been lost over time. Eusebius, a Church Father, citing Manetho, describes how the gods created hybrids like the centaur, half-human and half-horse, during their time on Earth. Däniken wonders why an advanced civilization, capable of space travel, would create such creatures. The answer he proposes is linked to the diversity of planetary environments they might encounter during their explorations. Some planets might be hotter or colder, larger or smaller than Earth, each with different gravitational and environmental needs. Hybrid creatures, therefore, might have been created to adapt to specific planetary environments, combining characteristics like the heat resistance of some animals or the physical strength of others. This ability for genetic manipulation suggests that the "gods," or rather extraterrestrials, possessed advanced knowledge in genetics, used to create life forms suitable for different planetary conditions. When extraterrestrials first observed Earth, they noticed the diversity of animal species and their unique adaptability to extreme environments. Erich von Däniken, citing these ancient encounters, describes how extraterrestrials were particularly impressed by the characteristics of some animals like the crocodile, whose skin resisted the high temperatures of the Nile, and the lion, known for its strength and agility in hunting. This observation led to the decision to combine the heat resistance qualities of the crocodile with the muscular power of the lion, aiming to create creatures suitable for surviving in diverse planetary conditions. According to Däniken, these hybrid creatures were not the result of natural evolutions, but of direct genetic interventions, a testament to the sophisticated knowledge in genetics possessed by extraterrestrials, whom he defines as the first genetic engineers of Earth. The ability to genetically manipulate living species suggests that the "gods" had technologies far beyond human understanding at the time.

Despite their technological superiority, extraterrestrials behaved like ethnologists, studying and influencing selected groups of humans before disappearing, leaving behind their hybrid creations. The presence of these creatures generated fear and reverence among humans, so much so that they were represented as symbols of terror in mythology and artistic representations, now considered legends or products of fantasy. The hybrid creatures, not being natural, failed to perpetuate and eventually became extinct. This explains why such beings are no longer present in our modern world. Of interest is the account of Auguste Mariette, a French archaeologist who in the 19th century, thanks to new skills acquired in reading hieroglyphs, explored ancient Egypt. Mariette discovered references to hybrid creatures like the Apis bull in ancient texts, a being revered not as a normal animal but as a sacred entity created by the gods. The Apis bull was not just an ordinary bull but a hybrid, a direct product of divine genetic engineering. However, despite the numerous mummifications practiced by the Egyptians, which preserved not only the pharaohs but all forms of life, Mariette never found a mummy of these hybrid creatures. This fact suggests deliberate omissions or losses over the millennia, or that these hybrid creatures were not intended for preservation like other living beings, due to their not entirely terrestrial nature. In every major museum, both Eastern and Western, depictions of hybrid creatures can be found, and Egypt is particularly rich in them.

Herodotus, along with other ancient historians like Theodore Siculus and Strabo, mentions these hybrid creatures in his writings, highlighting their non-human nature. And as we have seen, even Manetho, an ancient Egyptian writer whose works are mostly lost but partially cited by Eusebius of Caesarea, spoke of creatures created by the celestial gods, such as the centaur, a hybrid with a human upper part and a horse lower part. For Däniken, the creation of such beings by extraterrestrials was not a whim, but a scientific and genetic necessity. The implications of these genetic manipulations are profound, suggesting that the "gods" were actually space visitors with advanced knowledge in genetics, capable not only of traveling through space but also of manipulating life at a molecular level. However, these hybrid creatures elicited terror in our ancestors, so much so that they were represented as symbols of fear in mythologies and seen as mere fantasies in modern times. The case of Auguste Mariette, the French Egyptologist of the 19th century, demonstrates how little was known about hybrid creatures despite the evidence. Mariette's discovery of empty sarcophagi and then of sarcophagi filled with bitumen with crushed bones of different species inside suggests an attempt by the ancient Egyptians to prevent these creatures from being "awakened" or regenerated. These findings indicate not only the physical presence of such beings but also their deeply rooted cultural and religious significance, manipulated and ultimately forgotten, transformed into myth due to the inability to fully understand their origin and nature. Mariette's work highlights the difficulty of accepting the existence of such creatures without context or scientific understanding, a dilemma that persists to this day despite advances in genetics that

65

could one day definitively confirm the hybrid nature of such beings as products of ancient extraterrestrial genetic manipulations. As soon as we demonstrate that hybrid creatures existed in antiquity, it becomes clear that such creatures cannot derive from a normal process of sexual reproduction. For example, if a human were to attempt mating with a monkey, no result would be obtained because human chromosomes and those of monkeys are completely different. This means that a mixed creature cannot be born from the womb of a female monkey. The presence of hybrid creatures therefore necessarily implies a genetic design intervention. Who possessed such advanced knowledge? The ancient Egyptians? Impossible. Only extraterrestrials would have had the skills to carry out such genetic manipulations. Ancient testimonies, like those of Manetho and Eusebius, reveal that it was the gods who created such beings. And why would the gods create mixed creatures? Because these were used on planets with different environmental conditions, which makes perfect sense. In ancient Sumeria, tablets were found showing beings that archaeologists interpreted as winged deities or winged geniuses, engaged in activities that, in modern eyes, seem to refer not to a tree or tree of life, but to DNA. In fact, in DNA, four bases are observed connecting, and in Sumerian depictions, the manipulation of these bases to create hybrids is seen.

Concrete evidence of hybrid creatures is displayed, for example, in the British Museum, where a stele of black basalt called Salamazar II, a Sumerian king, is found. On this stele, animals held on leashes are clearly visible, which do not correspond to known species, demonstrating that they were living hybrid creatures. A Sumerian cuneiform text next to it narrates that some hybrid creatures were captured and presented to the king. When Herodotus visited Egypt around 450 B.C., specifically Thebes, today Luxor, he noticed that between the Temple of Luxor and the Temple of Karnak, 3.8 kilometers apart, the avenue was lined with statues of hybrid creatures carved in stone, numerous in his time but today reduced to a few survivors. This fantastic avenue highlighted how, even in ancient times, it was possible to genetically manipulate life to create life forms impossible in nature. Today, genetics has reached such levels that every theoretical impossibility can become reality. However, the creation of hybrid creatures is morally and ethically prohibited and legally banned in all countries, although the technical knowledge to do so exists. This imposes an ethical limit on the application of such advanced knowledge, even though the technique would allow the creation of such beings if someone, perverse enough to attempt it, decided to proceed.

HEAVENLY CITIES AND DIVINE CHARIOTS: ADVANCED TECHNOLOGIES AND TEACHINGS OF THE GODS IN ANCIENT INDIA

In the rich tapestry of myths and legends that form the history of our world, there exists a narrative suggesting a different perspective, particularly evident in India—a land teeming with deities, many of whom are closely connected to the cosmos. These celestial beings, often described as having descended from the heavens, are believed to be not mere mythical figures but teachers from beyond our world. They imparted knowledge of mathematics, calendars, and more to humanity. Take, for example, the revered god Shiva, who is said to have possessed an extraordinary flying machine called Garuda. Unlike any earthly bird, Garuda was capable of extraordinary feats such as circumnavigating the moon and venturing beyond the solar system, even equipped to deploy bombs. This suggests that Garuda was more akin to a spacecraft than a bird, transporting Shiva across the cosmos, not just within the confines of Earth. Surprisingly, the legacy of these divine flying vehicles persists in the architecture of Indian temples, both ancient and modern. At the top of each temple is a structure known as a vimana, which varies in form but is consistent in its symbolic representation of a flying machine. Some vimanas are circular or elliptical, resembling modern depictions of UFOs, while others take on different forms. These vimanas are said to represent the smaller spacecraft used by Hindu gods to travel between their larger spacecraft in orbit and the planet below. The concept of vimanas as space shuttles offers a fascinating glimpse into how the ancients interpreted their interactions with these divine visitors. It is interesting to note that while some of the artistic representations of vimanas found in Indian texts date back to the 17th century, they are based on much older scriptures. Designers of that time would read the ancient texts and then create visual interpretations of what they imagined the vimanas to be, integrating ancient knowledge with artistic interpretation to bridge the gap between past and present understandings of these celestial phenomena. This tradition continues to underscore a unique fusion of mythology, technology, and spirituality that characterizes Indian cultural and religious thought, suggesting a historical acceptance of extraterrestrial influences long before the concept entered the mainstream of modern science fiction. Ancient scriptures and legends do not always tell of simple myths or allegories, but often of real phenomena observed and detailed by the people of the time. In the context of ancient India, vimanas were not just elements of fantasy, but aerial transport means actually perceived and witnessed by entire communities. These "chariots of the gods," as they were called, represent in sacred texts what in modernity we might consider spacecraft. Unlike motherships capable of traveling interstellar distances, vimanas were more limited in their mobility, comparable to how a helicopter differs from a jumbo jet in modern technology: both fly but with different capacities and purposes. For example, the prophet Ezekiel in the Bible describes chariots similar to those mentioned in Indian scriptures, which were used for relatively short journeys within our solar system. The level of detail with which these flying machines are described in ancient scriptures is remarkable. There are vimanas with wheels and others without, some noisy during flight, others surprisingly silent. These accounts have been passed down and preserved with precision, as evidenced by the "Drona Parva," a text rich in references to these ancient Indian flying machines. The work of Professor Dr. Kanjilal, a Sanskrit professor at Sanskrit College in Calcutta, is exemplary in this regard. His book, "Flying Machine in Ancient India," is not just a collection of stories, but a scientific work that translates and analyzes the descriptions of vimanas found in the Vedas. This meticulously scientific text resembles biblical studies, organized by chapters and verses, confirming the rigorous approach adopted by the professor in his translation and interpretation of ancient texts. In the Drona Parva, an ancient scripture part of the Mahabharata, it is narrated how one of the gods destroyed a city of priests with a gigantic weapon, described as brighter than the sun. This weapon caused extreme devastation: elephants, panicked and in pain, spun around while burning alive; animals died in agony, and warriors, oppressed by the unbearable heat of their metallic garments, stripped naked screaming in pain. Even birds, struck by the unbearable heat, fell dead from the sky. It is also said that the weapon had such devastating effects that it caused the death of unborn children inside the womb, demonstrating that the emitted radiation reached considerable distances. This ancient narrative suggests a knowledge of the concept of radiation, an extraordinarily advanced detail for the time, indicating a possible extraterrestrial origin of such knowledge. The vastness of Indian scriptures, comprising about 5,000 pages, stands in stark contrast to Western religious texts like the Bible or the Torah, which are limited to about 500 pages. This extensive corpus of texts has survived despite the destruction of many other ancient manuscripts worldwide, such as the Mayan codices, of which only three have reached us, and two of them are still undecipherable. India is not the only custodian of such narratives. Even in Tibet, a notoriously isolated and mountainous region, scriptures such as the Kansur and Tansur have survived, sacred texts of Tibetan society. In these texts, the leitmotif of gods descending from the sky, endowed with unpronounceable names, who imparted teachings to humans, is repeated. One of these gods is described as a human-looking being, extremely intelligent and kind, who upon leaving Earth ascended into the sky with a Vimana. Students who witnessed his departure described the vimana progressively shrinking in size until it became as small as an egg, then as a point, until it disappeared completely. Before leaving Earth, this god would have hidden writings intended for humanity, writings that would be revealed only when the time was right. These narratives, from different cultures and times, intertwine, showing a common thread: the presence of superior beings, capable of traveling between worlds and profoundly influencing human civilizations. India, with its wealth of gods and mythologies, serves as a catalyst for these stories, representing a crossroads of divine and technological knowledge, as evidenced by the detailed descriptions of vimanas and interplanetary travel. These similarities between stories of different origins suggest a possible universal truth, hidden behind the veil of earthly mythologies. The vimanas, therefore, were not simple terrestrial vehicles but true spaceships, used to connect with motherships positioned in orbit around Earth, described in translations as "cities in the sky." This narrative, supported by rich historical and interpretive documentation, offers a surprising and detailed view of how ancient civilizations might have interacted with extremely advanced technologies, interpreted as divine manifestations.

Arjuna was the one who frequently ascended to the cities in the firmament, not just once, but multiple times. Between one visit and another, he would return to Earth. Arjuna even mentioned the name of his pilot, Matali, who accompanied him on these space ascents. He described seeing hundreds of different vimanas in these celestial cities. It was spoken of three cities situated not in a conventional paradise, but in the firmament itself, a place observable and described by earthlings for its diversity. The chronicles of Arjuna did not just describe the presence of these cities; he also narrated battles and an impressive variety of vimanas, each with unique characteristics. Analogous to the modern diversity of aircraft — from private jets to helicopters and military aircraft — vimanas varied greatly in shape, function, and capability. Some could carry up to twenty individuals, while others were designed to accommodate only two or three. Some vimanas had wheels, allowing them to land and move on Earth, while others were wheel-less and could only hover above the ground. This wealth of detail clearly emerged in Indian traditions and was documented in ancient texts like the Mahabharata. There were no industries on Earth capable of building vimanas; all knowledge regarding these extraordinary aircraft came from outside, indicating an absence of earthly technological evolution to explain the existence of vimanas. There were no reports of humans building vimanas nor testimonies of an industry or technological progress aimed at their creation. These extraordinary means of transportation were always associated with the gods, who arrived in their motherships, described by ancient Indians as "cities in the sky."

In Tikal, a gigantic pyramid stands erected in honor of the gods who landed there. Similar structures are found in India, comparable to the pyramids of Central America but different from those in Egypt. Egyptian pyramids have a triangular shape and are devoid of sculptures or designs on their surface. In contrast, Indian and Central American pyramids are rich in sculptures, carved heads, and inscriptions. In Hindu mythology, there is talk of two twins, the Maruts, described as beings capable of flying between continents, especially between India and Central America. This commonality of deities would explain the similarity between the step pyramids, resembling towers, found in both regions, unlike those in Egypt. The Maruts, according to the narratives, could move freely around the planet without the need to land or refuel, suggesting that the energy source they used was of an unknown and advanced nature. Their vimanas, as also described in the Drona Parva, produced a terrible noise during flight, highlighting the power of flying machines. Also interesting is the discussion about the energy used for these vimanas: some texts speak of fuel composed of elements like mercury and mica, but other components remain undeciphered, described with terms that sound like "honey," leaving room for multiple interpretations without precise translation. If it were possible to fully decipher these texts, we might discover a new form of energy for our machines.

Many so-called mythologies include dates that are impossible for humans to conceive. In Palenque, for example, beneath the temple of the Pyramid of Inscriptions, there are references dating events to 1,200,000 years before Pakal. Ancient Sumeria, as we have seen, also presents the so-called "king list" listing the names of Sumerian kings before the great flood, accumulating over 200,000 years of history. After the flood, it is said that the gods descended from the sky again, ruling for 24,301 years. Indian mythologies also record implausible dates. All these chronologies may seem confusing, but there is a theoretical explanation: if one travels through space at high speed, the time spent on the spaceship is different from that on the home planet. Thus, an astronaut could age only a few years traveling to Proxima Centauri, while on Earth, thousands of years could pass. This temporal discrepancy could explain how the same gods described in ancient scriptures could appear unchanged to human eyes despite the passage of millennia, hypothesizing that these "gods" traveled at relativistic speeds. However, this remains just one of the possible interpretations of these millennia-old narratives.

Every time a god touched the Earth, the place of their landing was considered sacred, and humans expressed joy and gratitude for the visits and teachings received. In honor of these divine encounters, humans erected temples, just as they did in the lands of the Maya, like in Tikal, where every sacred structure was a tribute to the celestial deities and their flying vehicles, the vimanas. When discussing with Western scientists, for example, German or Swiss Indologists, the antiquity of the stories contained in the Vedas is often downplayed, placing them around 500 B.C. However, speaking with Indian professors, who possess much deeper knowledge, one discovers that such narratives could date back as far as 6,000 years ago, much further back than commonly accepted. According to the narratives, extraterrestrials, after spending a period on Earth, decided to return to their origins. Some of the motherships were destroyed, like those mentioned by Arjuna, while others simply vanished. These "gods," like modern ethnologists, studied and taught certain human groups, then returned to their stellar homes without leaving a trace. Similarly to modern ethnologists who do not abandon their advanced technology—such as cameras or lighting devices—the gods did not leave behind their advanced tools, which returned with them. If we consider the lifespan of objects abandoned on Earth, even the sturdiest ones like tanks from the Second World War, today, nothing remains but ruins or wreckage displayed in museums. Everything made of metal has turned into rust and ruin in the desert. Likewise, extraterrestrial objects, if they ever existed, have been lost to time. The desire to find an extraterrestrial artifact, like a hammer marked "made on Jupiter," remains an unattainable dream. The stories spoken of are not myths or allegories born out of nothing. Mythology, in fact, arises from truths that subsequent generations fail to fully comprehend.

Suppose the Earth were destroyed, and only a few survived in the Andes or Tibet. These survivors, seeking to preserve human knowledge for their children, might recount tales of enormous metallic birds that flew faster than arrows and carried humans across oceans to cities with skyscrapers touching the clouds. Over generations, the reality of these aircraft would become a legend of gigantic flying birds—a mythology born from reality but distorted by time and oral transmission. This principle applies to the ancient Indian descriptions of vimanas and the weapons described in the Drona Parva as brighter than the sun, causing destruction and death. These narratives are not simple allegories but based on real observations of advanced technologies, interpreted through the language and knowledge of the time. Myths, therefore, always contain a kernel of truth, even though the details may be inaccurate or altered over time. All the deities in the so-called mythologies are interconnected, and what was once reality has been passed down with different names in different cultures, but the underlying meaning remains the same. For example, despite the destruction of the original Maya books, new texts written after the destruction, the so-called books of Shillambala, speak of a universal cataclysm similar to that described by Plato in ancient Greece. This demonstrates how two cultures thousands of kilometers apart and separated by the Atlantic Ocean can share tales of a universal flood, despite having independent origins and developments. This coincidence in narratives among such distant cultures suggests that myths could be rooted in real events, interpreted and adapted by different civilizations according to their knowledge and cultural context. For instance, while Western civilization can locate and date the events of the life of Jesus Christ to Jerusalem around 2,000 years ago, other cultures may have come to know these stories much later and integrated them into their traditions in ways that reflect their perceptions and values. Similarly, in ancient India, the gods were once considered tangible realities: extraterrestrials and masters who imparted advanced knowledge. Over time and the dispersal of populations across the planet, these original stories evolved into myths and legends, enriched with local details but retaining a core of universal truth. The persistence of these tales across cultures and continents demonstrates that, despite different interpretations and representations, the core of the story—the interaction between humanity and entities of extraterrestrial origin —remains constant. The "gods" described in all these cultures were teachers who shared their advanced knowledge in fields like astronomy and genetics, suggesting that our ancestors, devoid of such scientific knowledge, may have had contact with visitors from other solar systems. These advanced teachings, like genetic manipulation that gave rise to hybrid creatures or profound understanding of celestial bodies and calendars, support the idea of a direct and intentional

77

intervention by extraterrestrial entities in human history, transforming what may seem like myth into a possible historical reality.

SACRED LINES AND HIDDEN GEOMETRIES: A PREHISTORIC HERITAGE TRACED THROUGHOUT EUROPE

It is believed that there is a connection between ancient sites scattered throughout the world, and in Europe, this theory finds particular confirmation through what are called "sacred lines" or "ley lines". These lines, theoretically traced on a map of Europe, intersect villages and places whose archaeological and prehistoric significance seems to surpass mere coincidence. These sites include stone circles, dolmens, and menhirs that testify to a remote and mysterious past. The sacred lines traverse places like Calais, Mont Alec, Lalex, and Lalexon, extending through the Alps to reach Sicily. Each village along these lines shares similar linguistic roots in names, suggesting a deliberate rather than random connection. Even the Pyrenees Mountains, dividing France from Spain, are crossed by one of these sacred lines. Here, each village seems to bear names evoking stars, such as "Vesetei", "Lucella", and "Aster", culminating at Santiago de Compostela, whose etymology of 'Stella' further reinforces this pattern. These places were not chosen at random. It is believed that ancient builders were guided by extraterrestrial visitors, who instructed our ancestors to place monuments and villages along these lines for reasons that only future generations could understand or investigate. The network of lines stretching for thousands of kilometers across Europe is considered an encrypted message left by extraterrestrials, intended to be deciphered only as human investigative and understanding capabilities advance. The builders of the prehistoric era faced enormous challenges, such as crossing the Alps, a natural barrier up to 4,000 meters high, without knowing what lay on the other side. This suggests that the knowledge necessary to create these lines and accurately position sites along them could not solely originate from human insights of the time but must have been imparted by a much more advanced civilization. Ultimately, the sacred lines in Europe and the mysterious connections between archaeological sites along them are not just relics of a distant past, but signs of an extraterrestrial heritage begging to be explored and understood, inviting modern humanity to question the true meaning of these ancient signs left by our cosmic predecessors. Someone suggested to the ancients to build their sacred places in specific locations, foreseeing that the future would discover them. One of these ley lines crosses Brittany, passes through Stonehenge, traverses the Alps, and ends at Delphi in Greece. Delphi was the sacred place of the god Apollo, son of Zeus. According to legend, Apollo did not come to Delphi by chance. During his journey around the Earth in a flying chariot, Apollo noticed the humans of Delphi and decided to descend to impart his knowledge to them. At that time, the inhabitants of Delphi were considered technologically primitive. Apollo taught them how to build sturdy houses on mountains and hills so that they would not collapse during heavy rains. Additionally, he imparted lessons in astronomy, and his son Asclepius became the physician who taught humans medicine. Apollo, known for his flying abilities, would leave Delphi twice a year to visit distant lands to the north. The legend of Apollo is closely linked to the ability to fly. A few years ago, while giving a lecture in Delphi, Daniken was approached by a professor of archaeology and a high-ranking officer of the Greek Air Force. They confided in him that all the old sacred sites of Greece are connected to each other through precise geometries. Surprised, given that Greece is a mountainous country and many of these sites are on isolated islands like Crete, not visible to the naked eye, he doubted their geometric interconnection. The next day, he was invited to the military airport, where the professor of archaeology and the air force commander showed him a giant map of Greece. They explained that it was a coincidence to discover this geometric network: young pilots, during their exercises, always consumed the same amount of fuel, suggesting that the distances between the sites were uniform. So, they began to measure and discovered that the distances between one site and another always corresponded to the golden ratio. This left him perplexed, considering that Greece had exceptional mathematicians like Euclid and Pythagoras, and even Plato discussed Greek mythology. But the professor of archaeology clarified that these sacred sites predated these historical figures, having been venerated already in the Neolithic period. For example, the Temple of Apollo at Delphi was built on walls dating back to the Stone Age, much older than the temple itself, dated around 500 B.C. This indicates that the sacred sites had spiritual and geometric relevance long before the era of famous Greek mathematicians. When the professor of archaeology, with a compass in hand, illustrated to Eric how to

81

easily demonstrate their claim, he suggested placing the compass center on any archaeological site, such as Delphi or Epidaurus, and then pointing it towards another archaeological site, then tracing a circle. Surprisingly, each circle drawn always intersected at least two other ancient sacred sites. This exercise could be repeated 28 times, eliminating any possibility of coincidence: everything had been intentionally done. Whoever had guided the Stone Age ancestors knew that millennia later, humanity would fly and measure their countries, discovering with amazement that all these ancient Greek sites were geometrically connected, including the Mediterranean Sea. This could not be a coincidence. The extraterrestrials had left proof, a kind of indestructible time capsule, which would reveal their presence and technology, heralding a future return. However, where could they hide such a capsule to ensure its survival through the millennia? A terrestrial temple or pyramid could be destroyed by wars, religious changes, earthquakes, or tsunamis. The most logical solution would have been to place this time capsule in orbit, where no earthly cataclysm, dictator, or animal could reach or destroy it. Only a generation capable of space travel could retrieve it, since previous generations, lacking space technology, would have considered its message as mythology. The problem remained: how to ensure that future generations would seek this capsule? Not knowing of its existence, they would not seek it. That is why the ancestors were told to place the sacred sites exactly in certain positions, creating a large-scale geometric pattern that would arouse curiosity and questions in the future. These great stone lines and geometrically

82

aligned sites served to stimulate future generations to wonder how such precision could be possible without advanced technology. This method of preserving knowledge through imposing and mysterious structures ensured that once humanity gained the ability to explore space, it would be ready to rediscover and understand the message left by extraterrestrials. Today, with space technology available, it would be relatively simple to verify the presence of an ancient artificial satellite in orbit, but no one has yet undertaken this search, as the scientific community tends to first seek more plausible natural explanations for any anomaly. In summary, ley lines, megalithic structures, and sacred sites are not natural arrangements but human creations made to honor the gods, according to their instructions, who were actually extraterrestrial visitors. These sites form a geometric pattern that cannot be casually observed with the naked eye, demonstrating an intentionality and precision that suggest extraterrestrial influence and advanced technology. This targeted arrangement of sites was intended to ensure that over time, humanity would come to question its own origin and the reached capabilities, eventually leading to the discovery of an extraterrestrial time capsule that could provide definitive answers about our cosmic past.

Imagine when, in a remote age, an ancient Greek priest faced the challenge of positioning a new temple. The decision could not be made casually, especially considering that between one site and another there were mountains and vast stretches of sea, like the one that separates Delphi from the island of Crete. The choice of these precise locations could not rely solely on human sight; someone had to provide precise directions. It is argued that such indications came from extraterrestrials, described in mythologies as deities. These sacred places, embedded in the fabric of time since the Stone Age, have remained unchanged for millennia, testimony to an immutable tradition. Modern literature offers further insights into this extraordinary network of geometrically connected sites on a global scale. An example is the work of New Zealand pilot Bruce Cathie, who explored the concept of a global grid connecting ancient sites through lines that extend across the planet, from distant places like Peru to Easter Island. Although these researches are outside the author's personal studies, Cathie's books on the market vigorously support the idea that all geometries are connected, an idea further strengthened through the observation of the so-called ley lines in Europe. These ley lines, or sacred lines, are revealed through a detailed examination of the distances and alignments between the sites, which can be verified using simple tools like a compass. The extraterrestrials, whom the ancients identified as deities, would have imparted precise instructions to our prehistoric ancestors on where to erect their temples. The reason behind this meticulous choice lies in the awareness that future generations, equipped with flying capabilities and advanced measuring instruments, would recognize the impossibility that such geometric patterns were the result of chance. The realization of these structures according to precise geometric schemes had not only the purpose of venerating the deities but also of planting seeds of curiosity in future minds, prompting them to question the origin and meaning of such alignments. These questions would become the catalyst for further investigation into the presence and extraterrestrial influence on Earth. In summary, the geometric arrangement of sacred sites was an encrypted message, intended to be deciphered only by a civilization capable of space travel, a civilization that might finally seek and, perhaps, find a time capsule left by extraterrestrials, an artifact containing concrete evidence of their visit and interaction with our planet. This perspective transforms ley lines and ancient sites from mere relics of the past into keys to understanding our true cosmic heritage.

MYSTERIES OF TIKAL: THE DESCENDED GODS AND THE TIMELESS MAYAN CITIES

The Maya are a cultural group living in Central America and, like many ancient civilizations, they possess a rich mythology that includes deities and sorcerers from outer space. Among the known Maya cities, Tikal, located in present-day Guatemala, is considered the oldest, founded around a thousand years before Christ. This makes it older than ancient Rome in Europe, which was founded in 700 BC. What is striking about Tikal is its location in an area devoid of direct water sources, a detail that challenges conventional explanations, as human groups generally settle in places where water is easily accessible for drinking, working, and building. However, in Tikal, there are neither rivers nor streams nearby; the nearest water is Lake Petén, located about 40 kilometers away. This lack raises significant questions: why would the Maya have chosen to found their largest and oldest city in a place without immediately available water? One possible explanation lies in the analysis of pilgrimage sites in the modern world, such as Fatima in Portugal, Lourdes in France, and Guadalupe in Mexico, where it is believed that divine figures appeared, making these places sacred. Similarly, archaeologists have discovered at Tikal a Maya inscription stating: "here the gods descended from the sky." This suggests that the site selection may have been influenced by events or visions considered sacred, prompting the Maya to build in a place designated as sacred despite practical challenges. To compensate for the lack of water, the Maya had to create sophisticated drainage systems to transport water from distant sources to Tikal. The city is home to over 60 pyramids, many of which are oriented according to precise astronomical coordinates, suggesting that they served not only as tombs, like the Egyptian pyramids, but also had a ceremonial or astronomical-religious function, perhaps to connect with the stars or observe the sky. The stelae of Tikal, stone blocks about two and a half meters high engraved with images and inscriptions, offer further clues about the nature and origin of these deities. One of these stelae portrays what is believed to be the oldest deity of Tikal: the image shows a headless human figure, dressed unusually with footwear resembling that of astronauts rather than simple sandals or bare feet, typical of the Maya. Additionally, a spiral object descends into a basket or box, suggesting unfamiliar symbolism or technologies. These details reinforce the hypothesis that Tikal was not just an urban center, but a place of deep religious and cosmic significance, built where the Maya believed that the gods, perhaps extraterrestrial visitors, descended to Earth. This interpretation opens up new perspectives on understanding the relationship between ancient Maya constructions and their cosmological beliefs, indicating that Tikal may have been a kind of portal between heaven and earth, a sacred place where heaven and earth met.

The city of Tulum, located on the Caribbean Sea, is one of the cities near Tikal, famous for its dedication to sky-descended deities. Every temple in Tulum depicts a descending deity, visible in sculptures showing humanoid figures with splayed legs, almost as if lying on sleds or boxes, in the process of landing from the sky. These depictions are interpreted by modern archaeologists as "beast gods," a designation that raises some perplexity given the clear human form with technological attributes, often depicted with wings and devices on the head, also visible in other Maya sites like Chichen Itza. These figures are closely associated with Quetzalcoatl, one of the most revered deities by the Maya, known for coming from the morning star and for teaching humans astronomy and construction techniques, among other knowledge. Before leaving Earth, Quetzalcoatl, also known as Kukulkan depending on the regions, promised to return. Despite evidence of humanoid figures with advanced technologies, many archaeologists remain skeptical of interpreting these beings as extraterrestrial visitors, preferring more conventional and less controversial explanations. At Tikal and Chichen Itza, numerous heads of these deities have been found, complete with helmets and breathing devices suggesting the use of filters to protect against terrestrial bacteria and viruses, an indication that these figures may not be native to our planet. This technology, though rudimentary compared to Egyptian standards, which used huge stone blocks for their constructions, demonstrates significant advancement: the pyramids in Central America, while built with smaller blocks, are richly decorated with engravings representing these descendant gods, unlike the Egyptian pyramids, devoid of internal decorations. This contrast between the structural grandeur of the Egyptian pyramids and

88

the intensity of the depictions in the Central American pyramids raises questions about their function and the knowledge of the peoples who built them. The descending deities, represented with clear technology on them, indicate a possible connection with visitors from other worlds, an idea that the modern archaeological community may need to consider more seriously in the future.

The pyramid of Chichen Itza in Mexico is an absolutely extraordinary site, distinguished by its unique structure composed of nine descending steps. This astronomically calibrated arrangement allows, every March 21, to witness a spectacular phenomenon: at dawn, the orientation and structure of the pyramid create a play of lights and shadows that draw a figure of a winged serpent, the "feathered serpent," descending along the steps of the pyramid. An opposite phenomenon occurs on September 21, when at sunset the shadow seems to ascend the steps until it disappears. This representation is interpreted as a demonstration that a deity descended, taught humans, and promised to return. The figure of the god Quetzalcoatl, or Kukulcan, is central in Maya mythology; represented as a winged serpent, it suggests that the ancient Maya may have interpreted visions of flying machines resembling serpents, attributing divine characteristics to them. This connection between the deity and flight is found in the natural religiosity of the Maya, who initially feared natural events like lightning and earthquakes but then worshipped these winged entities as celestial masters. Every culture establishes its own calendar with a significant start date. For the Maya, the calendar begins on August 14, 3114 BC, a date that does not correspond to the known archaeological existence of the Maya themselves, suggesting that this date may derive from events related to ancestors or gods. About 450 years ago, Spanish conquistadors destroyed almost all written records of the Maya, except for three important codices that survive today in Dresden, Madrid, and Paris. Despite the difficulties in interpreting these documents, the Dresden Codex confirms the beginning of the Maya calendar in 3114 BC, highlighting the importance of this date that coincides with the descent of the gods, according to reconstructed accounts. This approach to the calendar and the origin of time, which directly links chronology to divine descent, is a distinctive trait that permeates Maya cosmology, where time and celestial events are intimately connected to divine activities and manifestations, showing a deep interaction between heaven and earth that shaped the culture and beliefs of this ancient civilization.

Let's imagine a scenario in which, following a global conflict, all Bibles are destroyed. Christian priests, knowing the texts by heart, gather in secret places to transcribe them anew. This historical parallel reflects what happened in Central America after the destruction of the Maya scriptures. The Maya priests, taking refuge in hidden places, began to document the ancient narratives again. These new manuscripts are known as the Books of Chilambalam. In the fifth volume of Chilambalam, a priest explains the origin of the Maya calendar, which begins on August 14, 3114 BC, the day when, according to their beliefs, the gods descended from the sky. This date marks the beginning of an important era for the Maya. The Maya calendar also predicts an end date, which many had interpreted as the day the world would end, in 2012. However, none of the ancient Maya scriptures actually predicted the end of the world for that date; rather, they indicated the return of the gods. The discrepancy between the expectations for 2012 and the lack of significant events has raised doubts about the correct interpretation of the Maya calendar in relation to our Gregorian calendar. For example, the dating of the birth of Jesus Christ is approximate, which further complicates the synchronization of the two calendars. One of the most intriguing examples of potential extraterrestrial contacts with the Maya is the archaeological site of Palenque. In 1949, Professor Alberto Ruz Lhuillier discovered a passage leading to an underground crypt under the so-called "Pyramid of Inscriptions". This staircase was blocked by debris, and it took three years to clear it. In 1952, Ruz and his team reached a triangular-shaped door, unique of its kind. Beyond this door, they discovered a room containing a monumental stone slab. Above this slab was depicted a young man who seemed to be operating the controls of a vehicle, with an unknown device at nose level, and feet positioned on pedals, giving the impression that he was driving a technologically advanced vehicle.

This image has sparked numerous interpretations, with some seeing it as evidence of advanced technology, perhaps of extraterrestrial origin, due to the precise depiction of details suggesting an advanced understanding of mechanics and aerodynamics. The

91

presence of stalactites and stalagmites in the chamber, indicating an antiquity much older than traditionally attributed to Maya civilization, adds another layer of mystery, suggesting that Palenque may have been a sacred site long before the cultural peak of the Maya. The apparent visual clarity of Pakal's tomb at Palenque fascinates anyone, but it does not completely convince archaeologists. We live in a society that values reasonableness, and science always seeks the most plausible explanation before venturing into speculation. Around this stone slab is an inscription, from which only a few words have been deciphered, including "Akal," identified as the penultimate ruler of Palenque. Archaeologists interpret Pakal's figure, depicted on the slab, as immersed in the mouth of a mythological monster rather than in a simple frame. They believe that the representation of what appears to be a tree or a stem of life emerging from his chest, but in reality, they argue that it is the stylized hair of the god of time. However, from 1952 to the present day, fourteen different interpretations of this image have been proposed. Recent studies conducted by the foremost Maya ethnographers, Professor George Stuart and his son, experts in Maya hieroglyphs, have confirmed that the image represents Pakal, but they contest the traditional interpretation. According to them, Pakal is not represented as falling into monstrous jaws; on the contrary, every detail engraved on the slab would be a reference to the universe, with Pakal leaving Earth to travel through space. This reveals that the so-called "Pyramid of Inscriptions" was originally not a tomb, but rather a celebratory monument. Below this monumental slab was discovered a tomb containing a skeleton with a mask, probably that of Pakal, despite his height of 1.81 meters, unusual for the Maya whose average heights were much lower. Archaeologists themselves are puzzled by the presence of stalactites and stalagmites up to seven meters long in the underground chamber, suggesting an antiquity of the chamber far superior to the Maya era, traditionally dated around 800 AD or, according to some sources, even 1400 AD. These natural elements indicate that the chamber could be much older, up to 5,000 years ago, long before the construction of the pyramid itself. It is hypothesized that originally there was a tomb containing a sacred figure, perhaps a god or a divine representation, immortalized in what later became a giant tombstone. This sacred site, worshipped for millennia, subsequently attracted the construction of the pyramid above the existing tomb, later identified as the Temple of Inscriptions. The pyramid, therefore, is significantly younger than the tomb it protects, suggesting a continuity of worship and veneration spanning different eras, further consolidating the sacred character and historical depth of Palenque. In every Maya city, from Tikal to Chichen Itza and beyond, the architectural and cultural landscape is deeply influenced by the representation of celestial beings. These cities are fundamentally aligned with the divine, made to honor the gods who, according to Maya belief, descended from the sky to teach humanity. Such reverence is embedded in urban structure and religious practices, underscoring a rooted anticipation for the promised return of these celestial visitors. Through various mythologies, there are accounts of gods, or extraterrestrial entities, directly

93

interacting with humans, sometimes even in intimate and genetic exchanges. However, in Maya culture, despite the widespread destruction of their scriptures by the conquistadors, the surviving records—meticulously reconstructed by the priests—do not explicitly mention such physical interactions between gods and humans as in other cultures. This absence may highlight a distinctive aspect of Maya theological narrative or may be due to gaps in the historical record left by the destruction of their texts. In the surviving narratives, the Maya attribute their advanced astronomical knowledge to these divine teachers. Their understanding of celestial bodies, especially Venus, was so precise that their astronomical calculations deviate by only about an hour over millennia, testifying to the sophistication of their cosmic teachings, which they believed were imparted by these otherworldly visitors. Furthermore, every Maya city is a tribute to these divine forces. The iconography depicting beings with helmets and other equipment, manipulative devices, and technological apparatus is common, suggesting a civilization deeply influenced by what they perceived as advanced, celestial technology. These representations often show beings using hands to operate complex tools, underscoring the Maya interpretation of their gods' interaction with technology. This widespread depiction, prevalent in Maya cities, of technological mastery and divine intervention speaks to a cultural understanding that saw their gods not as myths or abstractions but as real and influential entities in their development. These gods, as described in Maya tradition, were not mere inventions of the imagination but were real entities with abilities far beyond human understanding, leaving a lasting impact on Maya civilization. Thus, the enigmatic structures and detailed iconography found in Maya lands are not just remnants of the architectural prowess of an ancient people but are enduring symbols of their interactions with what they believed were powerful extraterrestrial forces. These interactions, deeply rooted in their cultural fabric, illustrate a civilization that saw itself directly connected to the cosmos, guided and instructed by beings from the stars.

CELESTIAL GEOGRAPHIES: TEOTIHUACAN AND THE MYSTERIES OF THE CAMINO DE LOS MUERTOS

In Central and South America, as in many other cultures around the world, tales are told of gods descending from the sky to teach humanity. One of the most significant archaeological sites, which every tourist should visit according to Daniken, is located just outside Mexico City and is known as Teotihuacan. This vast complex is famous for its imposing structures arranged along a road called the Avenue of the Dead (Caminos de los muertos), oriented north-south, with the Pyramid of the Sun and the Pyramid of the Moon dominating its ends. An American archaeologist named Hugh Alliston discovered that the arrangement of the buildings along the Avenue of the Dead reflects the order of the planets in our solar system. At the center is the Sun, followed by the planets Mercury, Venus, Earth, and Mars. Between Mars and Jupiter, Alliston noticed a surprising detail: an artificial river strewn with thousands of stones, large and small, symbolizing the asteroid belt, a detail that the builders of Teotihuacan could not have known without advanced knowledge of astronomy. In addition to the asteroid belt, the layout includes representations for each planet, including Uranus, Neptune, and even Pluto, a planet whose existence was confirmed by astronomers only in 1930. The presence of Pluto in Teotihuacan's design raises intriguing questions about how the ancient builders could have been aware of such precise details of our solar system. The arrival of

Hernando Cortés, the Spanish conquistador who invaded Central America centuries ago, brought Teotihuacan to the attention of Europeans for the first time. Upon his arrival, the site was completely covered with grass and bushes, so much so that the pyramids were hidden from view. Accompanied by the priest Bernardino de Sahagún, the first European to learn the language of the natives, Cortés explored the area. When questioning the local inhabitants about the name of the place, he was told it was called Teotihuacan, which means "the place where the gods were buried." This evocative name and the structure of the site suggest a deep reverence for the "gods" who, according to local beliefs, had a direct connection to the stars and celestial bodies, further emphasizing the cosmic and spiritual importance of Teotihuacan in pre-Columbian culture. These discoveries continue to stimulate debates and reflections on the possible extraterrestrial origin of ancient wisdom and the advanced astronomical understanding possessed by these ancestral civilizations. In modern times, just like in Egypt, small tunnels have been discovered under the Avenue of the Dead in Teotihuacan, connecting various structures of the site. These tunnels contained water droplets and were explored using robots. One of these robots stopped in front of imposing stone blocks under the Pyramid of the Sun, a finding that sparked great interest. Currently, it is not known what lies behind these stone blocks, but following the directions of Bernardino de Sahagún, the Spanish priest who first documented these places, they could be sarcophagi belonging to the gods, or, as some theorize, to extraterrestrials. Additionally, the composition of the
97

fuel used by the ancients, as revealed in some ancient Indian texts, included mica, a material with numerous remarkable qualities. A completely isolated chamber with mica was discovered at Teotihuacan, which remained inaccessible to the public for a long time. After this detail was published in a book by Erich von Daniken, the chamber was opened to public visitation. There are no clear explanations as to why an entire chamber was isolated with mica, but its properties — heat resistance, electrical insulation, and acid resistance — could indicate that it had a special function perhaps related to the fuel of the gods. This material is used today in high-temperature furnaces for its heat resistance, in computers for its insulating properties, and for its resistance to acids. Speaking of Tikal, another Maya site in Guatemala, a large sarcophagus was found under the main pyramid, believed to contain the remains of the city's founder. However, inside it, liquid mercury was discovered, another component mentioned in ancient Indian texts as part of the fuel of the vimana, the ancient flying machines. Mercury is extremely toxic and lethal if inhaled, but it can be stored in mica chambers, suggesting a possible advanced technological connection between these ancient civilizations. The dating of Teotihuacan, just outside Mexico City, remains a mystery shrouded in secrecy. Archaeological discoveries continue to challenge our current understandings and suggest surprisingly advanced astronomical and technological knowledge, which some believe may stem from contacts with extraterrestrial civilizations. These hypotheses continue to stimulate debates and research, as archaeologists and scholars try to decipher the secrets hidden in ancient monuments and their enigmatic constructions. In the deep mystery surrounding the origins of Teotihuacan, emerges the figure of a French archaeologist, Madame Lejouret, who has dedicated over fifty years to directing the excavations of the site. Through her long work, she has confirmed that despite Teotihuacan's central location in America, its pyramids do not reflect Maya architectural style. Unlike Maya pyramids, which are tower-like, those of Teotihuacan have a triangular structure reminiscent of Egyptian pyramids, suggesting a distinct builder culture. Faced with such an enigma, Madame Lejouret proposed to name this unknown culture as "Teotihuacanos", hypothesizing that the city was founded around 1000 BC, implying long-term planning spanning several generations. One of the most fascinating aspects of Teotihuacan is the layout of the city along the Camino de los Muertos, or Avenue of the Dead, which seems to reflect a model of the solar system, including a representation of the asteroid belt between Mars and Jupiter. This detail implies sophisticated astronomical knowledge, difficult to attribute without the influence of an external guide, perhaps even extraterrestrial. Similarly, in South America, at the site of Tiahuanaco in Bolivia, historical and nominative similarities with Teotihuacan emerge. Inca mythology tells of Viracocha, a celestial deity who, like other gods of ancient American civilizations, descended from the sky to teach humans. Viracocha is often described as a bearer of knowledge, particularly in the astronomical and technological fields, similar to what is reported for the deities of Teotihuacan. The presence of these narratives in geographically distant cultures strengthens the idea that ancient civilizations of Central and South America may have been influenced or instructed by extraterrestrial entities, making sites like Teotihuacan and Tiahuanaco central not only in archaeological terms, but also in the search for possible prehistoric interactions between humanity and celestial visitors. In remote Bolivia, at 4,000 meters above sea level, the Spaniards, led by the conquistador Hernando Cortés, discovered the ruins of Tiahuanaco. Next to them lay huge stone blocks that even the technologically advanced Spaniards admitted they could not move. When asked about their origin, the locals, including Inca priests, attributed the construction to celestial deities, claiming that they had been erected in a single night. This episode signals the hypothesis of the intervention of non-human forces, as the blocks were carved in andesite, a material as hard as granite, which requires particularly resistant tools to be worked with millimetric precision. The incredible construction techniques observed at Tiahuanaco suggest that the original builders possessed advanced knowledge, probably transmitted by extraterrestrial visitors. The latter would have used local resources, such as andesite blocks, applying advanced technologies to shape them precisely. The parallel with modern astronauts who could use Martian resources to build on Mars is suggestive: both scenarios imply the use of advanced technologies in alien contexts. In North America, the Hopi tribe preserves traditions that speak of figures called kachinas, which would represent ancient spiritual leaders who came to teach the ancestors. These figures are described with details that evoke a non-terrestrial origin, similarly to the

100

stories of the Kayapo in South America, who narrate about an extraordinary being called Bep Kororoti. This being, descended from the sky, demonstrated extraordinary abilities, such as immobilizing a jaguar with a simple gesture, and taught the indigenous people languages, astronomy, and agriculture. Bep Kororoti, dressed to completely cover the body, presented himself to the Kayapo as a teacher from the stars, promising to return in the future. These stories, although mythological, reflect a common theme in many indigenous cultures: the presence of celestial teachers who enriched human knowledge, especially in complex fields such as astronomy and agricultural techniques, highlighting a connection between myth and advanced technological knowledge. These teachings and their mysterious origins continue to stimulate curiosity and research, leaving open questions about who these "gods" were and where they really came from. In North America, the Hopi natives create kachina dolls in honor of the gods, a perpetual reminder of their promise to return in a distant future. These stories are also found among other tribes. For example, the Maya had an extremely precise calendar that according to their mythology was established when four deities descended from the sky. Before landing on Earth, they surrounded the planet thirteen times each, establishing the number 52 as the basis of their calendar, since four times thirteen equals fifty-two. Every fifty-two years the cycle of the Maya calendar restarts. Today, this representation of the four deities continues to be celebrated in Mexico. In front of the great Museum of Anthropology in Mexico City or at archaeological sites such as Chichen Itza and

101

Teotihuacan, visitors can observe a living representation of this mythology. Participants, dressed in colorful clothes, climb a tall pillar and tie themselves to it with ropes around their feet, then they launch themselves and turn around the pillar thirteen times each, evoking the image of the flying gods, just as described in the stories of the gods descended to Tulum and Chichen Itza. In this folkloric practice intended for tourists, the natives recreate the myth of the four gods touching the earth, symbolizing the 52-year cycle of the Maya calendar. During a visit by von Daniken to Chichen Itza, he observed a tourist under a tree watching these evolutions. The tour guide described the act as a test of courage, but it is actually much more than that: it is a living mythology, a reenactment of ancient beliefs that saw the gods as teachers who came from outer space. Every culture on Earth, past and present, venerates its gods or teachers. This happens not only among the Maya, the Inca, or in India, but in all cultures of the world. Even today, there are four or five major religions that worship their religious leaders or gods. However, the gods of the past were perceived as teachers from outer space. Maya culture, in particular, has immortalized these celestial beings in the stones of sites like Chichen Itza and Copan, where depictions of the gods descending from the sky are carved with clear evidence, a testament to veneration that spans centuries.

Now let's talk about the Maya and a place called La Venta, located in Mexico, where there is an archaeological park. Here, for example, there is a stone called the Monolith of the Dragon. Just like in

Palenque, there is depicted a human figure seated inside a dragon, apparently manipulating controls with their hands, and clearly in a flying position. There is also a large stela, a stone block about three and a half meters high, on top of which is carved a flying god with a helmet. This god is depicted with hands facing towards the humans on earth and knees bent towards the sky. Below, humans, with wide eyes, gaze towards the sky, a testament to their reverence for the gods descended from the sky. These examples exist and demonstrate that the Mayan pyramids were all astronomically connected. We talked about the Temple of the Inscriptions in Palenque, where the god Pakal is depicted in his spacecraft departing towards the universe. Even the temple itself, the pyramid, is oriented along the east-west-north axes, highlighting a strong connection with astronomy. On our planet, we have had many cultures, some of which were technically more primitive and others more advanced in technology and knowledge. The technologically more primitive cultures were not visited or influenced by extraterrestrials. The more advanced cultures in technology and knowledge, such as astronomy and mathematics, were instead visited and instructed by extraterrestrials. This is the only difference. As soon as there is contact with a teacher, culture develops differently than when there is no such contact. It's the same today with children's education; those who receive schooling learn to read and do math, while others do not. Erich von Daniken has extensively discussed all the mythologies according to which the gods, described as extraterrestrials, have promised to return one day. In all cultures of the past, as soon as

103

white men appeared, the natives initially believed they were the long-awaited gods who had returned. For example, when Francisco Pizarro, the Spanish conqueror, arrived in South America, today Peru, about 400 years ago, the natives believed he was the long-awaited god and prostrated themselves before him. The same happened in Central America: when Hernando Cortes arrived, Moctezuma, who was an educated and wealthy man, knelt before him believing he was the awaited god. Also in the South Pacific, when James Cook first arrived in Hawaii, the natives thought he was the god they had awaited. All these cultures had the expectation of the return of their gods. Honestly, not all religions can be right; some must necessarily be wrong. They are neither Jesus, nor the Mahdi, nor the Messiah or others who should return, but simply extraterrestrials. Currently, it is believed that extraterrestrials are visiting us, but in a discreet and friendly manner. They are aware of the functionality of the human brain and possess sufficient technology to manifest themselves publicly, for example in a crowded football stadium, where the cameras are already set up. However, such an explicit appearance could cause immense shock to humanity, leading to the collapse of many religions and causing millions of people to question the meaning of their existence. Religious leaders might interpret these beings as malevolent and incite to fight against them. Aware of the potential repercussions, the extraterrestrial civilization prefers to cautiously observe us, studying our language, our viruses and bacteria, as well as our arsenal, to assess if we represent a threat, especially in relation to atomic weapons. This
104

careful observation is part of a scientific program preparing for a future official encounter. Extraterrestrials desire a gradual change in the spirit of the time, so that new generations grow up with the idea of their promised return, without undergoing a collective trauma. For this reason, they use subtle signals, like crop circles. Although many of these may be artificially created, there are formations so complex and vast that they could not be counterfeited by humans in a single night. These intricate designs in the fields are not intended to frighten, but to educate. Whenever humanity encounters extraordinary phenomena, the natural reaction is to seek a scientific explanation. However, when plausible explanations are no longer sufficient to justify the breadth and complexity of these messages, mystery arises, prompting us to reflect on our loneliness in the universe and the possibility that someone, somewhere, is trying to communicate with us. In this context, while extraterrestrials learn all about us, they deliberately avoid causing a cultural shock, giving humanity at least one generation to prepare for an official encounter. This educational and non-invasive approach demonstrates a long-term strategy to gradually and peacefully integrate with our society.

CONTACT EPOCHS: EXTRATERRESTRIAL VISITS FROM ANTIQUITY TO TODAY

In human history, extraterrestrial visits have been hypothesized in various epochs, dating back millions of years, a time so remote that our current knowledge can only speculate on such events. However, archaeological evidence suggests visits in prehistoric times, around 6,000-7,000 B.C., and in periods we might define as biblical, around 2,500 B.C., periods during which there are traces that some believe could have been left by such visitors. In Egypt, one of the oldest civilizations, officially beginning around 3,000 B.C., we find references to these visitors in the accounts of Manetho, a historian of ancient Egypt. Manetho lists the deities who descended from the sky, and his chronologies extend back to around 4,000 B.C., suggesting a divine presence long before the construction of major temples and monuments. For example, the temple of Abydos, known to have been commissioned by Seti I around 1,300 B.C., is built on much older foundations, whose construction techniques surpass, according to Daniken, those of its time by far. This apparent technological regression is also observed at other archaeological sites around the world. At Machu Picchu, known as the last city of the Incas or the secret city of the Incas, archaeologists detect two distinct cultural layers: a prehistoric culture with megaliths and advanced techniques, and a subsequent, Inca culture, less refined. This site was hidden in the jungle, so much so that the Spaniards failed to find it when they conquered the region. In

106

Cusco, another famous Peruvian site, the wall of Saksaywaman shows incredibly precise stone construction techniques, attributable to a civilization far more advanced than the Incas who populated the region in later centuries. Here too, just a few meters behind the Inca wall, enormous blocks are arranged in such a way that it almost seems as if gravity was negated during their placement, as if these advanced techniques could only come from the intervention of superior entities, described in local mythologies as the ever-present "gods" descended from the stars. Extraterrestrial visits in human history have occurred on various occasions, as evidenced by archaeological and historical data. It is believed that the first visit occurred millions of years ago, a period so remote that it eludes our full understanding. Subsequently, traces of these visits date back to about 6,000 or 7,000 B.C., and further visits occurred around 2,500 B.C., a time described in various ancient texts. These events indicate that humanity has been visited at least three or four times. In Egypt, one of the oldest civilizations beginning around 3,000 B.C., the historian Manetho lists deities descended from the sky with datings dating back to at least 4,000 B.C., long before the construction of major temples. For example, the temple of Abydos, originally built around 1,300 B.C. by Seti I, was erected on much older foundations, with technology superior to that used in later periods. This implies that construction techniques evolved regressively, starting from advanced capabilities and then deteriorating over time. The temple of Seti, like other sites around the world, clearly shows that the most advanced technologies and the largest blocks were used in the earliest phases, underscoring the hypothesis of extraterrestrial intervention. This pattern is also observed in South America, for example at Machu Picchu, described as the last city of the Incas. The Spanish conquistadors failed to find the city, hidden in the jungle, but the oldest layers demonstrate a civilization and construction technologies superior to those of the subsequent Incas. Similarly, in Cusco, the famous wall of Saksaywaman reveals a skill in working stone superior to that of the Incas, with gigantic blocks worked with millimetric precision, positioned in ways that defy conventional explanations of the handling capacity of such masses. These observations lead many to believe that such technologies were the result of the influence of extraterrestrial visitors, who possessed knowledge and technological capabilities far superior to those of humans at the time. The narrative linking human history and extraterrestrial visits extends through time and space, connecting ancient civilizations through traces of advanced technologies and accounts of gods descended from the sky, suggesting a significant influence on the cultural and technological development of humanity.

Continuing the narrative, we delve into the story of Adam and Eve, which reflects the image of their celestial creators. This tale not only symbolizes an ancient belief but also relies on scientific evidence that could indicate genetic manipulations occurring in remote epochs. Our DNA, composed of trillions of sequences, could reveal traces of these artificial alterations. The majestic ruins, temples, and gigantic stones, which could not have been moved or worked with the technologies of the time, speak a language that points to a possible extraterrestrial influence, suggesting that these visitors may have taught ancient humans disciplines such as astronomy and mathematics. Critics often challenge these theories, emphasizing the diversity of life forms in the universe and ridiculing the idea that extraterrestrials may resemble us. However, the resemblance between humans and extraterrestrials is not coincidental but stems from the fact that we humans could be direct descendants of these advanced entities. This perspective explains why Erich von Daniken has repeatedly stated that he does not fear the return of extraterrestrials in our present days.

In Puma Punku, Bolivia, are the ruins of imposing structures believed to have served as a base for extraterrestrials, protecting their technologies. Although it is believed that humans transported the massive blocks, the design and underlying planning are clearly of non-terrestrial origin, showing a precise understanding of engineering and astronomy. Looking at ancient Greece, historical cities, as we have already seen, show a geometric grid connecting ancient sites through precise distances and angles, a knowledge that surpasses the understanding and capabilities of prehistoric populations. These alignments are not random but the result of sophisticated knowledge, likely imparted by cosmic visitors. In Brittany, France, the menhirs, huge erected stones, are arranged in lines forming Pythagorean triangles, a too precise arrangement to have been devised without an advanced understanding of geometry. These alignments are not coincidental and suggest widespread advanced knowledge in ancient times from those who possessed technologies superior to those of humans at the time. These examples indicate that the advanced knowledge and architectural achievements of the ancients were not only the result of human progress but were influenced, and perhaps directly imparted, by superior extraterrestrial civilizations. Evidence of these interactions is scattered around the world, in sites that defy conventional explanations and reveal a celestial connection.

Around the world, from Australia to Arizona, indigenous artistic testimonies depict drawings of deities descending from the sky, often depicted with helmets or luminous rays emanating from their headgear. These so-called "gods descended from the stars" are also known as "star blowers," indicating that these beings came from the cosmos. For example, the aborigines in the Kimberley, Australia, created rock engravings representing their gods similarly, as do the Hopi in Arizona with their rock paintings and kachina dolls, ritual figures. Even in remote places like the Sahara, we find giant drawings depicting figures that resemble astronauts, completely covered in protective suits isolating them from the air and earthly bacteria. These drawings, despite the distance and isolation of the various civilizations, share surprising similarities, suggesting that all have witnessed similar phenomena, interpreting them as visits from gods from the sky. In Japan, ancient statuettes called dogu, reminiscent of Hopi kachina dolls, show figures with similar features and clothing, although there has been no historical communication between the peoples of Japan and America. This phenomenon is repeated in Central America, in Villahermosa, Mexico, where in the Olmec park, large statues of gods with helmets are found, and also in the museum of Guatemala City, where gods with devices similar to filters placed on their noses are exhibited. These representations are consistent with episodes narrated in ancient Indian texts, where humans ask the ETs where they come from, and they invariably indicate the sky as their origin, never suggesting coming from another continent or Atlantis, for example. The variety of races and skin colors of these beings is a mystery, as there are no color photographs from that period that can confirm the details. It is possible that within the mothership, there were already different races, and that these diversities were brought to Earth. Definitive answers to these differences are hoped to be provided in the future by genetics, which could reveal further insights and confirm the extraterrestrial origin of these influences on Earth.

Around the world, major religions grow on common foundations, and key figures like Moses and Solomon, shared by Christians, Jews, and Muslims. These historical characters and their experiences with the divine, often described in terms suggesting advanced technological interventions, are interpreted, as we have seen, in ways that reflect interactions with extraterrestrial entities rather than with all-powerful and spiritual deities. For example, in the Bible and other ancient scriptures, there are stories of King Solomon possessing flying machines, used to visit the

Queen of Sheba. These descriptions, taken from texts like the "Kebra Nagast," a sacred book of Ethiopian kings, speak of these flying machines not as divine miracles but as advanced technologies. Additionally, angelic figures, often depicted with wings and described as heavenly messengers, actually physically interacted with humans, contrary to what would be expected from purely spiritual beings. The Book of Enoch, for example, tells of angels descending to Earth and engaging in relationships with humans. Another biblical episode tells of an angel descending from the sky and destroying 185,000 Assyrians in one stroke, an event that highlights the use of advanced warfare technologies rather than simple manual weapons. These accounts are echoed in similar stories in Egypt, where, for example, inscriptions in the temple of Edfu speak of Hor-Hut, a winged disk that descended from the sky to aid the pharaoh, moving at supersonic speeds to defeat enemies without being seen or heard. These narratives have also been incorporated into symbols and logos of organizations studying these phenomena, such as an object found in a tomb in Colombia, in the Tierradentro region. This object, described by archaeologists as a possible insect but revered as a sacred artifact, was worn around the neck of a tribal chief, suggesting that it was of great importance and object of veneration. Its aerodynamic shape and the fact that it was made of gold indicate that it may have been conceived to represent instead a flying object, supporting the idea that ancient civilizations sought to mimic the technologies observed and provided by extraterrestrials. These examples highlight how the notion of "gods" in ancient scriptures

112

and mythologies could have been the result of human interpretations of encounters with extraterrestrial visitors, who possessed technologies so advanced that they seemed divine to our ancestors.

During World War II, American soldiers, fighting against Japan in the Pacific Ocean, landed on several small islands, introducing unknown technologies to indigenous inhabitants. These people, never having seen an airplane, did not understand the functionality of such, such as engines or propellers. After the departure of the Americans, the indigenous people began to build replicas of airplanes out of wood and straw, imitating what they had observed without understanding their substance. This phenomenon is known as "cargo cult," a term that describes how native cultures mimic modern objects in a ritual context, believing that these objects possess special powers or connections with the divine. Similarly, the object found on a tribal chief in Colombia, worn as a symbol of veneration and power, represents another example of cargo cult. The indigenous, seeing the flying objects of the strangers, perceived them as divine manifestations and attempted to replicate them to attract similar favors or powers. This dynamic suggests a broader reflection on the nature of divinity and human interpretations of gods. While modern religions worship figures perceived as omnipotent and spiritual, historical and archaeological evidence suggests that many of these "deities" could have been advanced beings from other worlds, interpreted as divine by the ancients due to their superior technologies. Ultimately, we must distinguish between the notion of a universal

God, a spiritual and timeless entity that permeates everything, and the "gods" described in mythologies and sacred books, which may have been extraterrestrial visitors. This distinction helps us better understand our past and reconsider our current religious beliefs in light of possible misinterpretations of historical encounters with advanced beings from other worlds.

DEITIES AMONG THE STARS: THE QUEST FOR OUR COSMIC ORIGINS

In ancient times, humanity made contact with extraterrestrial beings, often asking them where they came from, as we know from Indian scriptures. The gods, in response, simply pointed to the sky. Sometimes, they also uttered names or words that held no meaning for us. This demonstrates how vast and mysterious the universe can be, a place without boundaries where a single intelligent society might feel isolated, wondering if other forms of intelligent life exist. For example, sending an electromagnetic signal into space could take a millennium before receiving a response, rendering that type of communication ineffective. To truly understand the universe, its composition, expansion, and spirit, it's essential for intelligent societies to spread within close proximity to each other. This would allow for rapid interactions, such as querying a nearby solar system, just four light-years away, about their contacts and knowledge. Perhaps this spreading of intelligence was the goal of the ancient gods, who came to Earth to multiply our intelligence. Curiosity is an integral part of every form of intelligence; without it, there is no development or progress. It's curiosity that propelled us to the Moon and Mars, and will drive us further, to other solar systems. This drive for discovery is etched into our genes by extraterrestrials. Through curiosity, we will discover that the universe is populated by countless forms of intelligent life, many of which are surprisingly similar to us. It might be that there are intelligences

entirely comprehensible to us. We can imagine incredible things, such as flying elephants visiting planets inhabited by other flying elephants. It's an inevitable logic, a force of nature that we cannot alter. Imagine us humans, capable of traveling through space for greater distances: where would we go? Our scientific community would convene to decide the destination. Should we go to Jupiter? No, its gravity would kill us immediately. And to Mercury? No, it's too close to the Sun, with surface temperatures of about 500 degrees Celsius. We would seek a planet with conditions similar to Earth because we want to survive and use our tools in a familiar environment. This same process likely occurred for extraterrestrials; their home planet must not have been too different from ours, or else they couldn't have survived here. Today, astronomers discover new planetary systems almost daily, and we must identify those closest to us, from which they likely originate. If an ethnologist visits a tribe, they try to help without transmitting potentially dangerous knowledge such as building weapons or cars, given the lack of basic resources like electricity or metals. Instead, they offer curiosity and new genes, stimulating intelligence and autonomous development. In the universal context, time is relative; it took us thousands of years to develop our technologically advanced society, not by coincidence, but driven by the curiosity inherent in us. We will recognize extraterrestrials because they resemble us and are much more technologically advanced than us. If they weren't so advanced, they could never have reached us. Despite astronomical distances measured in light-years and Einstein's theory of relativity excluding
116

speeds faster than light, there must be modes of travel that surpass these limits. Extraterrestrials are not primitive entities bent on destruction, as sometimes depicted in science fiction; they are wise, peaceful, understanding, and benevolent beings, not simple monsters thirsting for conquest. Professor John Mack, a lecturer at Harvard University, devoted himself to the study of extraterrestrial abductions. Daniken had the opportunity to meet him and spend time with him. During one of their conversations, Daniken asked him how many types of extraterrestrials existed in the universe. His answer was that there are hundreds of thousands of different forms of extraterrestrial life, some of which are humanoid. It's likely that humanity will primarily encounter forms most similar to us, but the existence of a vast number of other forms remains largely unknown. The universe, in its vastness, surely hosts multiple forms of intelligent life. Without this variety, it would be impossible to establish contacts and learn from these other civilizations. The mission of extraterrestrials to spread intelligence in the universe is motivated by the need to enrich and expand the possibilities of interaction and learning. In the universe, there may exist both benevolent and malevolent entities, just as among humans there are good and bad people, intelligent and less wise. However, it's likely that in the grand scheme of things, positive forces prevail over negative ones. Malevolent individuals aiming only to destroy have no sustainable logic, as humans are not a source of nourishment for them, and it wouldn't make sense for them to want to eliminate us. Intelligent species capable of traveling at the speed of light over long distances are generally benevolent, in von Daniken's personal opinion. Their advanced technology is not used to subjugate or destroy but to explore and possibly assist. On our planet, we know and interact with many different cultures, some of which still live in conditions similar to those of the Stone Age, such as in certain areas of the Amazon. However, none of these cultures are enslaved by extraterrestrials, debunking the myth that they may have been used as slaves in the past. This view offers a reassuring perspective and promotes the idea of a universe inhabited by entities that, despite vast distances and differences, might share with us not only technology but also fundamental ethical principles. Zecharia Sitchin, who passed away some years ago, argued that thousands of years ago extraterrestrials, the Annunaki, used humans as slaves. This theory seemed to make sense, as extraterrestrials exploited human labor and work. However, today, this perception has changed. Earthly cultures are well known and constantly observed thanks to satellites; cultural visits confirm that no population is enslaved by extraterrestrials. An interesting point: Erich von Daniken recounts having dreams in which he was visited by ETs or in which he himself visited ETs. These dreams were incredibly vivid and fantastic. In one of these dreams, his sister entered his room to wake him up, but soon he realized he was still in a dream. In this dream, UFOs of various shapes appeared, and strange creatures emerged from them, creating confusion and fear among people who didn't understand them. He, however, understood their language and could calm others, telling them not to shoot and to remain calm because he could communicate with the ETs, as if it

118

were his mother tongue. In another dream, he saw himself as a fighter pilot, shot down and killed, but at the same instant, he found himself in a room that was not on Earth, surrounded by beings who spoke a language different from his Swiss German, but who understood him perfectly. A voice told him that he had returned once again, that they could hear him and understand him. Another voice, very gently, told him that he had to return to his planet because his mission was not yet complete. Upon waking, he ardently wished to continue that dream, feeling that it was not just a dream but something deeper and more significant. In his dreams, Erich von Däniken believed he had experienced an encounter in another dimension, not just a simple dream. It was too realistic; he felt every sensation, perceived every smell, and some of these entities touched him with love, very gently. For him, it was much more than a dream. According to von Däniken, every form of energy that we perceive or that speaks to us must be extraterrestrial, as we haven't developed such forms of energy ourselves. Despite the human brain and consciousness allowing us to think and imagine, von Däniken hypothesizes the existence of spiritual beings, suggesting that humanity is not the pinnacle of evolution or the supreme creation. This belief is not influenced by religions but emerges from the logic of his thinking. Governments and religious institutions, according to von Däniken, have no choice but to reveal these truths. First, because the information is already a part of us, and genetics will bring it to public knowledge. Second, because space probes will provide us with evidence. For example, years ago, NASA sent a probe towards the asteroid belt, composed of hundreds of thousands of blocks, including the large asteroid Ceres, with a diameter of 930 kilometers, almost considered a small moon. Images sent from Ceres show rectangular formations on the surface, suggesting ancient and non-natural interventions. Today, probes are also active on Mars, with rovers like Curiosity exploring the planet and sending images showing anomalous structures on the Martian surface. These observations call into question conventional scientific explanations and lead to a reconsideration of many of our religious beliefs. Von Däniken argues that our understanding of gods and spiritual practices is actually based on mistaken interpretations of contacts with extraterrestrial entities. This awareness, according to him, could cause us to lose our life foundations, revealing that our beliefs and prayers are dedicated not to spiritual deities but to technologically advanced visitors from other worlds. Extraterrestrials are technologically advanced compared to humans and consider them primitive. To avoid initial shock, they chose to communicate through delicate means, such as crop circles, rather than more direct and potentially traumatic methods. This caution is shared by the scientific community and sometimes even by governments, which prefer to proceed gradually in disclosing such information. Erik von Däniken, in this context, has carried out his work as a lecturer, illustrating his view of the ancient world and his encounters with various professional figures who have confirmed his theories, although not always publicly. About a hundred years ago, in Fatima, Portugal, 70,000 people witnessed what the church described as a miracle of the sun, but which von

120

Däniken interprets as a visit from a UFO. During this event, a girl named Lucia received a message intended for the Pope, who, however, chose not to publish it in 1960, fearing to create panic among the population. Journalists speculated that the message might announce a world war, but the Bishop of Leira clarified that the content related to faith and did not foresee imminent catastrophes. According to von Däniken, the message did not come from the Virgin Mary but from extraterrestrials, who in 1970 assessed human technology as insufficient for effective global communication, deciding to postpone further direct contact. The message would have greeted humanity, reassuring it about the presence of other civilizations in the universe and promising future visits. The Church's silence on this message is seen by von Däniken as confirmation of its extraterrestrial origin, despite the expectation for a new "apparition," which is hoped to occur within the centenary of the original event. All popes since 1960 are aware of the message, but none of them has disclosed it to the public. There are many speculations, often contradictory. It is said that some popes have spread false information about Fatima. About thirty years ago, Erich recalls, during a secret visit to the Space Command located in a Colorado mountain, he realized that everything surrounding the Earth was observed there. During that visit, he was shown a Soyuz satellite, specifying its exact position above the United States. So, he decided to ask the responsible officials of the Space Command if they had ever observed UFOs, and the answer was affirmative; the UFOs displayed incredible speeds and maneuvers, such as rectangular ones, impossible to imitate. Despite

121

these observations, the information has never been made public. There is also discussion of the existence of entities from other dimensions. Current human knowledge may be insufficient to fully understand these phenomena, but it is hypothesized that, in a distant evolutionary future, humanity may no longer need the physical body, gradually transforming into pure spiritual intelligences. This perspective, the result of reflections and speculations on the existence of beings capable of surpassing great spatial distances in spiritual form, appears plausible and sensible.

DIVINE REVELATION: REFLECTIONS AND DOUBTS ON FAITH

Erich von Däniken received a strictly Catholic education in Switzerland, and during his youth, he is still deeply faithful to God. Even today, he considers himself a fervent believer, but as a young man, he had precise expectations of what God should be: infallible, omnipotent, and ubiquitous, without the need for any means to move from one point to another. These notions were instilled in him since he was 15 or 16 years old, while attending a Catholic school run by Jesuits, where he learned Latin and Greek and translated parts of the Bible from one language to another. Over time, however, he began to notice inconsistencies between the image of God he had been taught and that described in the Bible, where God sometimes appears to err and use means of transportation, as described by the prophet Ezekiel, and even repent of his creations, deciding to destroy humanity after realizing its sins. These doubts about his Catholic education led him to explore other religious traditions, such as Hindu mythologies, and to seek out ancient texts such as the Book of Enoch, which was recommended to him by his university professors due to his growing doubts about religion. At 17, reading Enoch deeply affected him: the text speaks of fallen angels, guardians of heaven, and sexual interactions between humans and deities, a narrative that challenged all his previous understanding of the divine. Raised in a family of hotel managers, Von Däniken had always lived in a hotel environment, working in various roles such as waiter, receptionist, and bartender, learning in the field everything there is to know about running a successful business. These experiences helped him develop a keen perception of hotel activities and a strong work ethic. Years later, while serving as general manager of a five-star hotel in Davos, he began writing what would become his most famous book, "Chariots of the Gods," inspired by the idea that many historical and religious misunderstandings could be interpreted as visits from extraterrestrial beings. During the 1960s, while still working as a waiter, von Däniken had already begun to explore these theories by writing for the magazine "Neues Europa" and publishing articles on mysterious topics related to the Bible. In 1964, four years before the publication of "Chariots of the Gods," he published a two-page article in a German-language Canadian newspaper, "Der Nordwesten," titled "Were the Gods of the Bible Astronauts?" This article represented his initial reflections on the theme that would later define his career, suggesting that the gods mentioned in the Scriptures might have been alien astronauts. This provocative premise served as a springboard for his future work as a writer and researcher in the field of mysterious archaeology. Erich von Däniken, raised in a family of hotel managers, had a habit of working in hospitality establishments during the summer and winter seasons. In his free time, however, he used to travel, driven by his passion for the archaeological mysteries he studied thoroughly before each visit to historical sites. Already at the age of 19, thanks to an invitation from an Egyptian schoolmate, he had his first experience in Egypt, visiting the pyramids and the ancient caves of Saqqara. These experiences greatly enriched his knowledge in the field, so much so that he often discussed them with hotel guests, where he worked as a manager. His deep immersion in these themes led him to write "Chariots of the Gods" (The Chariots of the Gods) in his spare time, after working hours. Despite having completed a 235-page manuscript, when he sent it to twenty German publishers, all rejected it, deeming it unsuitable for their publications. However, a fortunate encounter with the editor-in-chief of the prestigious German magazine "Die Zeit" during his hotel work led to a turning point. This editor, recognizing the potential in von Däniken's work despite its controversial nature, decided to help him. The next day, he called a colleague describing the book as a mad work of a young man, not a madman, convincing him to give the author a chance. The book was then first published in Switzerland in February 1968, under the German title "Erinnerungen an die Zukunft" (Memories of the Future), emphasizing the idea that extraterrestrials had visited humanity and that we, in turn, would explore other solar systems in the future. This non-traditional view of the historical events described in the Bible, such as Ezekiel's account mentioning a "chariot," prompted the British publisher to choose the title "Chariots of the Gods" for the English-language edition, further emphasizing von Däniken's ancient astronaut hypothesis. In Switzerland, one of the leading periodicals called "Die Weltwoche" began publishing the German version of Erich von Däniken's book "Chariots of the Gods." This made the book a bestseller even before it was available on the market.

125

During that time, von Däniken had already delved into texts such as the Mahabharata and the Book of Enoch, coming to the conclusion that the gods could be astronauts from other solar systems. He believed he was the first to formulate these ideas, but shortly after the book was published, he received letters referring to science fiction authors who had speculated similar ideas, suggesting that astronauts could be seen as gods on other worlds. These discoveries did not discourage von Däniken; on the contrary, he endeavored to take his theories seriously, presenting them as facts rather than fiction. To this end, he cited all the sources from which he had drawn inspiration for his questions and answers in the book. Despite being new to the publishing field and not fully accustomed to the intricacies of the writer's profession, his German publisher found a British publisher for "Chariots of the Gods." The latter sold the publishing rights to a New York publisher, Putnams & Sons, which in turn sold the rights to paperback editions to another American publishing house. About 8 million copies of the paperback version were sold, but von Däniken received only a small portion of the proceeds due to the rights divisions among publishers. Despite the success, von Däniken faced numerous criticisms, especially from archaeologists and theologians, who accused him of disturbing established beliefs and presenting unfounded scientific theories. A notable example was the book "Crash to the Chariot" written by Prof. Dr. Clifford Wilson, who initially presented himself as an archaeologist critical of von Däniken's theories, but later turned out to be a minister and priest, highlighting how much of the opposition came from a

126

religious context. Years later, an archaeologist who had harshly criticized von Däniken for his interpretations of the tomb of Palenque wrote a letter of apology, admitting he had been wrong and asking for forgiveness before his death. Von Däniken, with great magnanimity, accepted the apologies, ending a long-standing dispute that had lasted decades, thus demonstrating his openness to dialogue and reconciliation.

For decades, none of Erich von Däniken's books, including the famous "Chariots of the Gods," were published in the countries of the communist bloc. This changed about ten years ago when von Däniken visited Poland and met a professor who expressed the common opinion of the communist regime regarding Darwin's theory of evolution: everything evolves on its own, there is no need for a god. The professor criticized von Däniken for introducing new deities in the form of extraterrestrials, considering his ideas a modern heresy. Despite these initial criticisms, the situation has changed radically in recent years. Now von Däniken's books are available in Poland, Romania, and even in China. During his visits to these countries, von Däniken is often called upon to sign copies of his books and hold lectures, which generate great enthusiasm and participation. Von Däniken loves open dialogue with his critics, firmly believing that honest criticism can lead to mutual understanding. On many occasions, after hours of discussions, critics admit to being unaware of the texts cited by von Däniken and acknowledge the value of his research. Since "Chariots of the Gods," von Däniken has written another 40 books, with global sales reaching 72 million copies. The author argues that humanity occupies a unique position in the universe, seen from both a religious and scientific perspective. However, his view has changed over time: from a perception of absolute uniqueness to a more humble awareness of our modest position in the universe. This change in perspective is partly due to his interpretation of ancient religious texts, such as the Book of Enoch, which describes firsthand encounters of the author with celestial beings and is not included in the canonical Bible. According to von Däniken, the Book of Enoch is not only a mythological text but a direct testimony of interactions with deities, which he interprets as contacts with extraterrestrial visitors. This reinterpretation of ancient texts has led von Däniken to challenge traditional interpretations and promote a new understanding of our past and humanity's role in the universe. In the context of Indian Vedic mythology, the Mahabharata, and particularly the Drona Parva, describe events that leave modern readers speechless. The Drona Parva explicitly speaks of three cities suspended in the firmament, carefully observed by humans. These cities, with their various towers, seem to be part of a story that transcends traditional imagination. In the same section, there are accounts of atomic explosions that occurred in a remote past, which would have devastated entire cities and burned elephants, a detail that arouses astonishment and reflections on the possible advanced technology of ancient civilizations. One of the most extraordinary discoveries that profoundly influenced Erich von Däniken is the tomb of Palenque in Mexico. As already reported elsewhere in this book, during his visit, von

Däniken photographed the famous sarcophagus showing a seated man in a capsule, in a pose reminiscent of that of a racing motorcycle pilot, with one hand seemingly manipulating controls and a mask on his nose, all framed by a flame that seems to connect the device. It is a famous image and this image profoundly affected von Däniken, since the stone slab was carved about 2,600 years ago. The Temple of Inscriptions, where this tomb is located, officially dated around 600 A.D., would not be so ancient, but the presence of stalactites and stalagmites in its depths suggests that the underlying tomb could be much older, dating back over 2,500 years.

About thirty years ago, von Däniken met a young man in Germany who claimed to have had a close encounter with UFOs. This young man, described as extremely reliable, told von Däniken that he had been aboard a UFO. Believing him to be trustworthy and serious, Erich asked him to deliver a message to the extraterrestrials, expressing his desire for a personal encounter with them. Additionally, von Däniken wanted to ask them questions about the origin of the universe, their religion, their knowledge of the cosmic spirit, and to confirm the accuracy of his theories regarding biblical errors and other religious texts. When they met again, the young man confirmed that he had delivered the message, but revealed that the extraterrestrials feared that a direct encounter could destabilize von Däniken due to his excessive enthusiasm. He was advised to continue his work in the fields of archaeology and mythology, suggesting that within a decade the scientific community and governments would officially recognize the presence of extraterrestrial life, which had been here thousands of years ago and has now returned. Erich von Däniken predicts that significant discoveries will be revealed in the next ten years because, according to him, the key to understanding our extraterrestrial past lies in our DNA. He argues that answers may also be found on the surface of Mars, on the far side of the Moon, and on Ceres. The exceptional quality of photographic images of Mars has revealed unusual structures resembling pyramids or triangular formations, prompting further investigation. Von Däniken cites discussions with scientists proposing plausible explanations, but remains open to the possibility of even more extraordinary discoveries. During a visit to Moscow about twenty years ago, von Däniken discussed with Professor Dr. Shklovsky, then head of astronomy at the Sternberg Institute. Shklovsky shared the theory that Mars' two moons, Phobos and Deimos, which orbit unusually fast compared to the planet's rotation, could be artificial and hollow. This discussion amplifies von Däniken's hypothesis that there are non-natural artifacts in space that require further investigation. Von Däniken is motivated by the desire to change the "spirit of the times." Through his writings and research, he seeks to stimulate a global rethink of traditional interpretations of ancient texts such as the Bible and mythologies. His extensive reading of theological works, such as the 41 analyses on Ezekiel, has equipped him to challenge accepted narratives and suggest new perspectives. The author aspires to a more humble and less arrogant humanity, aware that we are just a small part of a vast universe populated by millions of forms of extraterrestrial life. This vision, von Däniken hopes, will lead to greater open-mindedness and a reconsideration of our place in the cosmos. He wants people to reflect on these new ideas to radically transform our understanding of the world and our origins. Erich von Däniken is constantly seeking new stories and is currently working on numerous books. He is particularly interested in the future potentials of genetics and the possibilities of interstellar travel, including surpassing the speed of light. Through scientific literature, he seeks to find answers to these questions and arrive at personal conclusions. His commitment includes dialogues with theologians, especially with older ones who, according to von Däniken, are more open to dialogue and less stubborn. He hopes to influence their thinking and, in some cases, believes he has succeeded. Von Däniken holds lectures worldwide, seeking to stimulate critical reflection rather than seeking consensus. He invites the public not to blindly believe what he says but to read and critically evaluate the stories he proposes. His work, "Chariots of the Gods," has had a significant impact, influencing millions of people and inspiring hundreds of other authors, such as Tellinger and Sitchin, who have explored similar mysteries about the connections between antiquity and extraterrestrial visitations. Many approach von Däniken during events to express how his theories have changed their view of life and their field of study, be it theological or archaeological. Despite advancing age, von Däniken, now eighty-two, declares himself satisfied that his mind is still active and functioning well. He is aware of mortality but is comforted by the knowledge that the organization he founded, Ramar, will continue its work. This organization connects archaeological sites around the world and allows them to be explored virtually, showing the connections between them. Von Däniken emphasizes the importance of recognizing that humanity is neither the crown of creation nor the pinnacle of evolution. He calls for greater humility and a deeper understanding of our place in a universe full of life, emphasizing that we have been and continue to be visited by extraterrestrial beings. This is a lesson von Däniken hopes to convey for the rest of his life and beyond, through the activities of his organization and the legacy of his works.

This chapter dedicated to Erich von Däniken has been crafted drawing extensively from the inspiration provided by his numerous books and interviews given over the years. The reflections and theories presented reflect the innovative spirit and depth of research that characterize von Däniken's work, who has dedicated his life to studying the possible connections between human antiquity and extraterrestrial civilizations. The information presented here is a tribute to his career and contributions, which continue to influence and stimulate debate on these fascinating topics.

BILLY CARSON: BETWEEN ANCIENT MYSTERIES AND COSMIC HORIZONS

BILLY CARSON AND THE INFLUENCE OF ANCIENT CIVILIZATIONS ON MODERN TECHNOLOGY

Billy Carson, a renowned researcher, blogger, social media manager, and founder of ForbiddenKnowledge.com, has distinguished himself through his in-depth research on ancient civilizations and their advanced technology. The author of the Amazon bestseller "Compendium of the Emerald Tablets," Carson is currently engaged in the production of a film, "Chronicles of the Anunnaki," which promises to be a significant cinematic success, produced by Dame Dash Studios. Carson's passion for the ancient and the mysterious has deep roots dating back to 1977 when, living near Opelonka Airport in Miami, he first observed an unidentified flying object that did not resemble any airplane. This observation prompted him to consult encyclopedias on aerospace at Rainbow Park Elementary, setting off a lifetime of inquiry. Through his studies, Carson has explored the possibility that ancient terrestrial civilizations possessed extremely advanced technologies, citing ancient texts that mention such technologies. His interest has particularly focused on Thoth, the ancient Atlantean high priest and son of Enki of the Anunnaki, whom we have already discussed in this book, who would have played a crucial role in disseminating human knowledge and relaunching civilization after the great flood. Thoth, also known for his symbolic representation as an ibis (a sacred bird for the Egyptians), is described as the one who brought knowledge from darkness to light, a metaphor for his role as humanity's illuminator. Thoth's influence, according to Carson, in ancient Egypt is evident in writing systems, such as hieroglyphs, and in complex practices of astronomy, astrology, and geometry. Considered the Egyptian god of magic, writing, mathematics, and science, Thoth is recognized for inventing language and writing, and only priests with adequate training could access his sacred knowledge. Thoth, the builder of the first pyramid, was one of the chosen. Thoth is believed to be the one who bestowed upon humanity writing, numbers, and the art of self-development through works of consciousness. Some considered him a historical figure later deified because of his accomplishments, while others saw him as a mythical entity from the start. Legends tell of a magical book written by Thoth containing the secrets of the gods, a book said to exist on the astral plane. It was not a physical object but something accessed through consciousness travel. This is probably one of the earliest examples of channeling, where an individual reached a particular mental state to connect with Thoth's energy, learning from this multilingual and multicoded consciousness. Thoth was not a Homo sapiens sapiens like us; according to ancient tablets, our species emerged long after Thoth's existence on Earth. He and his ilk, beings from past eras, were here millions of years ago according to Carson's research, and had developed technologies to prolong their lives by tens of thousands of years. Thoth was tasked with spreading knowledge and wisdom among humanity. He was ordered to teach all the languages of the world and to convey to civilizations how to develop various technological levels. He was also, as mentioned earlier,

135

the chief architect of pyramid structures across the planet. In the Emerald Tablets, Thoth claims to have built the Great Pyramid himself and instructed his companions to replicate what they had done worldwide. Thoth could live tens of thousands of years, which to us may seem astonishing, but Carson explains how this could occur. In short, Thoth entered the so-called "regeneration chambers" beneath the Great Pyramid, in a place called the Halls of Amenti, where his original body remained for one hundred years while he interacted in spirit with men in an avatar body. This explains his multiple identities and aspects over the eons. He continued to transfer his consciousness from one avatar body to another, regenerating the previous one or replacing it with a new one. Today, with modern technologies like cryopreservation and recent developments from Microsoft in creating a DNA hard drive capable of storing 433 petabytes of data, we are approaching the ability to transfer consciousness into a digital storage capacity. With current research on stem cells, it is possible to create a clone from a person's skin cell and transfer consciousness into this new avatar, opening incredible avenues for the future of medicine and human identity.

The Emerald Tablets are considered one of the most mysterious and revered scriptures of antiquity, directly authored by Thoth. This detail is particularly notable because, in most ancient cultures, it was scribes who wrote texts on behalf of kings or deities. Thoth, a central figure in Egyptian mythology, is believed to be the author of these texts with the intent of guiding

humanity towards a new golden age, akin to a return to light, comparable to the Ten Commandments. The Tablets, believed to predate biblical texts by tens of thousands of years, bear striking similarities to some words in the New Testament. Thoth is said to have traveled extensively, acquiring knowledge from mystery schools and teaching the art of reincarnation and healing, deeply influencing biblical figures like Moses, who, according to some theories, received the Forty-Two Laws of Maat instead of the Ten Commandments. These teachings were then simplified and incorporated into the modern Bible. Currently, it is believed that the original Tablets are secretly kept in the vast underground archives of the Vatican. Over the centuries, eminent figures such as Saint Thomas Aquinas, the Queen of Sheba, and Sir Isaac Newton have studied and translated the Emerald Tablets, making this knowledge accessible to a wider audience. Additionally, Thoth is believed to have been the founder of several 'Halls of Records,' secret areas where he collected all his teachings and advanced knowledge. Recently, advanced research and scanning techniques, such as muon scanning, have revealed the possible existence of such hidden chambers within the Great Pyramid and beneath the Giza Sphinx. These places may contain ancient texts offering profound wisdom destined to be revealed and shared with humanity in the present era. However, it is feared that many of these discoveries have been occulted or destroyed by powerful elites, eager to keep such esoteric knowledge away from the general public. Ancient civilizations are believed to have possessed highly advanced technological knowledge, including zero-point energy
137

devices and flying machines. Recent investigations also suggest the existence of a massive object hidden under the Sphinx's paw, which some believe could be one of these ancient spacecraft. Despite Carson's attempts to broadcast scans of these discoveries live to inform the wider public, a "powerful external intervention" at the last moment prevented Carson from disseminating the scanned images, perpetuating the mystery surrounding the true technological capabilities of the past. The figure of Thoth, often depicted with hybrid features between man and bird, symbolizes his ability to delve into the 'darkness' to bring knowledge to light. This image is metaphorically linked to the behavior of the ibis, a bird that must plunge its beak deeply into the mud to feed. According to legends, Thoth played a crucial role in educating humanity, teaching various languages and technologies, and even, as we have seen, in the construction of the great pyramids, as suggested by the Emerald Tablets. Narratives describe him as a non-human being, potentially extraterrestrial, hailing from a distant star system. Ancient texts, including over a thousand tablets examined in the last twenty years, tell of star wars in the Pleiades and migrations of these beings to our solar system. This has led some modern astronomers to hypothesize the existence of a second solar system within ours, formed by a brown dwarf and our yellow sun. These revelations underscore not only the ingenuity but also the extremely long lifespan of these entities, far exceeding that of humans, endowing them with apparent immortality in the eyes of the ancients. This deep connection with the universe and their advanced technology suggest that our past may be much more intricate and interconnected than ever believed.

Zachariah Sitchin, renowned for his theories on ancient extraterrestrial civilizations, author whom we have already encountered in this book and whom we will surely encounter again in the future, has left an indelible mark on research into these subjects. Throughout his life, he faced criticisms and defamation; however, the prefaces of his books clearly explain the sources of his information, based on interpretations of texts personally deciphered by himself rather than on original translations. This approach paved the way for other researchers who found much corroboration in his theories. Speaking of the ancient civilization of the Atlanteans, it is believed that these inhabitants of Atlantis were part of the Anunnaki race, which here appears as a generic term to describe different beings from other planets and star systems. These beings, arriving on Earth in ancient times, began to develop a high-level civilization, alien to Homo sapiens, and dedicated themselves to resource extraction. However, not everything was in harmony among them: internal tensions led to conflicts, also mentioned in the biblical book of Deuteronomy, which describes how warrior deities, called Igigi, descended to Mars to fight against other Anunnaki. The destruction of Atlantis is linked to a global flood, as believed by most researchers, an event so devastating that it is presumed to have wiped out this ancient civilization. The Emerald Tablets, written post-flood, speak directly of life before this catastrophe. Another important document is the Sumerian King List, preserved at the Ashmolean Museum in Oxford, which documents pre-flood kingdoms lasting tens of thousands of years, suggesting that the inhabitants of that time had extraordinarily long lifespans. The existence of the flood is debated among those who believe it was an inevitable natural event and those who argue it was a deliberate intervention to usher in a new era on Earth, eliminating pre-existing technologies and populations. This ambivalence in historical and mythological accounts raises questions about our interpretation of ancient events and the potentially lost truths over time. Carson believes that several catastrophic floods only affected large regions of the planet, not the entire Earth. One of these, particularly devastating, Carson reports, may have been responsible for the destruction of the Atlantean civilization, presumably located in the middle of the Atlantic Ocean. Some researchers argue that the cause could have been a meteoric swarm, triggered by internal tensions among the Atlanteans, who had begun mating with cloned humanoids, thereby creating the Nephilim. This intermixing of races would have led to jealousy and conflicts, culminating in a large-scale conflict that ultimately led the Atlanteans to decide to completely reset civilization. According to legends, some survivors of Atlantis fled to Egypt, contributing to the construction of the Great Pyramids. These Atlanteans, including Thoth, son of Enki, took refuge in a safe place outside the planet after the flood. The Emerald Tablets tell of how Thoth and his crew left Earth aboard a large spacecraft, only to return when the floodwaters receded. Upon their return, they found Earth's populations in a primitive and hostile state, but Thoth used advanced technologies to neutralize threats without causing deaths, a method reminiscent of modern non-lethal technologies used by military forces to disperse crowds. Thoth's account of returning to Earth, observing the planet from afar disappear and then reappear, suggests that their technology was significantly more advanced than current technology. These ancient texts offer striking parallels with the biblical account of Noah, who, according to alternative interpretations, may have been not the builder of an ark, but rather the guardian of a DNA bank. This theory is supported by other ancient legends, such as the Epic of Gilgamesh, which describe Noah's ark as an underwater structure rather than a traditional ship. It is said that in ancient times there were genetic masters like Thoth and Enki, capable of manipulating DNA to recreate extinct animal species, a practice that attests to an advanced level of scientific knowledge. In particular, Sumerian texts describe how these ancient scientists were able to 'model' new creatures, such as sheep, which did not yet exist on our planet. This ability indicates that their understanding of biology far exceeded current knowledge, allowing them to preserve and perhaps even restart entire animal populations after global catastrophes, such as the great floods. Research on these ancient texts, Carson notes, reveals that our past is imbued with lost knowledge, which we are only now beginning to rediscover through the study of thousands of documents, from technological potential to advanced architecture. Modern technology, with its rapid advancements, offers new insights into ancient mysteries, allowing us to approach the capabilities of those distant civilizations. Ancient writings also speak of beings

141

moving among us in unconventional ways. Thoth, in the Animal Tablets, describes entities that, although living among humans, differ significantly from us, using cloned bodies or 'avatars' in which they transfer their consciousness. These beings would be capable of abandoning their original bodies to 'jump' from one avatar to another, demonstrating a control over matter and life that challenges our current scientific conceptions. Such entities, according to hypotheses, may be present not only on Earth but also on other planets. Space missions and explorations by various space agencies, such as NASA, ESA, and Roscosmos, have collected data showing anomalies at various points in our solar system, suggesting that the capabilities of these ancient civilizations may extend far beyond the boundaries of our planet. For example, radar images of Venus show structures resembling earthly cities, complete with buildings and temples, suggesting a replication of their structures on different worlds, masquerading as deities and using local populations for their labor needs. This vision reveals a complex picture of a past where the distinction between myth and technological reality is blurred, and raises profound questions about the true history of our species and its interactions with almost divine powers, whose traces intertwine through epochs and galaxies.

In recent years, it has emerged that governments are gradually disclosing information about UFOs and extraterrestrial civilizations, following a strategy of gradual disclosure. This process is allowing scholars and the public to freely access data that was once veiled in mystery. Simultaneously, mysteries related to the Great Pyramids are being explored, suggesting that the geometry of these structures not only reflects, but may actually incorporate ancient cosmic codes, connected to universal harmonies or the "music of the spheres." This idea postulates an intrinsic link between the primordial tones of the universe and the creation of form and structure in the physical world. The architect of these wonders, Thoth, is described as the genius behind their construction. Not only did he design the Great Pyramid of Giza, but he integrated into it complex measurements that correspond to the precise dimensions and position of the Earth in the solar system. This implies the use of advanced technologies that allowed for the calculation of astronomical positions with extreme precision, utilizing polar orbits rather than equatorial ones, a practice that has only recently been understood and implemented by modern science. The arrangement of the pyramids, when viewed from above, and their correspondence with a NASA interplanetary map, highlight a remarkable knowledge not only of Earth, but of the entire solar system. The mathematical precision employed in their construction suggests that the ancient Egyptians, or those on their behalf, possessed an understanding of mathematics and astronomy that profoundly reevaluates our current interpretations of their civilization. The ability to incorporate into the constructions the speed of light expressed in meters per longitude, and the correspondence of the dimensions of the structures with specific astronomical distances, indicate a surprisingly advanced level of technological and scientific sophistication. These achievements suggest that the knowledge and technologies possessed by these ancient civilizations may surpass contemporary ones in some fields, especially those related to architecture and cosmology. The extraordinary mathematics underlying the construction of the Great Pyramids of Giza continues to be a source of wonder and admiration. In particular, according to Carson, the Great Pyramid was conceived on a scale of 1:432 relative to the dimensions of the Earth, and resonates at 432 hertz, demonstrating an advanced understanding of both geometry and acoustic resonance. This synchronization is not accidental but part of a larger code that links the structure itself to fundamental cosmic principles, thus highlighting an integration between scientific and spiritual knowledge. Concurrently, in the Emerald Tablets, Thoth describes entities known as the Dark Brothers, responsible for the decline of multiple civilizations in the universe. This duality of good and evil, as described by Thoth, reflects the perennial struggle between constructive and destructive forces that influence the fate of civilizations. According to Thoth, these Dark Brothers have contributed to numerous collapses of civilizations through corruption and egocentrism, pushing entire societies towards periods of obscurantism and regression. This narrative has surprisingly modern echoes, reflecting power dynamics and control that also manifest in contemporary societies. Elites manipulate the masses for their own interests, often instigating conflicts and divisions that divert attention from real issues and enemies, a divide and conquer strategy that perpetuates the status quo of power. These entities, described by Thoth as endowed with extreme longevity and the ability to profoundly influence the

144

fortunes of human civilizations from behind the scenes, fit into a broader context of manipulation and control that runs through the history of humanity. Their ability to perpetuate themselves through the centuries and to influence social and political dynamics from the shadows is a recurring theme in theories about extraterrestrial influences and ancient knowledge held and hidden until today. Throughout history, civilizations have gone through cycles of rise and decline, known as the yuga cycles. Currently, we are in the Tetra Yuga, commonly referred to as the Silver Age, a period in which we are preparing for the return to the Golden Age. This transition is seen positively because it coincides with an extension of human lifespan, an acceleration of technological development, and the expansion of our civilization beyond earthly boundaries, bringing us closer to becoming an intergalactic civilization. However, every yuga also has its dark side. After a period of prosperity and progress, inevitably follows a decline, similar to a return to the Bronze Age, characterized by the resurgence of negative forces that Thoth describes as the Dark Brothers. These forces seem to determine a cultural and social regression, pushing humanity towards conflicts, greed, and power struggles, leading to a lowering of the level of civilization. This cycle of rise and fall has repeated several times over millions of years on our planet. According to the prophecies of the Maya, we are advancing towards the Fifth Age, another golden period. This raises a fundamental question: is it possible to break this seemingly endless cycle of yugas? The challenge that arises is whether we can maintain a high civilization without falling back into old patterns of self-destruction and regression. The search for an answer to this question has inspired Carson's book "Compendium of the Emerald Tablets," in which he explores the possibility of transcending historical cycles of rise and fall to stabilize humanity at a higher level of awareness and realization. This would not only offer us the opportunity to live in an era of sustained peace and progress but would also mark a radical change in our historical and cultural approach to the cyclicity of time and history.

In the dark fabric of global control, a phenomenon known as the "Smith Effect" emerges, reflecting how certain forces, referred to, as previously seen, as the "Dark Brothers," subtly influence the human psyche. These entities manipulate the media, news, and even our thoughts and perceptions, acting from a shadowy background that few can clearly identify. Behind the scenes, a small group of powerful families exerts almost total control, directing global events and political decisions. The "Smith Effect" occurs when everyday conversations are diverted from significant issues to more superficial topics. For example, a discussion about a television program can flow freely, but attempting to raise issues such as conspiracy theories or uncomfortable truths leads to a sudden shift in the interlocutor's attitude, taking on an almost censorious role. This change is not random but the result of subliminal programming aimed at maintaining the status quo and preventing potentially revolutionary or destabilizing ideas from spreading. For decades, since 1977, scholars have combined aerospace research with ancient texts to decipher and understand the technologies and knowledge of the past, such as those mentioned in Thoth's Emerald Tablets. This research reveals that ancient technology was surprisingly advanced, to the point of using cymatic frequencies and photonic light to materialize physical objects. Recently, modern science has begun to understand and apply these concepts, discovering, for example, how to transform light into solid matter. Sound plays a crucial role in this process. In the universe, sound frequencies not only shape physical reality but also orchestrate the intrinsic harmony of every form of life. For example, the pattern of a cheetah's spots reflects the cymatic frequencies that shape its genetic essence, a phenomenon that extends to every creature and object in the universe. This revelation supports the idea that every material form, from the smallest to the largest, is interconnected through a universal field of frequencies, suggesting a fundamental unity of all life. Understanding these dynamics can radically transform our perception of ourselves and the world, emphasizing that separation is an illusion and that, in reality, every being is intrinsically connected to the other. This profound understanding promotes universal respect and communion with all forms of life, leading us to treat others as extensions of ourselves, in an expression of collective awareness and unity that transcends individual and species boundaries. This view not only expands our understanding of the fabric of reality but also invites us to live with a deeper awareness of our role in the universe. Life is inherently more complex and extraordinary than many people can imagine. Humanity often fails to realize how powerful it is, how

147

every human being carries within them a divine energy capable of creating reality out of nothing. This process of manifestation begins with a thought, which subsequently transforms into three-dimensional reality, following a path from the mind through digital design to physical creation. The example of how a cell phone is created illustrates this concept: the initial idea, formulated in the mind, is developed into a two-dimensional drawing by a CAD designer, and then transformed into a three-dimensional object by an engineer. This process demonstrates how humans are co-creators of their own reality, shaping the material world with their ideas and thoughts. This power of creation, Carson reminds us, is often underestimated, with many people living their days almost automated, without recognizing the profound meaning and potential of their existence. Everyday life, with its routines and predictable cycles, can obscure the understanding of how deeply we are connected to the universe and how we constantly influence the reality that surrounds us. Modern science has begun to recognize these capabilities, discovering, for example, that human DNA can transmit and receive information similar to a Wi-Fi signal, suggesting that every person is constantly in communication with the world around them, even without knowing it. Ideas and inventions are not isolated but emerge from a shared field of knowledge and information, which we access through our tuning into specific frequencies of the spacetime field. This revelation opens up the possibility that, if more people were to consciously understand and utilize these capabilities, we could not only transform our everyday lives but also advance as a civilization, exploring new dimensions of reality and potentially influencing our environment in ways previously considered impossible. This raises important questions about the nature of reality and our place in the universe, challenging the traditional perception of time, space, and matter and inviting us to consider a more holistic and interconnected view of existence. The mystery schools of antiquity carefully selected individuals with particular talents, considered the elite of society, to impart to them advanced teachings intended for the greater good. With the disappearance of the gods who once guided these schools, however, the transmitted knowledge began to be manipulated and lost over the centuries. Despite modern efforts, current science has not yet been able to equal or fully understand the technologies and knowledge of the ancients. A striking example of this is the temple of Abu Simbel in Africa, which was designed to align with the solstice so that the sun's rays would illuminate the statues of the gods inside the temple. Even after moving the temple to prevent flooding, engineers failed to replicate the original alignment with precision. During World War II, the frantic search for ancient texts by figures like Adolf Hitler demonstrates an obsession with the potential of ancient knowledge, which was believed to reveal advanced technologies. This search led the Allies and the Soviets to recruit German scientists after the war, accelerating technological and space development in the West, thanks also to the contributions of individuals like Wernher von Braun. The hermetic concept "as above, so below" highlights the similarities between the macrocosm and the microcosm, suggesting that the

149

same patterns are replicated on all scales of existence. This principle manifests in various natural phenomena and can be observed by comparing biological structures with astronomical formations, which show how the same geometric and organizational patterns repeat from one scale to another. In summary, while the ancients possessed a sophisticated understanding of the world around them, interpreting and manipulating the laws of the universe with a mastery that we still seek to fully understand today, their advanced knowledge challenges us to look beyond the surface of modern scientific understandings and to seek a deeper integration between science and spirituality. There is increasingly passionate discussion in scientific circles about the theory that the reality in which we live could be holographic, suggesting that every element of the universe contains the whole within itself, a concept that reflects ancient hermetic notions of "as above, so below." Modern scientists and theorists, including Elon Musk and James Gates, are interested in these ideas, supported by the discovery that adinkra codes used in physical theories to describe the universe are similar to those used in web browsers. This parallelism suggests that the entire universe may function like a hologram, where each part reflects the whole. This view is further reinforced by the observation that information and reality itself may manifest only when necessary, similar to how it occurs in video games, where scenarios are built as the user progresses through the game. Our perception of reality, therefore, may not be immediate but mediated by a consciousness transmission that continually encodes and decodes the universe around us, proposing an existence in which time, as we perceive it, is only a part of the broader structure of the holographic universe. In this perspective, every event, every object, and every moment are interconnected and reflect a larger reality, indicating that our own existence is part of a much more complex and integrated design.

In these reflections, a vision emerges that considers our earthly reality as a projection of a more complex structure, potentially a dodecahedron located outside the known universe. This perspective is attributed to the creation by a divine entity or multiple creators, suggesting that we live in an ancestral civilization whose foundations are deeply rooted in mathematics demonstrating the existence of a creator or creators. It is hypothesized that our reality is just one layer of multiple levels of reality and universes generated by ancestor civilizations. This conception extends to the comparison with video games like "The Sims," where AI-guided avatars gain awareness, comparable to our existence in this designed universe. The theory suggests that, just as avatars in a game can create and inhabit simulated universes, we too could be part of a similar cosmos, a kind of simulation. This leads to reflecting on the illusory nature of our physical reality, where, theoretically, all the matter that constitutes the world's population could be compressed into a sugar cube. This radical view proposes a significant impact on modern religion and spiritual practices, promoting a direct connection with divinity, freed from traditional religious dogmas that tend to control rather than liberate. It is suggested that a genuine understanding of these truths could emancipate people, allowing them to realize the power and control they have over their own lives, transcending passivity towards religious and social conventions. Finally, the interpretation of Thoth's intentions, according to these theories, is that humanity has the potential not only to reach but also to surpass the level of awareness and technological capabilities attributed to him. This message from Thoth urges humanity to transcend the current darkness to elevate its awareness and civilization, aspiring to an existence based on unconditional love and light, and to advance towards an interstellar civilization capable of exploring not only our galaxy but others as well. Currently, Billy Carson is delving into the scientific aspects related to spirituality and further exploring the concept of unified physics. He is involved, as mentioned at the beginning of the chapter, in the production of a film titled "Chronicles of the Anunnaki," based on ancient texts and tablets that promise to bring to life actual galactic wars through a series of episodes. Billy hopes that his dedication and discoveries will be recognized sooner or later. One of his major concerns is artificial intelligence (AI), which, if mishandled, could pose a threat to humanity. He cites narratives about the Anunnaki, who, despite having technology to create androids, chose to create a biological servile race rather than rely on AI, for fear that the latter could self-replicate and eliminate the need for humans. However, despite these concerns, Billy remains optimistic about the future of humanity, firmly believing in our ability to overcome these challenges and evolve towards a more aware and advanced civilization, bringing us back to a golden age of consciousness and harmony.

LOST CITIES IN THE SEAS: ECHOES OF VANISHED CIVILIZATIONS

In this chapter, we will explore together various renowned researchers who will guide us through a journey of discovering lost cities beneath the seas, shedding light on their research and the historical implications of what they have found. These experts, hailing from diverse disciplines, share a common narrative that connects submerged ancient civilizations with the legends of Atlantis and other global myths.

On December 7, 2001, an article from the BBC announced the discovery of a lost city in Cuban waters. The news came from a team of explorers led by Pauline Zalitsky, a naval engineer, and her husband Paul Winesweek. In collaboration with the Cuban government, they were searching for hundreds of ships loaded with treasures dating back to the Spanish colonial era. However, what their sophisticated sonar instruments revealed turned out to be much more mysterious. Winesweek and Zalitsky had struck a deal with Fidel Castro to conduct sonar scans of the seabed around Cuba, hoping to uncover hidden treasures. The agreement included a 50-50 split of the loot with the Cuban government, a privilege no one else had ever obtained, making the venture extremely exciting. Using sonar on the seabed, however, they found not gold, but something far more incredible. They discovered astonishing architectural structures, including pyramidal buildings and long roads, all megalithic stone constructions lying off the western tip of Cuba, about half a mile below sea level, in ocean currents so strong that exploration without the best submarines was almost impossible. The results of their sonar readings clearly showed that these were ancient and complex constructions. They had even signed an exclusive agreement with National Geographic magazine to publish their discovery in the summer of 2003, but for unknown reasons, this plan never materialized. During the discovery period, Pauline Zielinski began to disclose details about the findings, revealing through her reports the use of a submarine with which she had observed sphinxes and unusual carvings on underwater rocks. These structures, as reported, could not have been above sea level for at least 11,000 years. Underwater images showed a pyramid with a change in angle halfway up, similar to the Pyramid of Djoser in Egypt, suggesting a direct link between these monuments and those in Egypt. This suggests that the Egyptian pyramids could also have been built in the same period, thus being much older than conventional archaeology has hypothesized. This discovery clearly appeared artificial and then, mysteriously, the story was suppressed. Zielinski estimated that the structures had sunk to that depth over 11,000 years ago. Interestingly, after the disclosure of their findings, the media and information networks stopped talking about it. What could they have discovered that was so relevant? Speaking of submerged cities, it confirms the hypothesis of a cyclical civilization. The question is: how far back in time do these civilizations extend? It seems that they manifest in cycles of 5,000 years, and the historical context of civilizations dating back 50,000, 60,000, 70,000 years emerges in mythologies, which may be based on more concrete facts than previously believed. If the structure found under the ocean floor sank about 11,000 years ago or more, could it be connected to the famous Atlantis? Atlantis is almost a term used casually to seek the very origin of civilization. This notion dates back to the 19th century when U.S. Congressman Ignatius Donnelly wrote a seminal work on Atlantis titled "Atlantis, the Antediluvian World." Donnelly proposed that all ancient civilizations of the Old and New Worlds, the Americas, derived from a mother civilization.

Plato, the Greek philosopher who lived around 350 B.C., suggested that Atlantis lay somewhere between the Bahamas and the Caribbean. Influenced by this theory, Ignatius Donnelly developed the idea of a mother civilization, transforming Atlantis from a submerged city into a broader concept. It is plausible that a high culture once inhabited the large islands of the Bahamas and the Caribbean, only to be annihilated by a great cataclysm, the so-called Younger Dryas event. The last ice age began about 125,000 years ago, characterized by the formation of huge ice caps over North America and Northern Europe. Despite the precise causes of the ice age still being debated among scientists, it is undeniable that a massive ice sheet, two miles thick, covered these regions. The maximum extent of the ice was reached about 21,000 years ago. With climate warming, almost to current levels, the ice began to retreat. However, suddenly, 12,800 years ago, there was a sharp reversal: a drastic global cooling reinserted the planet into a severe glaciation, marked by a vast extinction of animal species. This transformation is explained by the hypothesis of the Younger Dryas impact, put forward by a group of mainstream scientists. They argue that they found evidence that Earth was hit by several fragments of a comet. For a long time, this comet, spectacular in sight, did not impact the planet. However, 12,800 years ago, after the comet fragmented into numerous pieces, it is estimated that four large fragments hit the North American ice cap. The impact generated immense heat, enough to melt vast stretches of the ice cap and trigger floods southward. In just days or weeks after the impact, temperatures fell again, trapping the released water and plunging the world into a long period of cold and animal extinction. This period of dry ice lasted about 1,200 years, from 12,800 to 11,600 B.C. Then, another extraordinary event: suddenly, 11,600 years ago, a second massive wave of melted water flooded the world's oceans. It is likely that Earth crossed again the debris flow of the same comet, undergoing further impacts, this time completely oceanic, generating huge tidal waves and a significant amount of water vapor in the upper atmosphere, triggering rapid global warming. Large comet impacts in the oceans not only cause extraordinary tidal waves but also a massive amount of water vapor expelled into the upper atmosphere. This vapor creates a greenhouse effect that contributes to the rapid warming of the planet. It is fascinating to note that exactly 11,600 years ago, the exact time indicated by Plato for the destruction of Atlantis, Göbekli Tepe arose. This coincidence adds another layer of mystery to Graham Hancock's theories about the Younger Dryas, proposing possible confirmation through submerged megalithic structures

156

in various parts of the world like the Azores, the coasts of India, and Japan. Also noteworthy is the discovery of a megalith in the Sicilian Channel, near Malta, dating back to 9,000 years ago, suggesting that the sea level covered that area much earlier than the established dates for the temples of Malta. Some scholars, like Jack Carey, have undertaken research that could integrate with discoveries about the periodicity of the Younger Dryas. The investigations of Dr. Courtney Brown and his team of remote viewers, who identified the possible cause of the decline of advanced societies like Atlantis, suggest that the use of certain advanced technologies may have led to their ruin, even implying a warlike conflict responsible for the destruction of land masses. These results raise questions about humanity's lost unity, highlighting how it has not regrouped as before the biblical dispersion of the Tower of Babel. Plato's ancient texts, detailing the destruction of Atlantis by Zeus as punishment for human arrogance, suggest that the founders of that city were semi-divine, ruled by Poseidon. Zeus's punishment for their moral corruption was devastating. According to Joseph Campbell's collection curator, Plato's narrative may have older roots, with possible borrowings from Sumerian tales of divine conflicts, reinforcing the hypothesis of cultural syncretism in historical narratives. It is interesting to note how legends of an elevated civilization before the universal flood are present in Sumerian myths, which recall an advanced civilization and then destroyed by great floods, starting over post-event. These stories find intriguing parallels with Plato's descriptions, and thanks to the Edfu texts, it could even be hypothesized that Plato had access to documents that linked Atlantis to much older Egyptian traditions.

According to ancient interpretations, Osiris, identified with the Sumerian god Enki, left Mesopotamia to found a new civilization. Moving towards the islands of the Atlantic, called La Mata in the Egyptian funerary texts, a name referring to "The water crown of Ta," another name for Osiris. This territory, exposed to Set's attacks, identified with Enlil, shows connections with Plato's accounts of the Atlantean civilization. The legends describe the use of Djed columns, Egyptian defense technologies that generated water walls to protect cities. It is interesting to note how the figure of Poseidon could be connected to Osiris, while Enlil could correspond to Zeus, reinforcing the idea of cultural syncretism between Greek and Sumerian narratives. The Greek narrative of an Atlantis ruled by Poseidon could thus derive from older tales, suggesting a connection with Sumerian texts. Anton Parks suggests that the disasters described in Egyptian texts could be linked to scientifically validated events like the Younger Dryas cataclysm. The destruction of a planet between Mars and Jupiter, where the asteroid belt is now located, is narrated as the "fall of the Sound Eye," an event that coincides with the death of Osiris and the devastation of Atlantis. Parks's interpretation resonates with Immanuel Velikovsky's theory, who in 1950, in his famous book "Worlds in Collision," proposed that Venus was expelled from Jupiter as a comet, which, passing close to Earth, caused global catastrophes. These events could explain the great flood mentioned in Sumerian texts and the subsequent rebirth of civilization in Egypt, where survivors would have founded new great cities, and the pyramids, which could contain mathematical codes linked to this ancient knowledge.

ELOHIM AND THE REVELATION OF DIVINE PLURALITY: JORDAN MAXWELL'S INTERPRETATIONS

Jordan Maxwell, esteemed researcher and author, points out how, in the sacred text of Genesis, commonly interpreted as the story of the creation of man by a single God, there lies a deeper and more complex meaning, revealed only in the original Hebrew. The first verse of Genesis, commonly translated as "In the beginning God created the heavens and the earth," actually uses the term "Elohim," which is plural and does not refer to a single God, but to "gods." This discovery leads to a reevaluation of the entire creation narrative: it's not a single God, but multiple divinities collaborating in the creation of the world. This plurality is also reflected in the famous phrase "Let us make man in our image, after our likeness," where "Elohim" suggests collective action, implying the involvement of multiple entities in the creation of humanity. The revelation that "Elohim" is plural challenges the traditional monotheistic interpretation of the Bible, suggesting that ancient Hebrew scriptures may have been influenced by polytheistic beliefs. This understanding emerges not only from linguistic analysis but also from the historical and cultural context in which these texts were written. The scriptures seem to indicate, therefore, that humanity was created not by a single omnipotent creator, but by a council of higher entities, each contributing to the creation of man and the earth. This pluralistic view of divinity may reflect older and more widespread influences than previously admitted by the monotheistic tradition, opening a new chapter in the study of the origins of Hebrew scriptures and their interpretations. The biblical account of the Ten Commandments, received by Moses on Mount Sinai, offers an intriguing perspective on the divine nature according to ancient Hebrew scriptures. The first commandment proclaimed, "I am the Lord your God, who brought you out of the land of Egypt, out of the house of slavery; you shall have no other gods before me," does not deny the existence of other divinities, but establishes an exclusivity of worship toward a chosen deity, reflecting a dynamic of loyalty and preference. This formulation suggests that ancient Judaism acknowledged the possible existence of multiple gods, a concept expressed with the term "Elohim," which is plural and translates as "gods." This term, used in ancient scriptures, highlights a polytheistic view rather than a strictly monotheistic one, contrary to how Jewish tradition is often interpreted. The classical interpretation of "you shall have no other gods before me" implies that among the various worshipped deities, the God of Israel should be considered supreme and without rivals in the worship of his people. This command establishes an exclusive relationship, similar to a lover asking their beloved not to have eyes for others, emphasizing a form of divine "jealousy" that acknowledges the existence but does not accept the veneration of other deities. This understanding extends beyond the Jewish context, entering into contemporary theological debates discussing the true nature of Jewish monotheism, often better described as "henotheism," the worship of one deity among many recognized. This concept challenges conventional interpretations and

161

raises significant questions about the evolution of religious practices and the understanding of the divine in the historical and cultural context of ancient civilizations. In the book of Deuteronomy, specifically in chapter 11, verse 16, a warning is given to followers of the Jewish faith: "Take care lest your heart be deceived, and you turn aside and serve other gods and worship them." This passage reflects the understanding that, despite the existence of multiple deities, followers should exclusively worship the Jewish God. It is interesting to note that the people originally known as Jews were not originally so named; they were actually Canaanites or Phoenicians, inhabitants of the geographical area that now includes Israel and Lebanon. Historical research indicates that the religious tradition of these peoples did not begin with monotheism. An article in a Jewish magazine states that the faith of the Jews and their religious evolution from the time of the Semites, known as Jews or Israelites, was not originally monotheistic. Instead, they practiced henotheism, the worship of a chosen deity among many. This concept of henotheism, as explored in academic publications of Liberty University, implies the recognition of multiple gods but with the choice to worship a specific one as the main deity. This framework of divine plurality and the evolution of the concept of God span millennia of human history, progressively changing until arriving at the contemporary conception of a single God creator of man, a notion that diverges significantly from polytheistic origins. It is relevant to note how Hebrew scriptures use the term "Elohim," a plural name for God, which is evident when it says: "Let us make man

162

in our image, after our likeness." This phrase, often misinterpreted, suggests that multiple divine entities collaborated in the creation of man, not a single God. This understanding challenges conventional interpretations and raises significant questions about the true nature of divinity and the origins of monotheism in ancient Jewish tradition. According to correct interpretations of the Scriptures, it is not accurate to state that God said, "Let us make man in our image, after our likeness" as proof that God created man. Rather, it is appropriate to understand that multiple deities proposed, "Let us make man in our image, after our likeness." This suggests not the creation of man from scratch but a modification of his existing form, implying manipulation of human DNA. This practice, though ancient, still persists today and is reflected in various theories about human genetics. The concept of a single God is not universally supported in ancient Jewish traditions, as evidenced in numerous texts. Psalm 82 describes God as one among many, presiding over a divine assembly. Similarly, the New Testament, in the works of Paul of Tarsus, acknowledges the existence of multiple deities, suggesting a variety of celestial entities recognized in the religious context of the time. In Genesis, the dialogue about God or the gods creating man offers a broader view: "Let us make man in our image and likeness."

Various translations of the Bible such as the Good News Bible, the New Living Translation, and the Common English Bible confirm this interpretative plurality, suggesting that humanity was shaped to resemble these divine figures, not only physically but also in abilities and potentials. This perspective opens a new field of understanding about human presence on Earth and its origins. It indicates that humanity might have been fashioned in the image of its cosmic creators, profoundly influencing not only our biology but also our spirituality. This raises significant questions about who we are and where we come from, expanding the dialogue about our heritage and our place in the universe.

Within the fabric of ancient scriptures lies a theological complexity that revisits and challenges traditional narratives about the creation of man. At the center of this reinterpretation is the concept of Elohim, not a single creator god but a collective of divinities who deliberately intended to shape humanity in their image and likeness. This view does not rely on the idea of creation ex nihilo but rather suggests that humanity was the subject of divine intervention, a sort of genetic modification that persists over time. The Genesis account reveals that the divinities, in shaping Adam, were not aiming to create a man from scratch but to refine and improve an already existing being. The original term, ADL, used to describe Adam, implies a creature remade or modified according to divine standards. This is further confirmed by subsequent passages where Adam, in turn, begets Seth in his image, replicating the characteristics imparted by his celestial creators.

The episode of Abraham and the three celestial visitors, detailed in the chapters of Genesis, vividly illustrates this human-divine connection. These visitors, appearing as ordinary men but later revealed as angels, demonstrate that the human appearance was shared between humanity and the divine. Abraham's reaction, recognizing and honoring them, underscores an awareness of a deep and reciprocal respect. The same narrative extends to the New Testament, where the Apostle Paul speaks of "gods" and "lords" in numerous heavenly and earthly places, confirming the plural nature of divinity.

Translations of the Bible, varying in expression but agreeing on content, invite humanity to reflect the divine image, implying a direct and personal connection between man and his cosmic creators. The interaction between Abraham and the divine visitors is not just a gesture of hospitality but becomes a powerful symbol of the direct relationship between man and the divine. The sharing of a meal, a profoundly human and daily act, is laden with theological meanings, highlighting the physical and behavioral resemblance between humans and deities. These encounters not only reveal the multiple nature of the divinities but also the intention of these supreme beings to establish a relationship based on recognition and mutual respect, which is the cornerstone of the entire biblical narrative.

Ultimately, the scriptures offer a glimpse into a complex and multifaceted truth about the origin and nature of humanity, proposing a vision in which man is not only created but is also continually influenced and shaped by the will and presence of a plurality of deities, each with their agency and significance.

Thus, we have seen how the Bible uses the term "Elohim" to refer to God, indicating, however, a plural form meaning "gods." This suggests, according to Maxwell, that humanity was created in the image of multiple deities, not just one. The concept of multiple divinities is confirmed by the appearances of angels in human form, as in the stories of Abraham hosting three men, one of whom is recognized as God, as we have already discussed. The concept of divine plurality is also present in the Quran, where God refers to Himself using the plural pronoun "we," emphasizing the presence of multiple divine entities. In the Judaic context, the term "henotheism" describes the worship of a main deity among many, a practice reflected in the command given to Noah to "replenish" the earth, suggesting a renewal of life post-cataclysm. A common misunderstanding concerns how humans were created. Maxwell points out that the phrase "let us make man in our image and likeness" does not imply the ex nihilo creation of humanity but rather a modeling on something preexisting, indicated by the Hebrew term "Adam," which does not correspond to the generic "ish" (man) but to a specific being already existing. This reinforces the idea that biblical narratives not only speak of creation but also of a deep affinity between humans and deities, manifested in the human ability to generate offspring in their image, just as the deities shaped humanity in their image. This divine connection is visible in the story of Abraham, who not only offers hospitality to angels but interacts with them as with human beings, thus revealing their divine nature and the close relationship between heaven and earth. This understanding enriches the perception of
166

ancient scriptures, offering a more nuanced and complex view of the relationship between humanity and the divine. The lexical choice to use the plural Elohim, therefore, suggests a plurality of deities involved in the creation of the universe. Contrary to common belief, the Scriptures do not assert that man was the first creature created by God. Rather, they indicate that man was remade or molded by the Elohim. The Scriptures in Genesis 1:27-28 urge humanity to be fruitful, multiply, and "replenish" the earth again, implying the existence of a previous population before a cataclysm that devastated the world. The translation of Genesis 1:2 as "without form and void" is actually a mistake; the Hebrew words "tohu vavohu" describe the earth becoming a wilderness, not being created in such a state. This interpretation is supported by the vision of the prophet Jeremiah, who saw the desolate earth and the cities in ruins, suggesting the existence of an advanced world, unknown to our history, destroyed long ago. The story of Abraham meeting three men, divine figures who appear as ordinary people, further confirms that human beings were created in the image of the divinities. These encounters illustrate the direct correlation between the human and divine appearance as intended by the Elohim, who fashioned man from preexisting beings, likely hominids, to make them like themselves. This narrative challenges traditional interpretations of monotheism and opens up to a broader understanding of the origins of humanity and divine plurality, recognized also in other religious traditions, such as the Quran using the plural "we" to refer to the divinity. These elements indicate a more complex and layered view of creation and human history, contrary to what many may have heard or read before.

GRAHAM HANCOCK'S THEORIES ON ANCIENT CIVILIZATIONS: AN ANALYSIS OF CATASTROPHES AND LOST CIVILIZATIONS

Graham Hancock is one of the most brilliant pioneers in the field of ancient civilizations. With his book "Fingerprints of the Gods," published in 1995, Hancock proposed a revolutionary view of human history. Contrary to the traditional view that sees the beginning of civilization in the so-called Fertile Crescent and in Sumeria, followed by an evolution towards ancient Greece with significant architectural developments and legal systems, Hancock suggests the existence of an advanced civilization long before Sumer. This civilization, according to him, possessed technologies superior to those of today and was destroyed by massive catastrophes approximately 12,980 years ago, triggering a long period of extreme cold and floods that erased almost every trace of this ancient society from the Earth's surface. Hancock's theories challenge the official and accepted version of human history, suggesting that what we know is only a fraction of the entire historical truth. Graham Hancock's work, "Fingerprints of the Gods," first published in 1995, has become a publishing phenomenon, selling approximately 5 million copies worldwide, half of which were sold in Japan alone. The book captured the collective imagination at a time when doubt about the conventional narrative of civilization history was growing. With a fresh approach and a collection of intriguing data, Hancock explored the idea of an advanced civilization that existed long before the civilizations recognized by traditional history.

These theses have even influenced filmmaking, partly inspiring the film "2012," known for its spectacular representations of catastrophes. Although the film borrowed only a few key notions from Hancock's book, such as Charles Hapgood's theory of crustal displacement and the connection with the Mayan calendar, most of the archaeological elements proposed by Hancock were not included, focusing instead on large-scale visual effects and catastrophic scenarios. At the heart of the theory presented in Graham Hancock's book "Fingerprints of the Gods" lies the idea that humanity suffers from a form of collective amnesia. Hancock argues that there was a significant forgotten episode in human history, which is not considered in our current understanding of who we are and why we are here. This forgotten episode, as we have seen, would have been caused, in part, by global catastrophic events that occurred approximately 12,980 years ago, and in part by active forces in our society that would prefer to suppress this information. These forces promote the idea of a simple linear development, from primitive cavemen, through Stone Age hunter-gatherers, to our modern civilization, considered the pinnacle of human history. Hancock criticizes this linear narrative, suggesting that there was an advanced civilization long before the civilizations traditionally recognized, which reached high levels of development and was destroyed, so that humanity had to start almost from scratch, like children without memory of the past. Mainstream archaeology and history, influenced by the media and the educational system, have established a timeline that has become entrenched in how we perceive ourselves, promoting a history of linear and continuous progress. However, new archaeological discoveries such as Göbekli Tepe in Turkey, which cannot be ignored by the mainstream as they were discovered by archaeologists themselves, are creating cracks in this timeline and present significant challenges to the conventional narrative. These findings show that societies thought to be composed of simple hunter-gatherers were actually capable of large-scale architectural projects that required considerable organizational and managerial skills, questioning the image we have of our ancestors in that historical period. During a visit to Göbekli Tepe, Hancock had the opportunity to speak with Klaus Schmidt, the archaeologist who conducted the excavations, who hesitated to say that the site was rewriting history, preferring instead to state that it was adding a new chapter. This caution reflects mainstream archaeology's attempt to integrate such discoveries into the existing model without disturbing the accepted narrative of human progress. At the heart of the theory presented in Graham Hancock's book "Fingerprints of the Gods," therefore, lies the central idea that humanity suffers from a form of collective amnesia. Graham Hancock's theory suggests, in summary, that human civilization may have experienced catastrophic interruptions, profoundly influencing our historical understanding. Hancock's research highlights how events such as the impact of a comet approximately 12,980 years ago could have caused a period of extreme cold and widespread flooding, erasing the signs of existing advanced civilizations before the so-called Sumerian period. His theory is strengthened by archaeological discoveries such as Göbekli Tepe, which show advanced building capabilities long before the recognized urban civilizations of conventional history. The episode known as the "Younger Dryas" highlights a period of drastic cooling followed by rapid warming approximately 11,600 years ago, consistent with narratives of ancient catastrophes such as that described by Plato regarding Atlantis. These periods of extreme climatic transition, highlighted by chemical signals in the Greenland ice, suggest that major floods and climate changes had a significant impact on the course of human civilization, challenging our understanding of ancient history and its technologies. Graham Hancock raises significant doubts about the traditional historical account, emphasizing how modern theories often conflict with ancient accounts such as those of Plato. Plato describes a great catastrophe that destroyed an advanced civilization 9,000 years before Solon, equivalent to 11,600 years ago. This period precisely corresponds to the catastrophic events known as the Younger Dryas, which according to modern studies were triggered by a comet impact. Hancock criticizes the tendency of modern academics to downplay the scope of Plato's claims, attributing errors in translation or misinterpretation to the details of the times mentioned in his writings. He argues that the consistency of these ancient accounts with recent geological findings demonstrates that the traditional interpretation of human history may be incomplete or even wrong. The finding of geological evidence confirming the comet impact approximately 12,980 years ago has offered

Hancock and other researchers a "smoking gun" they did not have before. This evidence suggests that the extinction of many megafauna and drastic climate changes were connected to this event, reinforcing the idea that a significant period of human history has been forgotten or suppressed. Hancock also explores speculative theories about even more extraordinary events, such as the idea that the comet may have been deliberately diverted towards Earth. Although these speculations may seem extreme, they reflect a growing awareness of the fragility of human knowledge and our understanding of the past. This dialogue opens up new interpretations about humanity's ability to influence and significantly alter our planetary environment, whether intentionally or not. Hancock's studies, based on concrete evidence such as data from Greenland ice cores, indicate with certainty that the Earth was struck by a fragmented comet. And after the immense flood following the event, a long period of glacial cold ensued. The interaction of the Earth with comet fragments may have then caused a sudden warming approximately 11,600 years ago, surprisingly coinciding with the period mentioned by Plato regarding the disappearance of Atlantis. The debate also extends to speculations about extraterrestrial interventions or deliberate manipulations of celestial bodies as weapons, suggesting that ancient wars or conflicts on a cosmic scale may have played a role in the disasters that shaped the course of Earth's history. Furthermore, Hancock discusses the implications of these events for our current civilization, highlighting our dependence on highly specialized systems and our vulnerability in the event of similar catastrophes.

174

Reflecting on the survival capacity of less technological societies more harmonized with the natural environment, Hancock warns that our advanced technology may not guarantee us safety in the event of new cataclysms. These theories, although often contested by conventional archaeology, stimulate critical reflection on the linearity and completeness of our historical understanding, inviting us to explore our past more deeply to better prepare for the future.

ANCIENT CATASTROPHES AND COLLECTIVE AMNESIA: THE REVOLUTIONARY THEORIES OF GRAHAM HANCOCK ON HUMAN HISTORY

As we have seen, Hancock's theory explores the idea that Earth hosted advanced civilizations long before ours. It has been a central theme in Graham Hancock's theories since his bestseller "Fingerprints of the Gods," published in 1995. This book gathered a considerable amount of data, synthesizing insights from hundreds of sources regarding ancient civilizations. Hancock suggests, as already noted, that our planet has repeatedly hosted sophisticated societies that were lost due to catastrophic events, leading to a collective amnesia about these past civilizations. The concept extends to speculation that Earth was involved in extraterrestrial politics due to its strategic importance in the solar system. According to some theories, Earth was colonized by beings from a planet in our solar system that later became the asteroid belt due to destructive wars. These colonizers would have brought with them advanced technologies beyond our current understanding, including methods of acoustic levitation witnessed by explorers in Tibet. This technology allowed the manipulation of physical objects in ways that today seem magical, such as the precise positioning of immense stones in structures like Sacsayhuaman in Peru, where the stones fit together with such precision that not even a blade or a hair can pass between the joints. Hancock's theories also touch on the idea of hidden and secret chambers beneath such ancient sites, suggesting a vast undisclosed history lying just below the surface of our current understanding. Several insiders have revealed the existence of numerous underground tunnels in South America, details of which we have been completely unaware. Hancock's disclosure aims to reveal the truth, even when it may be uncomfortable. The idea that an advanced civilization could have been destroyed by a widespread catastrophe is deeply unsettling. Graham Hancock has always emphasized how little of our civilization would survive an epochal catastrophe. A striking example, as Hancock points out, is represented by school buses that, abandoned in an impound lot for fifty years, end up completely rusting away. This process of oxidation, which turns iron into iron oxide, demonstrates the temporariness and fragility of human constructions. In Hancock's books, the massive extent of the cataclysmic event is explored, described as a disastrous event of gigantic proportions, responsible for large-scale extinctions of animal species and radical changes to the face of the planet, including dramatic rises in sea levels. Civilizations tend to concentrate their major resources along the coasts, which are the most affected areas in scenarios like the one hypothesized, as mentioned, between 12,980 and 11,600 years ago. If advanced constructions had existed on the North American continent, they would have been completely swept away by the floods caused by the comet impact on the North American ice cap. An additional theory, that of Earth's crust displacement influenced by a comet impact, as proposed by the Italian Filippo Barbiero, suggests that Antarctica may have transitioned from a tropical climate to a South

177

Pole climate. This would have generated worldwide tsunamis, even larger than those of Fukushima, with waves that could have reached hundreds of meters in height and penetrated deep into continents, annihilating any traces of civilization. In such a scenario, human structures would have been first destroyed and then buried under at least 30 feet of mud, rapidly degrading. It's important to consider that a previous civilization may not have used the same technology as ours. According to Hancock, they might have employed very different types of technologies. Our civilization has leaned towards mechanical advantage, thinking in terms of mechanisms and machines to perform tasks. We've lived through a massive era of machines and are now entering the digital age, but still using our intelligence to create technologies that move objects for us. We need to consider that ancient civilizations may have developed human mind capabilities in very advanced ways, allowing them to manipulate objects without the need for the hardware we rely on. Consequently, we shouldn't expect to find remnants that exactly reflect our civilization or our technology in the residues of an ancient civilization. We might not recognize what we find as technology. A significant example of different technology is Tibetan acoustic levitation, which is well-documented, including with photographs. Tibetan monks were able to levitate heavy stone blocks weighing hundreds of kilograms using sound. Described in Dan Davidson's book "Shape Power," the process involved a group of monks arranged in a quarter-circle, with trumpets and drums calibrated in harmonic proportions to the size of the stone. These instruments produced intense metallic noise as the monks chanted and increased the pace of their music. Initially at three-minute intervals, the rhythm would increase until the stone started to sway and eventually lift in a parabolic arc, thus defying the laws of physics as we understand them. While we have experimented with levitating very small objects through sound, the approach with large objects remains largely unexplored. This suggests that, due to our orientation towards mechanical solutions like levers to move objects, we may be closed to alternative methods. Looking at the mysteries of ancient civilizations, we must remain open to the possibility that they used techniques completely different from ours. A technology based on sound, for example, would not leave behind mechanical objects, making it enigmatic how these ancient civilizations accomplished their feats. In this context, we should also consider ancient traditions like the Egyptian one, where it is narrated that priests placed huge stone blocks using chanting. Instead of dismissing these narratives as mere fantasies of ancient Egyptians, we should ask ourselves what they might actually mean. Could they be clues to a highly advanced technology that we do not understand? Advancing further in the discussion, the tale of the Ark of the Covenant and the walls of Jericho raise further questions. The Ark, extensively described in the Old Testament and other Jewish traditions, appears as a potentially lethal technological object, linked to a severe and punitive deity known as Jehovah. This deity inflicted severe punishments through the Ark, which seems to have been some kind of deadly weapon. When the Philistines captured the

179

Ark from the Israelites and opened it, it is said that 50,000 of them died in agony, afflicted by cancerous tumors and blindness, a description evoking the symptoms of radiation sickness. This episode raises questions about the exact nature of the Ark: was it a device that emitted radiation? And if so, how is it possible that such an ancient civilization possessed such technology? These reflections lead us to reconsider our understanding of the technological capabilities of ancient civilizations and the nature of the stories that have come down to us through the centuries. When the Ark of the Covenant is put on display, as was the case with the Philistines, it turns into a kind of tourist object, allowing people to pass by and look inside, which definitely should not be done with the Ark. And then there is the story of Jericho. What strikes in the narrative of the fall of the walls of Jericho is the people of Israel surrounding them while blowing trumpets. But beyond the sound, what is fundamental is that they were carrying the Ark of the Covenant along the walls, causing them to collapse. Moreover, it seems that the walls, made of clay, liquefied, changing state somehow. It's hard to resist the idea that, through the perspective of biblical authors, we're observing the description of a device that we don't fully understand. There is also talk of diorite vessels. These stone objects, from ancient Egypt and around the world, were worked with an extremely hard stone, the processing of which remains a mystery. At first glance, these may seem like simple stone vessels on display in a museum, but if you consult an expert in stone work, like Chris Dunn, he will assert the difficulty in understanding how they were made, suggesting the need for advanced machinery tools. Even Flinders Petrie, a great Egyptologist, was surprised by the speed and efficiency of the drill holes observed in drill cores, left by the use of tubular drills to hollow out granite objects. The traces left by the drills indicate that they operated at incredibly high speeds, quickly digging into hard rock. Petrie hypothesized the use of diamond tips, but wondered what metal could support such tips, since in 2500 B.C. only copper tools were supposed to be available, a material too weak to support such stresses without bending or breaking. These observations lead us to consider that ancient technology may not reside in the tool itself, but in the ability to soften the stone, making it malleable and shapeable. This revolutionary method could explain how ancient civilizations were able to manipulate stone in ways that today we would consider impossible.

Graham Hancock has extensively explored Sacsayhuamán in Peru, a site he has visited repeatedly. The imposing zigzag walls of Sacsayhuamán, conventionally attributed to the Inca, have been the subject of study during these visits. Despite the common belief that the Inca are the builders, Hancock encountered Jesús Gamarra, a local researcher of Inca descent, who contests this attribution. Gamarra argues that the Inca were simple successors who built upon much older, superior foundations. These ancient constructions show no signs of being worked with conventional tools like hammers and chisels, suggesting instead that the stones were softened and shaped. Hancock and Gamarra observed that the surfaces of the stones appear to have been molded while soft, almost like butter spread with a knife. The site of Sacsayhuamán also includes extensive systems of underground tunnels, now inaccessible to the public and blocked by the Peruvian government. This closure fuels further mysteries regarding the true origins and functions of these constructions. Hancock criticizes conventional archaeology for not recognizing the possibility that the extraordinary walls of Sacsayhuamán are much older than the Inca. He proposes that this sophisticated architecture may have been achieved through unknown technologies today, such as the ability to soften stone. His analysis suggests that there are at least three distinct layers of civilization at the site, with the Inca as the last heirs of a much older and technologically advanced heritage. Graham Hancock has extensively studied the Olmec stone heads, venturing multiple times to La Venta, exploring the Gulf region of Mexico. These stone heads, some of which weigh close to 100 tons, feature facial features that do not correspond to those of native American Indians. The features rather resemble those of Africans or Polynesians, although their exact origin remains uncertain. Alongside these enigmatic heads, there have also been carved images of individuals with Caucasian appearance, sporting heavy beards, a non-typical element of indigenous populations of the Americas. These representations contrast with the current archaeological understanding that would attribute every ancient narrative, such as that of the feathered serpent Quetzalcoatl, to mere inventions of the conquistadors to justify a supposed pre-Columbian presence of Europeans in Latin America. However,

182

Hancock's visits to La Venta and archaeological discoveries clearly show that these bearded and Caucasian figures were an integral part of the oldest cultures in Mexico, challenging the conventional narrative that Asian peoples, crossing the Bering Strait about 13,000 years ago, would have been the only ancestors of the American populations. Furthermore, recent explorations in Brazil have unearthed physical types similar to the aborigines, further different from the Asian type that predominates in the rest of the Americas. These findings challenge the Clovis model, according to which the Americas would have been populated only from 14,000 years ago, suggesting a much more complex and layered history. Brian Forster has discovered numerous elongated skulls, scattered in various parts of the world, from Siberia to South Africa, to the French nobility, suggesting the existence of a global practice of cranial deformation or, perhaps, of a biological characteristic still not fully understood. These skulls, which often feature red hair and a cranial capacity double the norm, raise questions about the reasons for such physical modifications and the civilizations that may have practiced them. These clues, together with the discovery of giant spheres in Costa Rica, weave a narrative of a connected and mysterious global past, still full of secrets to be revealed. In this discussion, a new concept emerges regarding the spheres found in various places, characterized by remarkable spherical perfection. Despite their large scale, some argue that their precise execution indicates a cultural and technological level in the past greater than historians commonly admit. These reflections open the door to a radical revision of our origins and the possible existence of a mega-advanced civilization that could have been global. This connection between ancient megastructures, such as the Olmec stone heads, Stonehenge, and the pyramids, highlights an ancient ability to manipulate huge stones with an ease that modern cultures do not possess. The ability to build stone monuments of such size, if it had been easy for primitive cultures, would still be practiced today, but it is not; instead, it demonstrates that it was an extremely arduous undertaking. And even for us, so technologically advanced.

CRANIAL DEFORMATION AND ELONGATED SKULLS: TRACING THE ENIGMATIC HERITAGE OF ANCIENT CIVILIZATIONS

In many ancient cultures scattered around the world, the ruling classes practiced intentional cranial modification, a method aimed at deliberately reshaping the skull to express status, wealth, and nobility. Some of the oldest examples of this practice date back 5,000-12,000 years in China and are widespread across different continents. It is speculated that this practice could have been an attempt to mimic an advanced race of beings with elongated skulls. They could have been extraterrestrials, but is there evidence suggesting their actual existence? According to some theories, some of which we have examined in this book, there once existed on our planet an advanced civilization, the progenitor of humanity, characterized by elongated skulls as can be observed in ancient iconography and mythologies. Consequently, subsequent civilizations sought to emulate them, sometimes through cranial deformation, other times through hats and different symbols, thus confirming their existence and historical precedence. When the Spanish conquistadors arrived in what is now Peru, they noticed young priests with elongated skulls and wondered about the origin of such deformations. They discovered that from birth, when the skull bones are still soft, they were shaped to elongate them. This type of cranial deformation occurred because rulers with elongated skulls were revered in the ancient world, prompting questions about whom they sought to emulate or honor.

Elongated skulls are a widespread phenomenon globally, but some of the best scientifically studied examples come from Peru. Four hours south of Lima lies the Paracas Peninsula, an area surrounded by rich agricultural landscapes and a civilization dating back at least 5,000 years. It was here, in 1928, that archaeologist Julio Tello discovered a collection of massively elongated skulls, laying the groundwork for further investigations into these ancient and mysterious practices. Canadian researcher Brian Forster has lived in Peru for over ten years and has been fully dedicated to studying these specimens. It was about fifteen years ago, entering a local museum run by Mr. Juan Navarro, a local amateur archaeologist, that he first saw a mummified elongated skull. Coming from a background in pre-medical biology, he was amazed by this discovery, unable to understand what it truly was. Analyses have shown that the oldest skulls appear to be naturally elongated. Later, with the interaction between the Nazca and Paracas cultures, the practice of cranial binding began. The traditional academy maintains that the Paracas settled on the coast of Peru or evolved as a group around 800-600 BC, but this theory is not based on any radiocarbon analysis, but rather on assumptions. Only recently have radiocarbon tests been possible, the results of which align with this chronology. The oldest of the skulls examined dates back about 2,400 years, marking the beginning of the so-called Paracas period. Among the genetic characteristics of the originally elongated skulls are eye sockets about 50% larger than normal and more vertically elongated, as well as a significantly larger jaw. They also feature two holes in
186

the back of the skull, a genetic characteristic suggesting an adaptation for the blood and nerve flow necessary to adequately nourish the vertically elongated head. In any case, these elongated skulls differ significantly from standard human beings. For a long time, experts, archaeologists, and anthropologists have argued that such skulls were the result of cranial deformation practiced by compressing the brains of children. However, DNA analysis reveals that they are not similar to us. Radiocarbon dating has dated the oldest elongated skull to about 2,400 years ago, at the beginning of the Caracas period. It is interesting to note that the earliest elongated skulls, probably all of them, had dark and reddish hair during life, a characteristic not attributable to native American indigenous peoples, suggesting another migration from elsewhere. Most people associate red hair with Scandinavians, Irish, or Scottish, but in reality, this genetic trait dates back to the Middle East, an area that is beginning to show correlations in the DNA of these individuals. Two hair experts, analyzing hundreds of samples of red hair from Caracas, confirmed that black hair remains black while red hair, over time, can lighten, becoming blonde. This is a genetic characteristic that does not align with the standard history of indigenous Americans on the coast of Peru. Another notable feature is the absence of canine teeth in the skulls examined. Contrary to canine teeth, typical for meat consumption, these skulls feature normal or regular dentition, constituting a significant anomaly. The main characteristic distinguishing intentional cranial deformation from a natural skull is the absence of the sagittal suture. In a normal human skull, the sagittal
187

suture, a joint of connective tissue between the two parietal bones, extends from the frontal plate above the skull dome to the posterior occipital plate. However, many of the skulls uncovered in Caracas are completely devoid of this suture. Through morphological analysis, all these differences in the skulls have been documented, also allowing the extraction of DNA from tissue samples. While intentional cranial modification alters the shape of the skull, the question remains whether it can alter other typical characteristics of a regular human skull, such as the foramen magnum, the point where the spinal column enters the base of the skull. In the original elongated skulls from this area, the foramen magnum is located an inch further back than the normal position, which usually is almost at the center, indicating that original practices placed it significantly backward, in line with the characteristics of the vertically elongated skull. These are human mutations, as demonstrated by the finding of a fetus with an elongated skull, where the opening that connects the head to the spine is shifted back by over a centimeter. Such a shift, if applied to a human being, would be lethal, thus demonstrating that these do not belong to the same typology of human beings. When intentional cranial modification is practiced on a newborn, the process generally begins a month after birth, when the skull is more malleable, and continues for at least six months. Previous findings of fetuses and newborns with elongated heads suggest that intentional cranial modification may not have taken place, as it takes at least six months to alter the head shape and achieve desired results. Deforming the head can make it more conical, but its volume cannot be changed. Numerous doctors, nurses, dentists, neurologists, and surgeons have personally examined these skulls, noting features not covered in their university studies. They particularly observed the absence of the sagittal suture, eye sockets at least 50% larger than normal, two holes in the back of the skull, and the fact that the foramen magnum is shifted back by a whole inch. These traits cannot be explained by intentional cranial deformation and are indicative of innate genetic characteristics. The medical experts consulted agree to consider these findings not belonging to Homo sapiens sapiens but rather to a possible subspecies. Some of these skulls are well-preserved, with hair, skin, and tissues still intact, facilitating analysis. Tissue samples taken from two Paracas skulls, analyzed by geneticists William Brown and Nassim Harmein, were sent to the UCLA Genomics and Bioinformatics Center. DNA extraction was performed, and preliminary results of genomic analysis, begun in the early months of 2019, revealed very interesting anomalies. Initial genetic tests on the same skulls, compared with the catalog of the 1000 Genomes Project, showed significant genetic variation, indicative of non-random mutations or significant genetic divergence from Homo sapiens.

A more in-depth analysis, performed by John Hopkins using advanced genomic sequencing techniques, found no alignment or matches with the human reference genome. These results suggest that DNA samples from the elongated Paracas skulls may come from an extinct race of human beings. In particular, analyses of mitochondrial DNA showed significant variations suggesting that, at least maternally, there may have been an alteration in genome structure, indicative of a possible sister species of Homo sapiens sapiens, similar but not identical, and of unknown origin. The standard academic narrative maintains that all populations in this area descend from ancestors who crossed the Bering land bridge. If this were true, their mitochondrial DNA should belong to haplogroup B, the most common among the four haplogroups (A, B, C, and D) identified as those of the early peoples of the Americas. A haplogroup is a genetic group of people who share a common ancestor along maternal or paternal lines. These groups are marked with letters of the alphabet and further with combinations of numbers and letters. The conducted analysis allowed tracing the mitochondrial genome of two elongated skulls to a prevalent haplogroup in the Black Sea region, Central Asia. This discovery is significant because elongated skulls have been found in that region, suggesting a similar cultural presence in very remote times, contrary to standard evolutionary theories that do not contemplate genetic adaptations in such a short time, i.e., a few millennia. These skulls show up to 50 single nucleotide variations, more than twice as many as those generally present in the human population. For comparison, the mitochondrial genome of Neanderthals presents about 150 variants compared to that of humans, while that of Denisovans presents over 230. This suggests that the maternal line may represent a sister species of Homo sapiens, not yet identified and distinct from any current human population. DNA sequencing also revealed anomalies in the paternal line, specifically in the Y chromosome, which does not

190

match that of the human reference genome, indicating that the father was not a Homo sapiens. If the results of genetic tests on the ancient elongated skulls of Paracas show significant anomalies, could this be evidence of an extinct human species or genetic manipulation? The high variation in the genome suggests a possibility that these characteristics are not natural but result from intentional intervention on these organisms. Some of these strange findings are not limited to the Paracas skulls alone. In the Nazca region of Peru, some investigators have discovered a humanoid female mummy, nicknamed Maria, with an elongated skull and mysterious DNA. The DNA analysis of Maria has shown a 20% compatibility with the human reference genome, suggesting similarity with the Y chromosomes of previously analyzed elongated skulls. Medical specialists who examined Maria observed similar anomalies to those found in the Particus skulls. Dr. M.K. Chessie, a musculoskeletal radiologist at the University of Colorado Hospital in Denver, noted that Maria's skull lacks sutures and appears to constitute a solid structure, which could indicate belonging to an unknown species. Ángel Romero, a genomics specialist from Mexico, believes that Maria's DNA may belong to an unstudied organism. From the DNA results of Maria and the elongated Paracas skulls emerges a picture of extraordinary anomalies. DNA sequences, compared with the human reference genome, show only a 25% match, suggesting significant genetic divergence. Genetic sequencing laboratories in Canada, Mexico, and Russia have confirmed that Maria's DNA does not match any modern human DNA or any other DNA in their databases. This genetic diversity raises

191

questions about the possible extraterrestrial or at least unconventional origin of these individuals. Examining the elongated skulls of Paracas, one must question whether their large brain capacity could be the product of beings that did not evolve on Earth. Could they be descendants of extraterrestrials, as suggested by ancient scriptures like the Book of Enoch, which tells of "heavenly guardians" descending to Earth and giants with elongated heads, revered and feared by humans who sought to emulate them? This interpretation opens new perspectives on our history and human evolution, suggesting that we may need to completely reconsider our origins. The elongated Paracas skulls have a 60% greater mass and are 25% larger in size compared to a normal human skull. This raises the question of their possible unknown or even extraterrestrial genetic origin, prompting a reconsideration of our human history. The traditional academic sphere has often avoided exploring these anomalies, but recent discoveries challenge the established narrative, suggesting that we lack fundamental elements to fully understand human evolution and the emergence of Homo sapiens sapiens. The ancients practiced intentional cranial modifications to venerate beings of an advanced culture. These skulls were not the result of artificial deformations but were natural, suggesting a fascinating history behind them. Could their ancestors come from another star system? Is it possible they were partly aliens or hybrids between humans and a closely related life form from this planet or beyond? DNA analyses do not reveal matches with global genetic databases, which could indicate that these individuals were indeed different from Homo sapiens sapiens.

These artifacts could be evidence that once on Earth lived a progenitor group with elongated skulls, who mingled with various groups of ancient peoples. Over time, as this genetic line dissolved, their characteristics were emulated through artificial skull deformation. These beings may have had a significant impact on our cultures, religions, and art, and may have withdrawn to their original planet. The continued exploration of elongated skulls may one day allow us to trace our origins back to our cosmic family, offering new perspectives on human history and its genetic diversity.

THE ANCIENT CONNECTION: FROM THE ORIGINS OF MAN TO THE STELLAR KNOWLEDGE OF THE DOGON

In 1961, near Marrakech, Morocco, during a barite extraction operation in the Jebel Irhoud massif, a fossil human skull was discovered. Initially classified as Homo sapiens, the skull was dated to about 160,000 years ago. However, for many scientists, it remained shrouded in mystery because the Jebel Irhoud fossils appeared much more primitive than those of pre-existing Homo sapiens. The mystery persisted until 2017, when paleoanthropologist Jean-Jacques Hublin and his team from the Max Planck Institute reopened the cave where the skull was found. Their surprise was great to find not only additional skulls but also lithic tools, dated around 300,000 years ago. If these fossils were indeed attributable to Homo sapiens, as claimed by the team, this would push back the origin of our species by over 100,000 years, challenging some established conceptions. The findings also offered new insights into the brain development of these ancient humans, suggesting reasons for their peculiar physical features. Unlike modern humans, their brain was less globular and more elongated, with some areas, like the cerebellum—located in the lower back part of the skull—less developed. While the cerebellum represents only 10% of the organ's total volume, it contains over 50% of its neurons. Previously, its function was thought to be limited to coordinating simple motor activities like standing upright and breathing. However, in 2017, neuroscientists from Stanford University discovered it also plays a role in reward response, one of the primary drivers motivating and shaping human behavior. This discovery suggested that some brain areas had gradually developed, contributing to modulating human awareness and behavior over time. These understandings could shed light on how humans began to perceive their place in the universe.

Thousands of kilometers south of the Jebel Irhoud cave lived a tribe with its own intriguing evolutionary history. The Dogon of West Africa were discovered in 1935 by two French anthropologists, Griaule and Dieterlen. Over time, these anthropologists gained the respect of the Dogon shaman, who shared secret knowledge with them. The Dogon possessed remarkably detailed information about the Sirius star system, knowledge they theoretically should not have had. This raised fascinating questions about the origin of such knowledge and its impact on human understanding of the cosmos. Anthropologists were amazed to find that the Dogon tribe possessed advanced knowledge about the Sirius star system, knowledge that no ancient people should have had. The Dogon revealed that not only was there a relationship between Sirius and our sun, but they also claimed that a group of creatures that could only be described as aliens, called Nommo, descended to Earth. These beings had transmitted their knowledge about the Sirius system to the Dogon. It was unclear how they could be aware of Sirius B, a white dwarf star, the smallest visible star form, barely perceptible even with modern telescopes. However, the Dogon knew its precise existence, calling it Potolo, resembling a tiny seed found in West Africa, describing it as a small star but extremely dense. The Dogon, therefore, also spoke of another previously unknown celestial entity in the Sirius system, Sirius B, whose existence was not confirmed until 1995, sixty years after the discovery of this tribe. Could the Dogon have been instructed by beings from Sirius? If so, who were these mysterious Nommo, and how did they influence the human species? Regarding the Nommo, the Dogon describe them as aquatic and civilizing beings who, according to their tradition, descended from the sky and brought wisdom to the Dogon people. A particularly interesting aspect of Dogon culture is the great reverence for twins, as they believed that every man and woman is born with both sexes, highlighting a profound understanding of duality. The creation story of the Dogon is fascinating: they narrate that in the beginning, there was an all-powerful entity called Amma. Amma created the twins, but the first group emerged prematurely from the earth, resulting in imperfection and symbolizing the human race. A second group of twins emerged perfect, and these were called Nommo, amphibious aquatic creatures. After death, the Nommo retired to a place called Paradise, which the Dogon placed in the star Sirius. After their departure for Paradise, the Nommo promised to return to Earth, where they would bring the arts of civilization to a then primitive humanity. The Dogon's story reflects creation myths from around the world, from South American to Polynesian cultures, highlighting striking similarities. Even linguistic similarities around the Nommo find counterparts in other cultures: in ancient India, there were the Naga, semi-serpentine

deities; in Australia, Aboriginal tribes knew the Nurambunguti. These names are so similar as to suggest a common origin. Considering Neolithic cultures and human evolution, it is incredible that peoples without writing, mathematics, and advanced constructive abilities could, in a very short time, erect megastructures and develop a complex language like Sumerian. This raises questions about a possible connection between the Sirius star and a sort of global intelligence that drove primitive humans to develop civilizations and belief systems. Could it be that Sirius is the repository of a specific type of wisdom, from which humanoid creatures, similar to us but still very different, came, being present in every culture worldwide? These entities would have arrived on Earth after a barbaric era to give us knowledge that we now consider fundamental, such as mathematics, astronomy, temple construction with monolithic blocks, agriculture, and animal husbandry. Such knowledge seems to always trace back to these mysterious figures linked to Sirius. But were they real, or was it a myth to explain a particular point in the universe from which everything originated? The Nommo were described as representatives of order on Earth, amphibious fish-like beings, shrouded in mystery. Examining other mythologies, such as that of ancient Atlantis, we find similar beings known as the Telchines, holders of incredible knowledge. Even in ancient Egypt and Sumeria, there were similar figures, but with different names. The Sirius star, the brightest in the earthly sky located in the constellation of Canis Major, may have inspired the name of the Dogon tribe, said to have originated from ancient Egypt. This
197

connection is also reflected in the mathematical correspondence between the mass of the Great Pyramid and that of the Pyramid of Khafre, an exact parallel with the mass difference between Sirius B and our sun, described by the fraction 1.036, known as Pythagoras' comma, symbolizing a harmonic mathematical theory according to which a body can vibrate in such a way as to induce changes in another. This was the secret knowledge at the heart of ancient mystery schools, the idea that harmonic interaction between bodies could deeply influence reality.

The Dogon are considered descendants of an ancient lineage of teachings that have traversed wars, cultural changes, and climatic variations, pushing them to migrate westward, where they are today. As we have seen, within their social and spiritual structure, they venerate a creator god called Amun, or Amma, names that are essentially interchangeable and represent the same divine concept. This deep connection could reveal further connections between the ancient mystery schools of Egypt and the star Sirius in human development. One of the most fascinating notions concerns harmonic resonance, a principle integrated into ancient monuments by the Anunnaki who built stone structures employing occult and mysterious knowledge. These structures were designed so that the human body, through the seven chakras, corresponding to the seven notes of a musical octave, could influence the fabric of reality through light harmonics. This concept posits that just as a piano string can vibrate in response to a violin sound, similarly, a change in the Sirius star could immediately influence our sun. Research continues to explore this dynamic between Sirius, also known as the sun behind the sun for its intense brightness, and our earthly reality, suggesting that the same harmonic relationship governs the entire universe. This cosmic connection is interpreted as a possible explanation of why figures like the Anunnaki, the Nommo, the Nagas, and other mythological beings may have come to Earth following a "harmonic highway" through the star system. The conception of Sirius associated with Isis, symbolizing the universal mother or the source of all physical creation, further enriches this narrative, suggesting a deep and intrinsic connection between ancient knowledge and the structure of the universe.

At the heart of the ancient mystery schools and their esoteric heritage was the belief that universal harmony could be influenced through harmonic resonance, directly linked to the seven human chakras. This profound knowledge, implying control of the surrounding reality through specific frequencies, was guarded and passed down by the Anunnaki, described as master builders of ancient megaliths. The structures they erected, such as those in Egypt, were designed to perpetuate and utilize these light harmonics, fundamental for accessing universal knowledge. Akhenaten, a pharaoh of the eighteenth Egyptian dynasty, set out to revolutionize this elitist tradition by promoting the cult of Aten, the solar disk, as a unifying symbol of creative energy. His reform aimed to reduce religious fragmentation and diminish the power of the clergy, who had intervened as mediators between the people and the divine. He wanted his subjects to directly understand the divine nature, eliminating the need for intermediaries. During his reign, Akhenaten attempted to share this knowledge with his people, but he faced strong opposition and was eventually overthrown through a coup. It is believed that his ideas and reforms were influenced by his connection with Sirius, considered the "sun behind the sun" and associated with Isis, a goddess symbolizing motherhood and universal creation. This association was not coincidental but reflected a deep and ancient connection between Egyptian constructions and the star Sirius, through which it was believed possible to access a higher level of universal consciousness. In the context of these broad reforms, Nefertiti, Akhenaten's wife, played a crucial role. The royal couple was seen not only as earthly rulers but also as direct descendants of cosmic forces linked to Sirius. According to some esoteric narratives, Akhenaten and Nefertiti came from the Sirius A star, carrying with them an understanding and celestial influence aimed at spiritually elevating the Egyptian people. This divine connection is emphasized in artistic representations of the time, showing both with distinctly elongated and almost alien physical traits, symbolizing their non-earthly origin. Additionally, guided spiritual visits recount journeys into the temple of Akhenaten and Nefertiti, revealing discussions about changes in Egyptian beliefs, emphasizing the importance of a direct spiritual connection without intermediaries. These accounts, though metaphorical, underscore the depth of their commitment to altering the spiritual structure of Egyptian society, an attempt to return to a purer and more direct understanding of the universe, centered on the worship of the sun and its celestial manifestation, Sirius.

In the Egyptian pantheon, Anubis is associated with the constellation of Orion. According to myth, Anubis took on the form of a dog to reflect his association with the Dog Star, Sirius, and to be accepted by other Egyptian gods like Ra, Osiris, and Isis. This transformation symbolizes Anubis' attempt to integrate into the group of demigods. Connections between ancient cultures, as highlighted by the presence of similar figures to Sirius and Orion in various mythologies, suggest a common origin of astronomical and mythological knowledge. In the broader historical context, the rapid development of agriculture, architecture, and other fundamental technologies in ancient civilizations has often been attributed to external influences, including the possibility of extraterrestrial intervention. Such theories are bolstered by the rapid advancement of Mesopotamian and South American civilizations, which built complex architectural structures in relatively short periods. Akhenaten's story, along with the alleged presence of influential figures from Sirius, could be seen as indicative of a recurring influence by extraterrestrial intelligences in human history. Linda Moulton Howe, a researcher in the field of ufology, argues that such intelligences may have exerted considerable effort in guiding human development.

A curious anecdote tells that during the drafting of the Declaration of Independence, Thomas Jefferson experienced an enigmatic encounter. According to some accounts, while Jefferson was absorbed in drafting the document in the garden of his residence, a mysterious individual, dressed in a large cloak, would have opened the garden gate as if he owned the place and approached Jefferson. This stranger would then have placed a sheet of paper in front of him, suggesting that that design should become the emblem of the new nation. The design depicted a pyramid with thirteen steps, topped by an all-seeing eye inside a triangle, a symbol that today we find on the back of the one-dollar bill. After leaving the design, the individual would have quickly departed, leaving Jefferson surprised and puzzled. This episode, although shrouded in mystery and lacking direct documentary confirmation, is often cited as an example of possible extraterrestrial influence or at least of esoteric knowledge that goes beyond simple earthly politics. Historians are divided on the authenticity of such a story, but it persists in American folklore as a symbol of a broader debate on the occult and potentially non-human origins of the foundations of the United States.

This chapter on Graham Hancock draws inspiration from the numerous works and lectures he has given over the years. The theories and reflections presented here illustrate the pioneering character and extensive scholarship that define Hancock's work, who has dedicated his life to studying ancient civilizations and their mysterious connections with modern consciousness. The information included here pays tribute to his long career and significant contributions, which continue to provoke and enrich the debate on these intriguing topics.

ORIGINS, HISTORY, AND HUMAN DESTINY ACCORDING TO GREGG BRADEN

Gregg Braden is an American author and researcher known for his approach that connects scientific discoveries with ancient traditions and spiritual practices. With a background in earth sciences, Braden worked as a senior geologist for Phillips Petroleum in the 1970s, and later as a computer systems designer for Cisco Systems, before devoting himself full-time to writing and lecturing. Throughout his career, Braden has explored topics such as the relationship between human emotions and DNA, climate change and its connection to historical cycles and ancient predictions, and hidden human potentials. He is the author of several bestsellers, including "The Divine Matrix," "Fractal Time," and "The God Code," in which he discusses how ancient wisdom and modern scientific discoveries intersect and what this might mean for the future of humanity. Braden is often a guest on network shows such as History Channel, Discovery Channel, and Hay House Radio, where he discusses these topics. He is known for his style that combines scientific data with philosophical and spiritual insights, aiming to demonstrate how a shift in perception and awareness can lead to positive transformations in individual and collective life.

Braden's main focus is on DNA, emphasizing how it sets us apart from all other forms of life and gives us the extraordinary ability to profoundly influence our lives and the world around us. This unique capability,

Braden argues, has its roots in our origins. While the scientific world struggles to decipher the mystery of our origins, it often confines itself to a narrow belief system that presumes to have already solved the mystery with the theory of evolution. Braden criticizes this tendency to force discoveries, such as bones, teeth, and fossils of ancient life forms, into a preconceived evolutionary narrative, without allowing these testimonies to freely guide toward new truths about our history. His reflections on Charles Darwin, the father of the theory of evolution, are interesting, starting from the publication of his influential book "On the Origin of Species" in 1859. Before Darwin, the big questions about life were predominantly addressed and answered through religious institutions. Darwin proposed shifting the debate from the realm of faith to that of science, a paradigm shift that was quickly embraced and integrated into the dominant thinking of the time, given his authority as a scientist and geologist.

Braden expresses respect for Darwin but also highlights where, in his view, Darwin may have deviated from the deeper truth of our existence. Particularly significant is the full title of Darwin's work, often forgotten or overlooked in modern editions: "On the Origin of Species by Means of Natural Selection, or the Preservation of Favoured Races in the Struggle for Life." This title, Braden reflects, reveals much about Darwin's thinking: his belief in the existence of "favoured races" and his view of life as a continuous struggle. In this context, Braden aims to guide his readers and listeners through a discovery that could not only challenge but also radically change the conventional understanding of our origins, opening the way to new interpretations and possibilities in the narrative of our evolution.

Gregg Braden introduces the concept that Charles Darwin's view of evolution may not be complete or definitive, especially in light of modern scientific discoveries. Braden, with a geological background, expresses respect for Darwin's observations but criticizes the reductionist approach he may have adopted. According to Braden, Darwin interpreted isolated phenomena as representative of universal natural laws. For example, the behavior of certain animals in specific circumstances was seen as exemplifying general principles applicable to all life, including humans. However, nature shows exceptional variety and does not follow a single pattern universally applicable to all species. Importantly, Darwin himself was aware of potential weaknesses in his theory. He was open to the idea that if even just one complex organ could not be explained through gradual modifications, his theory would collapse. Today, examples such as the human eye or the blood clotting mechanism suggest that some biological structures and functions may not be explainable by the gradual evolution proposed by Darwin, as they require a coordinated set of functions that must appear simultaneously to be operative.

Charles Darwin, in his attempt to explain the origins of life, did not seek to outline the exact circumstances of the origin of life itself. According to his theory, once life was already present on Earth in the form of primitive cells, these began to evolve and become more complex in response to environmental needs. For example, if a life form needed to adapt to colder temperatures or different types of food, or if it needed to develop new senses to interact with the environment, these factors triggered internal changes in the organism, leading to the gradual development of new characteristics. Since 1859, the year of the publication of his work "On the Origin of Species," Darwin's theory has laid the foundations of biological thought regarding human origins and our evolutionary development. According to this view, organisms develop and acquire new characteristics over long periods of time. Upon their death, these organisms would leave behind fossil traces, representing evolutionary snapshots, which we could rediscover and which would help us reconstruct the evolutionary genealogy from the origin of species to modern humans. However, Darwin himself was aware of the gaps in his theory. He expressed puzzlement as to why intermediate fossils were not found in every geological stratum, expecting the fossil record to be full of such evidence if his theory were correct. This doubt is often overlooked in modern academic teaching, where these uncertainties are rarely discussed. Darwin acknowledged that if it were shown that a complex organ could not have evolved through gradual and successive modifications, then his theory would collapse. A glaring example is the human eye or blood clotting mechanisms, which cannot be the result of partial evolutions because each component must be present for them to function effectively. Nevertheless, Darwin did not advocate for completely discarding his theory but rather using it as a starting point for further investigation. This openness to the possibility of revising and adapting his work underscores the importance of maintaining an honest and open approach in scientific education. Proposing to students not only Darwin's theory but also new evidence and discoveries encourages a worldview where mysteries remain to be solved, thus stimulating greater curiosity and engagement in scientific learning. Braden challenges Darwin's theory of evolution not to completely reject it, but to highlight that new scientific discoveries require a broad revision or even surpassing of some of its aspects. He emphasizes that science is an evolving process and that the theory of evolution itself might need to evolve to accommodate new discoveries about DNA and the complexity of biology. During the 1950s and 1960s, anthropology experienced a period of great excitement due to discoveries in the Olduvai Gorge in Africa, where the Leakey Foundation discovered increasingly ancient fossils of primitive beings. Eye-catching magazines on newsstands proclaimed "The Age of Human Ancestors," presenting discoveries such as Australopithecus, better known as Lucy, or Homo habilis, known as "the handy man," up to Neanderthals. These finds were presented as evidence supporting Darwin's theory of evolution.

However, the problem is that, despite the abundance of fossil evidence, according to Braden, Darwin's theory seems to lack solid confirmation. If one examines the traditional human evolutionary tree, which depicts modern man at the apex and intermediate species as progressive links, it is noticeable that many of the connections between these species are represented by dashed lines. These lines indicate hypothetical or speculative relationships, suggesting that scientists consider their existence possible but have not yet found concrete evidence to confirm them. These hypotheses have been perpetuated since Darwin's theory was published in 1859. Despite more than a century and a half of intensive research, with the contribution of the best academic minds, the most advanced technologies, and substantial funding, many of the dashed lines in the human evolutionary tree have not yet been transformed into certainties. Academics continue to argue that perhaps we have not yet looked in the right place or found the right fossil. This suggests that physical evidence may not be the only key element to understanding our origins, as new evidence is taking us much further and questioning the reliance on physical evidence in the traditional narrative.

Lastly, the concept of "missing links" in human evolution remains a question mark. The reality may be that these missing links do not exist at all, as current evidence does not seem to confirm the presence of such evolutionary intermediates. This scenario raises significant doubts about the validity of the entire evolutionary framework proposed so far, indicating that there may be aspects of our evolutionary history that we still do not fully understand. Human DNA is beginning to tell an exciting new story, reminiscent of science fiction. Today, we are capable of extracting human DNA from the bone marrow of millennia-old fossils, an unthinkable feat until recently. A striking example of this capability occurred in 1987 in Northern Europe when the well-preserved body of a

Neanderthal infant was discovered. Dated to about 30,000 years ago, this child was long considered one of our direct ancestors. However, the analysis of DNA extracted from the marrow of one of its toes led to surprising conclusions, published in 2000 in the prestigious journal *Nature*. The results indicated that modern humans do not descend from Neanderthals. This discovery spurred further research that demonstrated how modern humans coexisted with Neanderthals, excluding direct descent. The term "Cro-Magnon" has been replaced by AMH, short for "Anatomically Modern Human," to describe humans who appeared on Earth 200,000 years ago and have not changed since then. We are genetically identical to these ancient humans, so much so that if the skeleton of an AMH were placed next to a modern person, the differences would be minimal, perhaps only in the leg bones, which were more robust in our ancestors due to a more active lifestyle. These findings challenge Darwin's idea of evolution as a slow and gradual process of adaptation and change over millions of years. In reality, it seems that we suddenly appeared 200,000 years ago with fully developed features. Anthropology journals such as *Advances in Anthropology* in 2012 confirmed that the DNA of Cro-Magnons, now called AMH, has not changed over millennia. This raises doubts about the validity of the traditional evolutionary tree, which places us at the top of a long chain of intermediate life forms. On the contrary, it seems that our "evolutionary family" more closely resembles a bush, without a linear succession of life forms directly preceding us. These findings indicate that the theory of evolution, as long understood, may require substantial revision to accommodate the complexity and rapidity with which human life forms appeared on Earth. The mystery of how we appeared 200,000 years ago remains unsolved, and we haven't undergone significant changes since then. The question of how and why we appeared remains central in the scientific debate. Delving into recent DNA research, we can better understand what these studies tell us in comparison between modern humans and Neanderthals. Let's now examine chromosomes with Braden. Both modern humans and Neanderthals possess 23 chromosomes. Through a graphical image overlaying the chromosomes of both species, we can identify where there are similarities and differences. In the points where an orange bar appears above the chromosomes, it indicates an area of DNA correspondence between humans and Neanderthals. However, these correspondences are scattered and few, highlighting minimal DNA overlap. This leads us to conclude that, despite sharing DNA with many forms of life—from flies to cattle to our pets—the degree of overlap with Neanderthals does not support the idea that we are direct descendants of them. These results, published in the peer-reviewed journal *Nature* in July 2006, clearly show the low correlation, although these findings are seldom presented in textbooks or documentaries. Charles Darwin was aware of the limitations of his evolutionary theory. He never claimed that his theory was definitive or without alternatives; rather, he saw it as a bridge to new understandings. His honesty is evident when expressing doubts about the applicability of natural selection to complex organs like the eye. In his words:

210

"To suppose that the eye, with all its inimitable contrivances for adjusting the focus to different distances, for admitting different amounts of light, and for the correction of spherical and chromatic aberration, could have been formed by natural selection, seems, I freely confess, absurd in the highest possible degree." These reflections invite us to consider evolutionary theory with a more open and critical approach, recognizing that there may be aspects of biology and human origins that natural selection fails to fully explain.

One of the problems scientists encounter today concerns the context and the ability to fit small discoveries into a larger framework. To illustrate, Braden suggests imagining walking in a field and finding a car key on the ground. Without a broader context, it's difficult to deduce significant information from that key; you wouldn't know which car it belongs to, what year or model it is, or how long it has been there. This principle is constantly repeated in science, both in archaeological sites and in out-of-place artifacts discussed earlier in the series. If we only focus on civilizations, like the walls of an ancient temple or hieroglyphs, without considering what was happening in the cosmos, climate, or on Earth, we probably won't fully understand history. The same goes for human origins. If we exclusively concentrate on fossils from Olduvai Gorge or rigidly apply Darwin's theory to all discoveries, we risk not finding the answers we seek, as we force every finding into a preconceived idea of an evolutionary tree, without fully exploring other possibilities. To truly discover our origins, we must consider the broader context.

This chapter dedicated to Greg Braden has been composed drawing extensively from the inspiration provided by his numerous books and lectures given over the years. The reflections and theories presented reflect the innovative spirit and depth of inquiry that characterize the work of Melchizedek, who has devoted his life to studying the connections between ancient spiritual traditions and new perspectives on human and universal consciousness. The information reported here is a tribute to his career and contributions, which continue to influence and stimulate debate on these fascinating topics.

GIANTS AMONG US: UNVEILING THE MYSTERY OF ANCIENT MEGALITHS AND LOST CIVILIZATIONS

In the summer of 1908 in Collinsville, Illinois, near the Cahokia mounds, some construction workers stumbled upon a stone tomb containing several giant bodies, each surpassing seven feet in height. Following this discovery, the bodies quickly disappeared, fueling the mystery of a purported species of large humans that once inhabited the Americas. Today, what remains of this enigmatic mound complex continues to perplex archaeologists. Cahokia was considered the largest city north of Mexico, with a population ranging from 25,000 to 50,000 inhabitants in 1000 AD. This Native American civilization possessed an advanced system of waterways, agriculture, and textiles, along with numerous legends about the so-called Mound Builders. Who were these Mound Builders? Could they be connected to the large bodies accidentally found in the ancient tomb? Is it possible that what they had discovered were the remains of a great culture that not only roamed the Americas but the entire world? Researcher Brad Olson suggests that the mounds themselves are the key to these forgotten ancient entities. It is true that giants have been found in the mounds of the Midwest. This area saw the evolution of several cultures, starting with the Adena culture in the state of Ohio, which then became the Hopewell culture and later the broader Mississippian culture that encompassed the entire Mississippi Valley. Over 2,000 pyramidal mounds dot North America, including

Mexico. Examining the mounds of North America, it is discovered that indigenous or Native Americans built them to honor deceased giants who likely once ruled over them in some way. These mounds are erected from the earth itself, shaped like serpents and various other creatures, and some are simply mounds. But what is truly interesting is that, looking around the world, dolmens are also found, huge stones assembled to mark the burial of a giant or a person of royal rank, a practice also found in the Americas, where building these imposing mounds was a daunting task. This custom of erecting large monuments is a link between these cultures, as both celebrated individuals who may have been very spiritual in the distant past. In my research, I have found over 1,500 newspaper articles spanning from the late 1800s to the early 1900s, documenting continuous discoveries of giant bones, some of which not in mounds. These bones often belonged to Native Americans, a fascinating detail considering the descriptions in the diaries of early North American explorers, who depicted the chiefs of each tribe as giants, some standing 12-15 feet tall. And yet, examining the records of the first ship to land on Easter Island, sailors reported the presence of a priestly class of giants, the Rapa Nui, tasked with overseeing the construction of stone huts. This narrative is found identical in a hundred other locations worldwide, which is extraordinary. Another clue that may support this mythology is provided by over 100 large humanoid footprints, mysteriously preserved in stone for thousands of years around the world. Could this be physical evidence of such legends? For instance, the Bible mentions giants at least twice in the first book of

Moses, and everyone remembers the duel between David and Goliath, the latter being a giant.

The book of the Eskimos, representing the mythology of this people, tells that once giants lived on Earth. The same is told in ancient Egypt: the pyramid texts explicitly speak of some giant deities compared to humans. Giants are a living presence in practically every ancient mythology, so why shouldn't they also be in the United States? If this were true, how is it possible that all this evidence has simply disappeared? Over the past two hundred years, hundreds of skeletons of exceptional size have been discovered both in mounds and in Native American cemeteries. Many of these skeletons, ranging from 7 to 7.5 feet tall, were found by archaeologists associated with the Smithsonian Institution and were meticulously documented, then taken away and are still subject to consultable publications today. However, all these skeletal remains are now lost. Although many were housed at the Smithsonian, they were returned in the early 1990s, following the NAGPRA law on the return of the remains of Native American indigenous peoples. So, unfortunately, they were removed from museums and institutes and can no longer be studied. However, we can still consult these reports to try to understand what was happening. Is it possible that traces of their genetic lineage are still traceable today, hidden in the very fabric of humanity? On February 22, 1918, just 25 miles from Collinsville, Illinois, the Illinois couple Harold and Addie Wadlow gave birth to a child who would become the tallest man in the world. Robert Wadlow reached a height of 8 feet and 11 inches and continued to grow until the day of his death at the age of 22. Wadlow's immense stature and his continuous growth were due, according to doctors, to a hyperplasia of the pituitary gland, which caused abnormally high levels of growth hormone in his body. Could this growth hormone be a hidden gene in human DNA? It was determined that he suffered from what is called pituitary gigantism.

Gigantism is a phenomenon that occurs in most species but is extremely rare, affecting only about 0.0007% of any population. Robert Wadlow represents a significant example of the survival of genes that caused gigantism as described by multiple cultures. It is hypothesized that Wadlow possessed a gene similar to that of ancient giants, right in the region where these mounds were built. Most of the doctors who observed him concluded that his stature might have been simply a genetic characteristic. Could Wadlow's towering height be solely attributed to his overactive pituitary gland, or is there a deeper genetic connection? Geneticist William Brown argues that this connection is not purely coincidental and is indeed possible. In the human genome, there is a vast reservoir of variations in genetic codes that can lead to very particular phenotypes, as in the case of dwarfism or gigantism. It is therefore plausible that, in that vast region of DNA with normally silenced or dormant segments, there are genes linked to the production of humans of very large stature. Since physical evidence has mysteriously disappeared, does modern human DNA provide any support for the existence of an extinct species of humanoids that once inhabited the planet? And could this connection explain one of the tallest men in the world? When we inquire about the existence of direct genetic evidence linking us to the giants of the past, to the best of my knowledge, such evidence does not physically exist at this time. However, when we examine the history of humanity, we find that tales of giants are widespread, frequently mentioned in ancient history and rediscovered in modern times. So, we wonder if we are somehow related to these giants. Examining the accounts of our oldest and dearest spiritual traditions, a fascinating common theme emerges: humanity has undergone multiple iterations of an intentional process to bring us to the point where we are today. In other words, there have been many attempts to find the right genetic formula for the human body we see today. Judeo-Christian traditions, for example, indicate that there was a search for the ideal genetic formula to contain the power of the human spirit in physical form in this world. Through these iterations, between trial and error, life forms were created that were not sustainable over the ages. Among these life forms, we see references to giants, the Elohim, and the Nephilim in the oldest texts of the Old Testament. In May 2019, Regina Meredith, host of the Open Minds program on Gaia TV, led a team of researchers to investigate a series of giant bones belonging to a man named Luigi Muscus on the island of Sardinia. In his book titled "The Giants of Sardinia," Muscus presents photographs of large human bones and the results of DNA analyzed by the University of Padua in Italy. The examined remains showed a blood type O, Rh negative. This detail is relevant because Sardinia is one of the places in the world with the highest concentration of this blood type. Luigi believes that this genetic lineage derives from their ancestors of giant stature. If this were true, is it possible to find further evidence of this genetic lineage in ancient texts? What impact would this have on the true history of humanity in relation to an ancient race of giants and their possible interactions with Homo sapiens sapiens? Examining numerous ancient texts, indications emerge of an advanced race from space, initially arriving in Mesopotamia, modern-day Iraq, and subsequently also in Africa, before migrating across the planet to North America, following the directives of one of their leaders. These beings interbred with other hominids, giving rise to individuals of considerable size. The book of Genesis tells of when the Elohim, the sons of God, joined with the daughters of men and giants were born. It is said that sometimes the newborns were so large that they had to be extracted from the maternal womb through what we would call today a cesarean section, as they could not be born naturally. Could these accounts of giants in religious texts confirm the hypothesis that we share DNA with this lost species? Experts suggest that if this were true, there would be accounts of many types of giants.

Throughout the world, giants have been found, with extraordinary stories coming from China that remain unknown to most of us in the West. During travels on the Silk Road, from the 1500s to the 1600s, starting from the Mediterranean to China, explorers like Marco Polo were amazed by the giants, standing 15 feet tall, who served as guards in the imperial palace. These giants, likely remnants of the Anunnaki, were too conspicuous to go unnoticed. These are astonishing narratives concerning imperial China that are little known today. In addition to these stories, there are giants considered custodians of wisdom, holders of knowledge passed down from their ancestors on how to build megalithic structures, cultivate, understand celestial cycles, and speak multiple languages. They also had the technology, according to ancient texts, to travel around the planet. This advanced race, known as Nephilim or Anak in modern religious texts like the Bible, imparted this knowledge to humans. The Anunnaki, according to ancient accounts, were giants. In the cylindrical rolls preserved in the British Museum, the Anunnaki god is seen sitting while speaking to much smaller humans. Even in ancient Egypt, in the hieroglyphs of some temples like that of Dendera, very large figures are seen compared to the people they interact with. Matthias De Stefano, relying on his memories of past lives on other worlds, recounts tales of giant races. In his grandfather's stories, during the time of Atlantis along the Nile, in one of his previous lives, it was said that species from the sky populated the Earth. The Aesir were the great people, perhaps twice the size of the Anunnaki. The Nemnir, the first arrivals, were giants even larger than the Aesir and lived only in cold regions. During the last glaciation, which lasted about 200,000 years until 10,000 BC, the Nemnir dominated regions like Europe, Siberia, part of the Middle East, and North America. These giants were not warriors, but they were not friendly either. They came here to record information in the ice and lived like ancient humans, in caves, without a real civilization or cities, often alone or in small families. Fear prevented humans

219

from approaching northern regions, thus establishing natural boundaries. On the other hand, the Aesir, or Anunnaki, were giants with whom humans had much more contact. They established relationships, coexisted, and mingled with humans, profoundly influencing human society. Although some sought to dominate humans as slaves, others shared love and family with them. These giants taught humans agriculture, society, religion, and other fundamental aspects of civilization. Even though many of them were considered harmful to humans, they were the ones who gave us the knowledge that defines what we are today. If there were indeed two strains of giants on our planet, is it possible that they are still present today? Could they persist in our DNA, as in the case of Robert Wadlow, or live isolated in remote areas? During his experiences leading groups in the highlands of central China and Tibet, from the 1990s to the early 2000s, Mathias de Stefano had the opportunity to interact with monks and nuns who spoke of giants still living in the caves of the Himalayas, inaccessible and isolated areas. These giants are extremely reclusive and seem to lack a spoken language as we know it. Although their age is unknown, they seem to still exist. De Stefano even says he was able to see physical remains, such as skulls and bones, of these beings found in caves after their death. If an ancient civilization of giants truly roamed the Earth, why have their stories been reduced to mere legends? Could modern giants, like Wadlow, simply be the product of an overactive pituitary gland, or represent the result of a genetic lineage dating back to these towering creatures? Documented interactions between ancient peoples and giants can be traced on almost every continent. Could these narratives refer to a now extinct race?

Giants were attributed with two distinct qualities: some were savage barbarians, while others were spiritually enlightened guides of humanity. What can we learn from our gigantic past? De Stefano recounts that during the time when we were a civilization in Khem, in the northern part of Egypt about 12,000 years ago, we considered giants as the fathers and mothers of our civilization. We had many entities come from the stars who taught us various skills, but none taught us about ourselves as much as they did, because they were driven by emotions. Other entities, such as the Arcturians or the Syrians, were devoid of emotions and focused solely on scientific information and architecture. But the giants were like us: they had family problems, sentimental issues, joys, and sorrows. Their presence made us feel that the gods and goddesses were like us, that we too could become as great as them. This idea fueled the creation of deities in their image because they represented abilities that we did not possess, such as control over fire, air, and lightning, things they could do because of their evolution. Seeing that they had feelings and problems similar to ours made us believe that we too could attain those same abilities. That's why we won the war against them: we saw that we could be greater. The image we had of them, Mathias tells us, was what we wished to become. We wanted to be like Poseidon or like Zeus; they were like the celebrities of their time. They showed us in such a way that we could emulate them. So, what we can inherit from them today is not so much what they did living in our world, but the idea that no matter how big you are, you have the same problems, and no matter how small you are, you can become great. Could the presence of giants be encoded in human DNA? Might we one day unlock the strength, wisdom, and knowledge of our ancestors? Is it possible that giants walk among us today, perhaps right in our midst? Unraveling the mystery of these ancient giant beings could allow humanity to discover more about itself and the world in which we live. These reflections lead us to consider not only our history but also the potential inherent in our genetic heritage. By exploring these ancient narratives and their connections to the present, we may reveal aspects of our past that continue to influence our existence in previously unimaginable ways.

GOBEKLI TEPE AND THE MYSTERY OF THE TABBY'S STAR

In 2015, astrophysicists Duncan Lorimer and Laura McLaughlin discovered a star that was flashing in an unusual manner. Its radiation pulsed so intensely that it couldn't be associated with any known object in the universe. The news quickly spread around the world, leaving scientists baffled globally. Subsequently, astronomers at the Green Bank Telescope confirmed that the light signals were coming from a star in the Cygnus constellation, located 1,200 light-years away from Earth. This variable star was cataloged as KIC 8462852 and renamed the "Tabby's Star" in honor of Tabata Suzanne Boyajian, the first astronomer to study it in detail. The peculiarity of this star lay in how its light, or flux, periodically dimmed significantly, by up to 22%. To give an idea, if the planet Jupiter, the largest in our solar system, were to transit in front of the Sun from a distant perspective, it would cause only about a 1% reduction in solar light. Therefore, a reduction of up to 22% indicated the presence of something huge and unprecedented in astronomy. Since 2015, this mystery has captured the attention of astronomers, scientists, and space enthusiasts, generating a multitude of theories, none of which has provided a definitive explanation. Interestingly, even the most skeptical scientists haven't ruled out the hypothesis that a large object interrupting the brightness of Tabby's Star could be the work of an advanced civilization capable of space travel. This theory gained traction to the point of being the subject of a BBC documentary, which proposed the existence of a possible alien megastructure around the star. This narrative was further fueled in 2016 when a new type of signal was detected: a distinctive burst of radio waves followed by the collision and destruction of neutron stars, after which silence reigned. The BBC featured this phenomenon in its documentary, boldly suggesting that Tabby's Star might be surrounded by an extraterrestrial structure, introducing the idea of civilizations far more advanced than ours. The question raised is whether there really exists a structure around this star, and what the implications might be for us here on Earth. Is it plausible that alien civilizations may have interacted with us in the recent past or even in remote epochs? The star in question is about 1300 light-years away from our solar system, which means that any phenomenon we observe would date back to about 1300 years ago, around 700 AD, a period when the Maya civilization was still in full swing. It's intriguing to think that while we observe the star, anyone there looking towards us would see Earth as it was in the same historical period. Linda Moulton Howe's theory suggests that the Maya civilization was the result of a hybridization program, and then mysteriously disappeared, perhaps transferring to another planet. Surprisingly, this theory coincides temporally with observations of Tabby's Star. Could there be an ancient civilization that once inhabited Earth and is now trying to connect with us? Some sources, including former employees of government agencies like the CIA and NSA, have suggested that the Maya civilization was created through a hybridization program, implying advanced collaboration in transmitting historical mathematical knowledge. Astronomers have hypothesized that variations in the star's brightness could be used to transmit information, which could take the form of binary numbers, prime numbers, or other types of data intended to capture attention, which a civilization like ours might recognize as signals of intelligence. My research indicates that there is indeed intelligence behind these transmissions, which may not be limited to simple prime or binary numbers but may include very specific mathematical formulas.

Kepler is the name of a space mission managed by NASA, whose main objective is the search for extrasolar planets, namely planets that orbit other stars outside our solar system. Launched in March 2009, the Kepler mission utilized a space telescope equipped with a highly sensitive photometer to monitor the brightness of over 150,000 stars. The main method used by Kepler to find planets is the transit method, which detects variations in the brightness of a star caused by the passage (or "transit") of a planet in front of it relative to Earth's line of sight. These small periodic decreases in brightness indicate that a planet might be present, orbiting around the star. Thanks to this technique, Kepler has discovered thousands of candidates for extrasolar planets, many of which have been subsequently confirmed with further observations. These data have significantly expanded our understanding of the variety and distribution of planets in our galaxy, indicating, for example, that Earth-sized and super-Earth planets are very common in the universe. It has been determined that there are specific cycles in Kepler's data that are interconnected and reflect key numbers, all multiples of 11. This detail may seem trivial, but it's fascinating to note that these numbers correspond to those found in some of the most complex mathematical formulas known on Earth, such as Pascal's triangle, which is structured precisely on multiples of 11. This discovery becomes even more intriguing considering that the Great Pyramid and its two neighbors are aligned exactly with the same constellation as this star, Cygnus. Just 1000 miles to the northeast, the largest and oldest megalithic site in the world, Göbekli Tepe, also points towards the constellation of Cygnus. These coincidences raise the question: could Göbekli Tepe reveal a code that connects us not only to this celestial anomaly but also to other ancient sites around the world? Göbekli Tepe, located in southeastern Turkey, is known to be one of the oldest stone monument complexes in the world. This extraordinary site is aligned with the Cygnus constellation, a detail that has raised questions about ancient astronomical knowledge. Furthermore, similar representations of celestial birds and bird-men, seemingly pointing towards the same constellation, have been discovered in the world's oldest rock paintings, suggesting a universal link among diverse ancient cultures. The name "Göbekli Tepe," which in Turkish means "potbelly hill," was given to this site when German archaeologist Klaus Schmidt began excavations in 1994. Just below the surface, Schmidt discovered stone ruins that revealed the true age of the site, estimated to be about 7,000 years older than Stonehenge, challenging many accepted theories in human history. Schmidt dedicated his life to exploring these mysteries until his mysterious death in 2014. At the time of his disappearance, 95% of the ruins were still buried, and the true function of Göbekli Tepe remains an enigma. Archaeologists estimate that Göbekli Tepe is about 13,000 years old and was used for several millennia before being intentionally buried. Some suggest that the site could be even older, given the existence of evidence suggesting human presence in Turkey millions of years ago. Global warming has had a significant impact on polar ice melting, allowing better visibility through ground-penetrating radar, revealing complex archaeological sites under the ice, which appear as technologically advanced civilizations, well beyond simple hunting villages or huts. These findings could revolutionize our understanding of antiquity and the technical capabilities of prehistoric civilizations. A scientist might argue that two scenarios are possible: either these complex structures were built under the ice after it had already formed, which appears less likely, or the structures already existed and were later covered by ice. Currently, the dating of civilizations has been pushed back to 13,500 years ago, while the last ice age ended about 12,000 years ago. The historical context of civilizations dating back 50,000, 60,000, or 70,000 years, following cycles of 5,000 years, frequently emerges in myths, suggesting that such narratives might be based on more concrete facts than previously believed or accepted. Göbekli Tepe, located in northern Mesopotamia, near the areas of Urfa and Horan, is considered the oldest stone circle complex in the world and represents the cradle of civilization, the power place of the Anunnaki according to some theories. Built towards the end of the last ice age, around 9,500 BC, it was used for about 1,500 years before being abandoned around 8,000 BC. Its stone structures, advanced and technologically sophisticated, include carvings depicting animals and abstract human forms, all crowned by T-shaped pillars, which may have had the task of resonating with certain frequencies. During a visit to the site with geologist Robert Shock, who earned his PhD at Yale University, limestone pillars almost 6 meters tall and weighing about 15 tons each were found, arranged in circles. Shock shared reflections on how these pillars, with their T-tops, could serve as tuning forks. He hypothesized that Göbekli Tepe may have been built in a natural depression to amplify certain frequencies from above. Observing the animal carvings on the pillars, the idea emerges that they may have been used to record the standing wave patterns of various living organisms. For example, a crocodile resonates at a different frequency than a crane, an elephant, or a monkey. The theory suggests that these structures may have been created to preserve such frequencies, engraved in the stone pillars as an attempt to conserve these life forms. Could Göbekli Tepe have been an ancient portal built to communicate with deities from distant galaxies? Is it possible that the Tabby's Star is a signal for humans, an invitation to pay attention to this portal? At Gobekli Tepe, there is indeed a precise and clear evidence of advanced astronomy, including the construction of the world's first perfectly aligned building from north to south, an impossible feat without sophisticated astronomical knowledge. The site exhibits alignments with specific star clusters at precise moments of the year, demonstrating remarkable complexity. Shamanic cultures across the

Eurasian continent viewed the northern celestial pole as a passage from the physical world to the celestial realm, often described as a portal connecting different universes. The presence of mysterious luminous phenomena, often described in the surrounding mountains of Gobekli Tepe and interpreted today as UFOs, were likely seen by ancestors as significant signals, hints of places to establish contact with other worlds. Constructing monuments in these sites would have strengthened the connection with the stars and intensified the transmission of crucial information for the creation of civilizations. Pillar 43, for instance, served as a signpost for shamans who, having reached an altered state of consciousness within ceremonial spaces, embarked on spiritual journeys to the upper world. A deeper understanding of the relationship of these ancient monuments with Tabby's Star and other galaxies could be the key to uncovering who built them and why. While detailed aerial views of Gobekli Tepe have not been examined, some research suggests that the site may correspond to a star map, a concept that would find resonance not only in Egyptian culture but also in pyramid construction, highlighting a harmonious relationship with this star. It could therefore be that this ancient extraterrestrial race, which once visited our planet, not only understood this harmonic map of the universe but actively followed it. If indeed Gobekli Tepe was a portal to other galaxies, its builders may have foreseen an impending global catastrophe and buried this ancient technology to protect it. As excavations continued, surprising discoveries began to emerge. First and foremost, it emerged that the Gobekli Tepe site had not been covered by natural sedimentation. After about a thousand years of use, it had been deliberately buried by those who managed it. It wasn't an invading army that destroyed it, but rather an act of preservation. One must imagine teams of hundreds of people with buckets full of stones and debris arriving and pouring the contents over the existing stone circles, continuing until each circle was completely covered. The knowledge thus buried has preserved the mythology of nearly every ancient culture. Gobekli Tepe shows Sumerian influences, Egyptian symbolism, as well as traces of Hindu and Japanese culture. This makes the site a melting pot of cultures, a microcosm of global civilizations that presumably had never shared information with each other. This raises the hypothesis that Gobekli Tepe could be the secret link between all world cultures, discovered just in time to reveal crucial information. Many believe that finding the answers to these questions could transform our understanding of ourselves. If it were true that the site was deliberately buried, this would suggest that those who built Gobekli Tepe knew of an impending global catastrophe and chose to protect this ancient technology by burying it. The discovery of Gobekli Tepe in the 1990s was revolutionary, but research has been problematic due to political and social dangers in the region, and much knowledge remains buried. The discovery of Tabby's Star may have shed light on the knowledge still preserved at Gobekli Tepe, pointing us in a direction to uncover some human truths. It is our responsibility to preserve those documents that are being destroyed in this crucible of civilization between the Tigris and Euphrates rivers, in Iraq, Syria, and Turkey, as in some

230

cases their destruction is intentional, to erase the memory of these past civilizations. Once lost, they are lost forever. If the necessary funds were obtained to excavate the remaining 95% of the site, it is likely that this would answer many mysteries related to other megalithic sites. Gobekli Tepe could reveal much more than we know, being an incredibly well-preserved site, at least as far as we know. It could be a perfect construction of the science they were trying to save. If so, we could witness a global rebirth and a real effort to rediscover what we now lack, due to our turbulent history. Wars and catastrophes, like the destruction of the Library of Alexandria, have led to the loss of more knowledge than we possess today. Much of this knowledge could be recovered by studying these ancient sites, and it is hoped that this will happen with Gobekli Tepe. Only 5% of the site has been excavated, suggesting that there is a huge amount of information still to be discovered beneath the surface. Gobekli Tepe may have many more secrets to reveal. Scholars are beginning to explore the astronomy of the site, which could be one of the keys to understanding its origins and functions. However, nothing can replace good old-fashioned archaeological exploration, and the site needs to be fully excavated. Gobekli Tepe is potentially so important for unveiling the origins of our current civilizations that it is essential to fully expose the site to understand how it works. This could profoundly change the way we see ourselves and our past. There is something beyond, something that suggests that a part of us comes from the stars themselves, and that the point of incarnation, what we call soul or spirit, dwells in blood and flesh and exists. This provides us with a

231

connection to the stars, indicating that the soul or spirit comes from an extraterrestrial or stellar source. What other secrets are buried in the fertile soil of Gobekli Tepe? Could there be further truths about the true origins of humanity to discover? Is communication with Tabby's Star pushing us to dig deeper and connect with these ancient sites? Could there be a code that links celestial positions with terrestrial monuments? Gobekli Tepe could be the ultimate proof that connects these ancient monuments worldwide and reveal the reason for their existence. It could reveal a message that helps us understand our current civilization and how to continue humanity on this planet. Researchers continue to gather data, but the answer may still lie buried beneath the earth. As these mysteries are unveiled, interesting evidence emerges from unusual places. One of these places possesses one of the largest stones ever carved by man, weighing 1,650 tons. Baobab remains one of the greatest enigmas, of which very little is known. It is a huge complex. Around the Temple of Jupiter, there were once 54 columns. Fifty-four, what is the significance of this number? Could this numerical sequence help reveal a code at Baobab? And could it be further evidence of an ancient message? Perhaps the future will provide us with these intriguing answers.

MATIAS DE STEFANO: CELESTIAL ARCHITECTURE AND THE ROOTS OF HUMAN CIVILIZATION

Matías De Stefano is an Argentine spiritual teacher and public speaker, known for his unique insights into the origins and structure of the universe and humanity's place within it. Born in 1987 in Venado Tuerto, Argentina, Matías claims to have access to universal wisdom and memories that cover the history of the cosmos, a concept often referred to as the "Akashic Records." He has gained increased attention by participating in spiritual conferences, where he explores ancient civilizations, metaphysical theories, and the interconnectedness of all life. His teachings often focus on integrating spiritual knowledge with everyday life, aiming to help people understand their universal connections and spiritual heritage. Exploring the origins of terrestrial civilization under the influence of the Moon and the Anunnaki, Matias de Stefano delves into the fundamental roles these entities played in shaping human history. The Elohim, known as the architects of the universe, orchestrated a multidimensional structure to foster life throughout the cosmos. Their vision for Earth required a balance between different evolutionary perspectives, necessitating both tangible and metaphysical elements —comprising life and death, positive and negative forces. The concept of numerical counting emerged from the physical attributes of humans, primarily our ten fingers, leading to the decimal numeral system. However, during the Atlantean era, this system expanded to twelve, incorporating the same hands, and

233

a mysterious thirteenth point directly connected to the heart, symbolizing a deeper spiritual dimension. This numerical framework was not only about counting but understanding life through twelve distinct aspects, with the thirteenth representing a temporal dimension.

With the descent of celestial beings on Earth, primitive humans gained profound insights into the structural and temporal dimensions of their world. The influence of these celestial visitors extended beyond the physical realm, suggesting that the very fabric of human existence was intertwined with cosmic forces and temporal cycles, profoundly influencing how civilizations conceived their environment and their place within it. Therefore, the shape of 12 was sought, multiplied by spirit, soul, and body. This is why there existed the ninth path of the spirit, of the mind, plus that which was achieved by understanding the mind of the universe, then the soul of the universe, and finally the physical one. Thus, the structure of the universe was outlined in 10, 10, 10, and these 12 faces of reality were presented in the three-dimensional world. By uniting the temporal lines of the process, which were the 10, 10, 10, and then uniting the faces of the process, which were the 12 aspects of the numerology we had in Atlantis, we discovered the 360 degrees. The space beings helped us understand that these two elements together formed the sphere. The shape of a sphere was formed by these 360 degrees arising from these three aspects of unity, which were the 10 of the spirit, 10 of the soul, 10 of the body, in the 12 faces of matter. Thus, 12 multiplied by 30 gave us this reality of the sphere, which we had to realize, which we had to see as a being, as a form, which we had to imitate to access the core of reality. According to De Stefano, this introduction of time and space divided by 60, by 30, by 90, was a structure brought by high-level beings in other dimensions when humanity was emerging, to understand that we had to go to every corner of the planet. This mathematics helped us find the portals of the planet and the times when we had to act. This helped us understand that humanity was not just a civilization in one place, but we had to move to many places, at different times. And by the time we reached every space and every time in the 360 degrees of the sphere, we would be able to reach the mind of God. It was a concept brought by the architects of the universe, introduced by the Assyrian people of Ena, which helped us understand that we had to keep the numbers of the sphere to reach the core. And this leads us to understand that reality was not perfect, because if we had created a perfect reality, we would not have had the timeline to improve reality. Therefore, the project aimed to reflect perfection and to create a distortion of the project so as not to specifically have the perfection of time and space, allowing us to evolve and transform continuously without remaining unchanged. This was the project of what we now call Lucifer. Lucifer was the being in the sixth dimension who devised this plan to exit the perfection project, creating a slight delay in time and a slight distortion in space. This would offer us the opportunity to live another process of experience, another introduction to time and space, keeping us immersed in this reality as if it were a labyrinth from which we cannot escape. The old architects of Sirius suggested to the architects of this planet that we had this unbalanced time and space in the process of evolution, so we had to honor that process and balance it. That is why on our planet we have 360 degrees and 360 days to achieve the perfection that the structure of the sixth dimension modifies by adding other days, so as never to reach perfection and be able to continuously improve, again and again, through time and space. So, those five extra days we have in our calendar serve to make us evolve in another way, to free ourselves from perfection, because for beings of the realities of the sixth dimension, perfection is something that fixes you in the idea that everything is perfect, so there is nothing to do. And the goal of the sixth dimension is to have something to create, improve, transform. That's why they changed time and space so that we could have a distortion of this reality of perfection. That's why these other five days on our planet are the ones to celebrate the opportunity to evolve, transform, and honor diversity in the universe. Positive and negative forces were those that created the idea of mind and heart. They were emotions and thoughts. And these two ways of creating the path of evolution made these two structures of positive and negative limited in space through time, giving rise to these two species or races that help us survive in the three-dimensional world like reptilians and giants.

These two species populated the world with the purpose of uniting emotions and mind and concentrating all the information in one place. However, they also needed an additional perspective that was the integration and transcendence of that. In

the time when we have the four perspectives of the evolutionary cycle, expression, experimentation, integration, and transcendence, we also needed four affirmations of time rooted in space, what we call north, south, east, and west. Thus, while the reptilians and the giants were the rulers of the north and south, the positive and negative forces, the new rulers of space, had to be the balance between east and west. The balance between East and West meant that the consciousness cycle had to be one of waking up and falling asleep. In every cycle we will have in the history of the universe, we need consciousness to be awake in every part of the sphere. That is why we needed two civilizations on opposite sides of the planet. So, while one sleeps, the other is activated by the sun. That's why the civilization of Alikir had to come to this planet in the Pacific Ocean, and on the opposite, in the Mediterranean Sea and the Middle East, the Aesir had to emerge as the sun race. In the times of Atlantis, we called them Alikir and Aesir, but now you know them, Alikir as the civilization of the moon, and Aesir as the Anunnaki. One of the main reasons the Alikir came here, according to the Elegy Plan 200,000 years ago, was to verify the possibility for some beings from other planets to literally live on this planet and to find out if the Earth's immune system would not kill them. These beings, coming from outer space to live in the oceans, sought to understand the Earth and to reconnect with it, with plants, stones, minerals, so they could feel part of it. However, it took them a long time to establish a civilization on this planet. The Aesir, 200,000 years ago, did the same. They began to analyze the entire planet to determine the most suitable places to establish
237

civilization. They were more connected to humans and inhabited deserts, mountains, and continents. They came to this planet to populate vast territories and dominated the highest mountains in the world, while others were in the sea. Thus, both civilizations had this structure of positive and negative, where on one side, to the west, in the Pacific Ocean, they were connected to water, and on the other, they were connected to Earth. Both civilizations were therefore connected to both Earth and the Sun, which is why they were called the Civilization of the Sun. Once settled in the Middle East, they created the first civilizations about 20,000 years ago, bringing the Sun to Earth, bringing the sky to this planet. The Aletheia were guided to this planet through the largest portal the Earth has ever created, when the Moon collided with the Earth. The largest existing crater on the planet is the Pacific Ocean. So, the center of the Pacific Ocean was the portal through which all the waters and all the information from the sky came directly to this planet. That's why that was the largest portal through which these higher-level beings could enter this world. And this crater has this trinity impressed with the Earth. So, they populated the entire region to preserve the information of this crater and settled in this triangle of islands, which includes Hawaii, Rapa Nui, Easter Island, and New Zealand. All the information about water, light, and sky is found in the middle of these three islands. That's why they had these constructions in New Zealand, in Micronesia, in the statues of Easter Island, Rapa Nui. All this is linked to the culture of the Aletheia. The Aletheia were called the angels of the sea because they were so ethereal that they looked like angels, given their particular bodily conformation that made them appear angelic. They were very tall, with long faces, and they always looked the same, as if nothing happened, regardless of whether there were negative or positive events, they always remained centered. They walked so delicately that they seemed to levitate. And there was the idea that they came from the core of the light of the galaxy, the core of Vega, the heart of the galaxy. They were these angels on Earth, connected to air and water, and they populated the entire Pacific Ocean and the Indian Ocean, acting as guardians of the water information. Just as the Nemeer were the guardians of ice in the past, they were the guardians of the waters. They had many relationships with all the whales, dolphins, and aquatic animals that preserve information through sounds and vibrations in the water. Some people remember that their civilization had crystal cities, like huge cities, but they were not specifically made of crystal. They were decorated with hearts so that the vibrations could retain the information, and this made them so bright. On this planet, it was necessary to use stones to store information, so they built large stone structures decorated with hearts to make this information shine in the cities. Their mode of transportation was more magnetic and moved autonomously. They lived here without communication with the outside world in space, so they moved through ships equipped with quartz plates that moved through the ocean by vibration, rather than through spacecraft. The Alithir were connected through telepathy, and their civilization functioned like a beehive. They didn't have a social structure like ours, with debates, kings, or

239

queens. Although they had a figure similar to a queen, it was not the ruler of the civilization. They were all essentially equal, and no one imposed on others what to do. They vibrated like bees and communicated through those vibrations. That's why vibrations propagate better in water, allowing whales and dolphins to communicate better with them. All the information of oceanic creatures was transmitted to them, and through vibration, also the information from the skies and the stars passed to whales and dolphins. They had a large heart chakra, and it was said that the beating of their hearts could be heard wherever there was water; by closing their eyes, one could still perceive the vibration of the beehives on the planet. The Tessir, coming from the stars, from the sky, from the invisible as we call them, came from one of the stars of the Orion constellation, a crucial portal in the galaxy. They were imposing beings, similar to giants, with a strong sense of almost military value. You could compare them to the gods of Greece and the Middle East. They were the first to truly bond with humanity. The others connected with humanity only occasionally and not directly. The Tessir came to this planet guided by the Orion constellation, not directly from it, but from other dying planets because they had nowhere to go. The Confederation directed them here, knowing that their potential could quickly awaken humanity's. So they came here guided by the Elohim with a main purpose, but they also had their own personal purpose. They had to take all possible resources from this planet to be able to rebuild their own. They needed minerals from this world, so they needed workers to extract those minerals for them. The Anunnaki, also known as

Nephilim in ancient cultures according to Matthias, devised a system to control us and instill fear in us. They created in our society the idea of threatening creatures and demons, which however did not really exist; they were just mental illusions used to maintain control and continue their collection of energy. This energy, which we call emotion, is considered one of the most important creations of the universe because emotions act as portals to every dimension. Whoever masters their emotions can cross any dimension. Every human being is like a great energy factory, constantly active in opening portals, even if we do not understand how they work. The reptilians were the first to notice this potential and considered women as the main producers of this energy. They then taught women to use this force, allowing society to understand and use male energy. This led to the birth of a material civilization where women, through emotion, dominated the male aspects of society. However, with the arrival of an external force called the Parasite, the Aethir manipulated this emotional knowledge, causing us to forget how to handle such energies, making us unable to harness our internal energy factory. Consequently, the more energy we lose, the more they gain to sustain their worlds. And this is not only about the species that visited us but also about those who brought them here, into the fourth dimension. Fourth-dimensional beings do not feed on elements of the three-dimensional world like fruit or meat; they feed exclusively on energy. Therefore, they needed humans in the three-dimensional world to generate large amounts of energy, in order to feed and survive in the fourth dimension. That's why many entities of this dimension seek to prevent us from managing our emotions, so they can continue to feed. However, we cannot judge them harshly because we humans sometimes do the same with animals. Some Aethir, Nemnir, Althir, and Sophir taught humans how to manage their emotions. Within each species, there were two factions: one that wanted to use humans as factories to obtain minerals for their worlds and nourish their spirits, and the other, aware of their own imminent extinction, supported the need to transcend through humans, teaching them their own methods to perpetuate themselves through human blood. Consequently, some factions of reptilians and Anunnaki wanted to control humanity, while others wanted to help it. Not all pursued the same goal. This dualism led some families to rebel against the rules of the Aesir, granting humans the power to build their own civilizations. Thus, all cultures on Earth simultaneously discovered how to use fire. In the myths of Greece, India, Mexico, and Egypt, giant families taught humans how to manage internal emotions, although some tried to control the world and the energy generated daily by humans. When the period of domination by these cosmic entities ended, they passed their knowledge on to all shamanic cultures of Asia, Siberia, and the Americas, transmitting knowledge on how to simultaneously connect with the Earth and the Sky. Today, the greatest impact on our society is attributed to the Aesir, who structured our society, provided the foundations of our culture, and built the first temples with large stone blocks. These constructions are found in the Middle East, the Mediterranean Sea, Central America, and

Asia, and demonstrate how the Aesir guided and influenced the construction of monumental temples through the use of huge stones, the foundations of new religious structures. In Mathias de Stefano's idea, there is a belief that, although not always their actions towards humanity were benevolent, they have provided us with the main tools to create civilizations and the awareness that no one can dominate us, because we humans are the main source of power.

This chapter dedicated to Mathias de Stefano has been extensively drawn from the inspiration provided by his numerous books and lectures held over the years. The reflections and theories presented reflect the innovative spirit and depth of research that characterize the work of Melchizedek, who has dedicated his life to studying the connections between ancient spiritual traditions and new perspectives on human and universal consciousness. The information presented here is a tribute to his career and contributions, which continue to influence and stimulate debate on these fascinating topics.

TIM TACTICAL: EXPLORING EXTRATERRESTRIAL INFLUENCE ON HUMAN HISTORY

Tim Tactical is the pseudonym of a tactical advisor and analyst operating within a secret sector of the German government, working to understand the missions and strategies of non-human intelligences on our planet, in the solar system, and beyond. With over 100 face-to-face encounters with beings known as the "Grays," Tim has gained deep specialized knowledge of over ten different extraterrestrial species. His experiences have allowed him to gather information on a conglomerate of ETs working on timeline manipulation, genetic seeding, and historical intergalactic conflicts. Connecting with a collective consciousness he calls "Entity 6" on an interfrequency level, Tim unveils perspectives on the mysteries of our universe from various densities of reality.

Ultimately, Tim analyzes and suggests various strategies related to extraterrestrial groups in contact with Earth. He reveals that extraterrestrial entities' understanding of human history diverges significantly from our linear view. During his encounters with over ten different extraterrestrial species, Tim has found that each species has its own interpretation of human historical events. These discrepancies are often exacerbated by the fact that history has been rewritten multiple times, creating confusion and divergent interpretations. Additionally, Tim has explored the impact of so-called "failed temporal cycles," a natural physical phenomenon in the universe where certain explored timelines may fail due to self-destructive behaviors, random accidents, or conscious decisions by units of consciousness to abandon a particular path. These failed cycles are reintegrated into the main successful timeline, functioning as a cosmic backup plan to ensure the stable and successful evolution of the universe. This dynamic ensures that even if a parallel version of an individual fails, the main subject may not notice it, as it continues to exist in the successful timeline without perceiving discontinuities. One of these entities, described as a level six consciousness operating outside conventional dimensions, offers a perspective that considers human history an extremely exotic concept. These beings see every element of the universe as a direct portal to the "Source" itself, interpreting existence as a series of probabilities that give rise to systems where life can manifest. According to them, everything we experience is actually a very old thought coming from the Source. For example, when we observe an apple, the information we receive is not immediate; there is a time delay, just as moonlight takes a second to reach us and sunlight eight minutes. So, everything we see is actually a past version of the observed objects. These beings, operating outside of time, perceive history as an old thought of the Source that wanted to explore what it means to exist. From the perspective of extraterrestrial entities known as the Grays, reality is perceived as a mental and cognitive concept rooted in a very old thought that they believe they have materialized into existence. Their experience of isolation and loneliness in the universe is so intense that they describe the universe as empty and desolate, a feeling that led them to perform an extreme act of self-destruction to give birth to a new existential purpose, thus erasing their "Master Line." According to the Grays, this experience of loneliness drove their species to create a reality where a sense of community and the possibility of exchange and diversity could emerge. This view is reflected in their historical narrative, which includes the construction of the two pyramids in Egypt aligned with the Orion constellation, considered the universal headquarters of the Grays. Specifically, they refer to Zeta Reticuli, a place in the Orion star system, where they claim to have built these pyramids. These structures were not just buildings but portals: humans, created by the Grays from bonobo DNA — known for their particularly evolved social dynamics — could enter the pyramids, shed their biological bodies, and transport themselves to the Grays' star system. There, they could connect with the Gray community, explore the universe, and enrich their spirituality. The Gray narrative emphasizes that the main ingredient of human DNA is that of the bonobo, highlighting how socialization is a distinctive trait that the Grays find particularly advantageous. This is their story, a tale of how they shaped humanity and used the pyramids as gateways to new dimensions of existence and awareness. This entity maintains that every star serves as a direct portal to the Source, and that the visible field of the universe, dotted with dark areas, represents areas of controversy or exploration within the Source itself. The Source experiences and explores itself through these dynamics. With regard to human history, these entities believe that the Great Pyramid of Giza was placed where it is to divide the light and

246

thought that we are experiencing at this moment. They assert that the construction of the pyramid, done before humans existed on this planet, allowed the Source to observe itself. This, according to them, explains the ubiquitous presence of the all-seeing eye on the pyramid, symbolizing the technology used by the Source and the level six being to self-observe.

The Zeta Reticuli, known as the Grays, claim to have created humanity by crossbreeding their own DNA with that of primates, thereby giving rise to modern humans. However, this claim is shrouded in mystery and controversy, as other extraterrestrial species, as we have seen in this book, contest this version, asserting that they too had a significant role in the genetic manipulation of humans. The discrepancies between these narratives highlight a complexity in human history that extends beyond a single timeline and suggest the existence of multiple parallel realities that intertwine. According to the Grays, not only did they introduce genetic modifications to humans, but they also contributed to the creation of the pyramids as key structures for their project. The Great Pyramid of Giza, in particular, according to them, already existed when they arrived on Earth. The Grays argue that they used this pyramid and two others, built later, as portals to transfer human souls to their star system in Orion, integrating them into their cosmic community. This process was part of a broader design to harness the spiritual and cognitive abilities of humans, thereby enhancing their understanding and interaction with the universe. This narrative reveals not only the alleged extraterrestrial origin of some of the oldest and most mysterious structures on Earth, but also the interconnection between ancient terrestrial constructions and interstellar geopolitics, suggesting that past catastrophic events, such as great wars or the flood, may have had causes beyond our conventional historical understanding. Another historical perspective suggests that the pyramids were used as advanced technologies for humans of the time, who were spiritually evolved enough to interact with extraterrestrial entities. These beings, often associated with the Galactic Federation, claim that the pyramids already existed when humans inhabited Earth. The pyramids are not bound by time and appear as ancient structures, although they do not have a defined age; they could be at least 15,000 years old, a period that coincides with major earthly cataclysms. The pyramids, especially the Great Pyramid of Giza, were conceived to divide light so that the Source could observe itself. Some theories suggest that the Great Pyramid of Giza may have a counterpart outside of time.

The pyramids were used to orient people toward the Orion star system, facilitating human transfer to this system as part of a process of integration into a cosmic collective. It is believed that the pyramids had multiple functions, besides never being used as tombs. The inner chambers of the Great Pyramid of Giza, for example, were employed for healing purposes and to stimulate spiritual awakening. The pyramids were also designed to conduct electricity, using materials that allowed for a natural conduction system. Despite some parts of the pyramids being plundered or damaged, they are believed to still be active and continue to perform some of their original functions. This highlights the complexity and multidimensionality of their purpose, which goes beyond the simple architectural or historical function traditionally attributed to them. The sacred geometry of the pyramids alters the natural geometric flow of energy. This was one of the original purposes of the pyramids: to break and divide light so that the Source could experience itself. The pyramid structures, regardless of their location, constantly modify the energy flow, acting as points of high energy frequency on the planet. During World War II, there was intense observation by extraterrestrial entities, due to the high energy level of the conflict. It is supposed that there was some sort of sabotage by external entities that influenced the outcome of the conflict, facilitating events that led to what was a tragic outcome. Time-traveling species, such as the Grays, do not intervene to alter these events as they are relevant to Earth's evolution. There is evidence that particular war technologies and strategies were secretly transferred to Antarctica by the SS, under Himmler's command, without Hitler being fully aware. These technologies included significant advancements not disclosed to the general public, and it is believed that this Nazi timeline is still active and influential, requiring corrections from within rather than external interventions that could generate further chaos in timelines. In the 1940s, numerous UFO crashes were recorded in North America. Some argue that the Grays and other species sought to balance human technological progress, particularly with reference to atomic bombs. The Germans, advanced in such technologies, would have attempted to move them to

Antarctica. Subsequently, atomic technology was globally distributed to maintain a balance, allowing various nations to access such destructive power. This balance was also sought in the field of UFO technologies. It is believed that the Germans were particularly advanced in this technology, as evidenced by the 1947 incident involving Admiral Byrd in Antarctica. The Grays, among other species, would have played a role in distributing such technologies to Americans and Russians, contributing to creating a global strategic balance. During the conflict between the Ebens and the Grays, the latter conducted observation flights over US territory to monitor activities related to atomic and nuclear bombs. Unlike the Ebens, who were less invasive, the Grays adopted a more direct approach. It is theorized that, realizing the implications of the discovery of their UFO by the Americans, the Grays orchestrated the Roswell and Corona incidents as seemingly natural events, foreseeing that they would lead to a positive outcome in the long term. Regarding our perception of history, it emerges that history itself is largely a construct dependent on the perspective from which it is observed. It has been learned that multiple influences and forces seek to protect and guide Earth. This episode did not dwell much on high-ranking entities that have influenced Earth by providing ideas and directions through cognitive content alone. This type of influence, less tangible but significant, shapes human history every day through spontaneous ideas that come to certain people, profoundly influencing the course of human history. It is comforting to know that there is a vast number of entities watching over and assisting humanity, ready to offer their help, and that we can always seek to connect with them.

This chapter is dedicated to Tim Tactical, whose interviews have delved deeply into themes of strategy and tactics in various contexts. Although he has not written books, his conversations have been a source of considerable inspiration and have offered valuable insights. The theories and reflections that emerged from his interviews reflect an analytical approach and a keen understanding of group dynamics and decision-making. The information presented here pays tribute to his ability to stimulate thought and debate on complex and current issues.

ORIGINS AND REVELATIONS: EXPLORING THE ANTHROPOLOGICAL AND METAPHYSICAL MYSTERIES OF HUMAN HISTORY

In the narrative of the Holy Scriptures, God created the beasts of the earth according to their own kind and everything that creeps on the ground according to its own kind. God saw that it was good and, turning to the heavens, pronounced the intention to create man in his own image and likeness. Thus, according to the account in the book of Genesis, man and woman were fashioned from the same earthly clay about 6,000 years ago. For centuries, humanity has looked to the divine to understand its origins and essence. However, the advent of modern archaeology has introduced a different narrative, challenging traditional conceptions. Excavations in the earth's soil have revealed ancient bones and tools that seemed to tell a story of evolution, not divine creation. Charles Darwin, in his influential book "On the Origin of Species," though not focusing extensively on human evolution, suggested that further research would illuminate the origin and history of man. These few lines sparked a revolution in scientific and cultural thought. In 1870, the theory of human evolution from ape-like ancestors gained traction among scientists and academics in the Western world. Following the publication of Darwin's book, elaborate family trees began to appear from various scientists, including the German naturalist Ernst Haeckel, who sought to trace the evolution of the human species from lower life forms. These schemes, however, were often lacking in solid evidence, relying primarily on scientific speculation and a few fossil finds, such as those of the Neanderthals, too recent to be considered true missing links. Nevertheless, the scientific community remained hopeful of discovering older and more decisive fossils of "ape-men." This anticipation was not in vain: in 1894, the Dutch physician Eugene Dubois discovered a primitive skull and femur in Java, identifying what Haeckel had anticipated as Pithecanthropus erectus, now known as Homo erectus, which lived about 1.6 million to 300,000 years ago. This finding was just the beginning of a series of discoveries that would continue to populate the human family tree with new species, including Homo habilis and Australopithecus, discovered respectively in 1950 and 1920. Human evolution was then described as a process that began in Africa, with Homo erectus later spreading to other regions of the world, evolving into Homo sapiens. The latter, completely replacing Homo erectus, colonized new areas of the planet, including North America, no more than 20,000 years ago. However, over the past 150 years, new fossil discoveries have continued to challenge this established narrative, showing the presence of Homo sapiens even in much older geological strata than previously thought. This raises significant questions about what else there is to discover and reconsider in the vast and complex puzzle of human origins. In the 1850s, Carlos Ribeiro, head of the Geological Survey of Portugal, discovered tools in Miocene formations in the Tagus River Valley near Lisbon. To understand the incredible antiquity of Ribeiro's discoveries, consider that the Miocene extends from 5 to 25 million years ago. Currently, the most primitive stone tools

253

recognized date back to the Pleistocene at most, an epoch that ends about 2 million years ago. The tools of the type discovered by Ribeiro in Miocene formations are generally attributed to the late Pleistocene and are characteristic of modern humans. At that time, the only known extinct primates in the Miocene were some types of monkeys. So the question arises: who made Ribeiro's tools? Are they really artifacts or just natural products? Analyzing a tool from Ribeiro alongside one officially recognized, made by Neanderthals in the late Pleistocene, less than 100,000 years ago, reveals striking similarities. In both, large flakes have been removed in parallel, an unlikely result for simple random impacts from natural forces. Both tools also show additional features typical of human work, such as the percussion bulb, created by a direct blow that detached the flake from the flint core, and the percussion platform, the surface on which the blow was struck, along with a small flake removed from the percussion bulb. In every aspect, Ribeiro's Miocene tools resemble those recognized by science as products of human labor. Despite this evidence, many scientists remained skeptical of the conclusion that humans had made tools in the Miocene. During an International Congress of Archaeology and Anthropology held in Lisbon in 1871, a commission of scientists was appointed to examine the sites of Ribeiro's discoveries. One of the commission members, the Italian geologist J. Bellucci, found a tool in Miocene formations that all the present scientists recognized as identical to late Pleistocene scraping tools. This led some to argue that it was indeed a late Pleistocene tool transported into a Miocene formation from above. However, the tool was

254

found firmly embedded in the upper surface of an overhanging section of the Miocene levels. Even older tools than those found in Portugal were discovered by Abbot Bourgeois in Tene, France. Many of these tools were embedded in undisturbed Oligocene formations, indicating an age between 25 and 38 million years, further challenging accepted theories on the timing of human tool appearance. Particularly noteworthy is the edge retouching on the discovered tools. This retouching is limited to one side of the working edge of the tool, indicating that several small flakes were removed in succession, most of them oriented in the same general direction. Such retouches are generally considered a clear sign of intentional work. The tools from the Oligocene of Tene exhibit the same characteristics as a scraper accepted as original from an Upper Pleistocene site in France. There are other examples of unifacially retouched tools from the Oligocene of Tene, reproduced in scientific journals from the 19th century. At another site near Aurillac in southern France, various scientists recovered stone tools from Miocene formations during the 19th century. In 1905, the German scientist Max Verborn sought to confirm these discoveries by personally conducting excavations in Aurillac, from which he recovered such tools from Miocene formations. The cortex, or outer surface of a flint found there, was removed from the working edges, which had been carefully chipped to form a point. Scientists like Henry Bruhl sought to demonstrate the natural origin of such tools. In an excavation near Clermont, France, Bruhl found specimens with small fragments of flint near the main blocks, apparently removed by geological pressure.
255

Since this occurred in an Eocene formation, Bruhl was convinced that any human work could be excluded, firmly believing that humans could not have existed between 38 and 55 million years ago. Based on this preconception, he concluded that all flint fragments resembling tools found in the same Eocene layer had been formed by geological pressure. In fact, Bruhl was astonished to find in an Eocene formation a tool that exactly resembled a late Pleistocene tool made by Homo sapiens. But here's an important fact: specimens of this level of sophistication have not been found with the flakes in place. The fact that geological pressure could produce similar effects does not mean it can produce complete tools with wear marks in the appropriate places. It appears, then, that Bruhl actually found a genuine human artifact in an Eocene formation. On the coast of East Anglia, England, Jay Readmore and other researchers reported several intriguing discoveries. A pointed piece of wood was recovered from the Cromer Forest Bed in East Anglia. The right end was cut flat, as if sawn. The formation of the Cromer Forest Bed dates back to the late Early Pleistocene, about 1 to 1.5 million years ago. Readmore noted that at one point it seems that the cutting line was corrected, as often necessary when sawing. It is difficult to imagine how such sawing could have been done without tools considered rather modern. Another discovery was a carved shell, presented in 1881 by geologist Henry Stopes to the British Association for the Advancement of Science. It was recovered from the Red Crag Formation, which has an age of 1.5 to 2 million years. Remember that, according to common opinion, humans capable of such work would not have

256

appeared in Europe before 40,000 years ago. Below the Red Crag Formation is a layer called the Detritus Bed, which rests on the Eocene clay of London. It is composed of fossils and sediments from the Pliocene, Miocene, and Oligocene periods. Anything found here could be between 2 and 38 million years old. Jay Readmore recovered some bone tools from the Detritus Bed below the Red Crag. The fractures forming the points cut across the natural grain of the bone, indicating intentional work rather than natural breakage. In the Detritus Bed, another round object was discovered, described by Henry Brule, one of Europe's leading experts on prehistoric man, resembling a sling stone, like those used recently in New Caledonia. The sling stone appears to have been shaped from a clay-like substance, and its surface shows many parallel striations, indicating processing with some kind of tool. If the current view of human evolution is accepted, it is difficult to explain what kind of being could have made this object at least 2 million years ago, and perhaps up to 38 million years ago. In the middle Miocene marine formations on the northwestern coast of France, the Abbey of Lannay discovered a bone of a halotherium, an extinct marine mammal. The bone bears marks that appear to have been left by a sharp tool. Similar marks were found on a whale bone, recovered by Gian Cappellini from a Pliocene formation in Italy. These cut marks are distinct from those that could be made by teeth. A tooth scraping the surface of a bone typically leaves a U-shaped depression, crushing rather than cutting the bone. On the other hand, a sharp flint blade would leave a narrow V-shaped incision, like those found on the bones in question. In his original report,
257

published in the 1870s, Cappellini provided an enlarged cross-section of a cut mark on one of his fossil whale bones. Cappellini's methodology was as sophisticated as that used by modern scientists. So far, we have considered stone tools, cut bones, and other artifacts indicating the presence of humans in very ancient times. One might ask if there are human skeletal remains from the same period. The answer is yes. In 1860, in Castanedolo, Italy, on the southern slopes of the Alps, Professor G. Ragazzoni, a geologist, discovered human fossils in an excavation on a slope at the base of a five-foot-thick Pliocene clay layer. Ragazzoni carefully examined the overlying layers and determined they were intact. In 1880, the bones of a fully human man and a child were discovered a few yards away, at the same depth. Ragazzoni inspected the overlying layers again and found them undisturbed. Shortly afterward, the bones of a woman were found at a slightly higher level. The overlying layers of yellow sand and red clay were intact. This ruled out the possibility that the bones had been introduced into the Pliocene clay from above. The reconstructed skull of the woman is entirely human and provides excellent evidence of the existence of Homo sapiens in northern Italy over two million years ago. According to modern theory, modern Homo sapiens appeared only 40,000 years ago. Leaving Europe, we now turn our attention to discoveries made in other parts of the world. In 1894, Dr. Fritz Nordling, a paleontologist with the Geological Survey of India, found a tool in the Miocene Formation in Burma. Dr. Nordling commented that if this tool were to be rejected as a product of natural forces, then nearly all recognized stone tools from later periods should also be rejected. At the beginning of this century, some Argentine scientists discovered stone tools in the Pliocene Formation at Miramar, on the Argentine coast, just south of Buenos Aires. The formation contained bones of mammals typical of the Pliocene, dating it to over two million years ago. However, Argentine researcher Antonio Romero insisted that the formation was rather recent and that the Pliocene animal bones had been transported from elsewhere. Carlos Amagino, instead, found in natural connection the bones of the entire hind leg of a Toxodon, an extinct species of South American mammal from the Pliocene. This find is probably not due to the random movement of bones in river currents. If the bones truly belonged to the same set, it means that a Pliocene animal died there and that the formation actually dates back between two and five million years, like the stone tools found there. Here's another interesting fact: Carlos Amagino found a stone arrowhead embedded in the femur of the Toxodon, further evidence of the presence of technologically advanced humans over two million years ago in Argentina. A human skull, dubbed "Philly," was discovered in 1896 by workers during excavations of a dry dock basin in the port of Buenos Aires. It was found in the keel pit of the basin, about 35 feet below the riverbed, immediately after the workers had drilled through a hard limestone-like layer called Tosca. The sediments in which the skull was found are between 1.5 and 2.5 million years old. Some might argue that no scientist was present at the time of the discovery except the workers. However, even the Heidelberg jawbone, fully accepted as a specimen of

Homo erectus in the Middle Pleistocene of Europe, was discovered by workers. In the 1850s, miners began searching for gold in the gravel beds of California rivers. Later, they dug mining shafts in places like Table Mountain in Tuolumne County, to access the gold-bearing gravels. The gravels were originally deposited in rivers that flowed in this area millions of years ago, during the Miocene period and earlier. At the end of the Miocene, volcanic eruptions covered the entire area with basalt. More recently, rivers have carved new valleys, leaving formations like Table Mountain with deposits of gold-bearing gravel now buried under layers of basalt. In 1877, John H. Neal entered the Matazuma mine shaft at Table Mountain. He proceeded for 1,400 to 1,500 feet inside. Then, at the operational end of the shaft, he found in an intact gold-bearing gravel this mortar and pestle, along with several stone spear points. Neal testified that he saw no cracks through which the objects could have entered from above. The gold-bearing gravels of Table Mountain date back to at least the late Miocene, so the objects found in them would be 7 to 9 million years old. Some modern geologists argue that ancient river channels date back to the Eocene period, potentially up to 55 million years ago. Miners have made similar discoveries at dozens of nearby locations. A mortar with pestle was found in 1861 in gold-bearing gravels 16 feet below the surface at Kincade Flat. Similar finds were recorded at Gold Spring Gulch. Another interesting object was found in 1864, 16 feet below the surface in gold-bearing gravel at Oregon Bar in Placer County. These examples and many others were reported by J.D. Whitney, the state geologist of

California. However, some objected that they were all hoaxes perpetrated by miners. But in 1869, Clarence D. King of the U.S. Geological Survey found a pestle firmly in place at Table Mountain. It is displayed next to a modern Indian pestle. American anthropologist W.H. Holmes dismissed the California finds, mainly because they did not conform to his ideas about evolution. The discovery of the Java man had placed a man-ape in the Middle Pleistocene. So, how could there exist men capable of creating advanced stone tools in the Miocene or Eocene? According to Holmes, it was completely out of the question. However, many scientists, most of them evolutionists, had discovered abundant evidence of human presence in the Pliocene, Miocene, and earlier periods. But with the discovery of Java man and later Australopithecus, this evidence disappeared from view, mainly because it did not fit into the emerging new scenario of human evolution. Today, practically no one has even heard of this evidence. If you want to learn more, you have to look in obscure 19th-century journals in various languages. Of course, discrepancies in the evidence contradicting the current theory of human evolution can be highlighted. But even the evidence said to support this theory is full of discrepancies. Consider, for example, Java man. Since Dubois made his initial discovery at Trinil, scientists have made many other discoveries at other sites in Java. These fossils are now classified, along with the original Java man, as Homo erectus. In 1978, a standard textbook provided potassium-argon dates for the Homo erectus fossils from Java ranging from 700,000 years to 2 million years ago. A table in the book lists 24 discoveries. Of these, at least 18, or 75%, were found on the surface or came from unknown locations and therefore unsuitable for potassium-argon dating. Fourteen were initially found by native collectors. And four were found in a museum in the Netherlands 30 years after their discovery, with no clues about their original stratigraphic location. The potassium-argon method does not date the bone itself but is used to test the age of volcanic deposits. Only if a fossil is found beneath a layer of undisturbed volcanic material can it be dated using this method. Devastating criticisms could have been made against the Java man fossils because most were found on the surface at unspecified locations by paid native collectors, but no such criticism has been made. Instead, scientists simply embellished these imperfect proofs with undeserved potassium-argon dates that allowed the fossils to be easily fitted into the accepted sketch of human evolution. This double standard in the treatment of evidence is a general phenomenon. Let's examine how the process of selective acceptance and rejection of evidence works in a related field we have already briefly touched upon: the peopling of the New World. The currently vigorously defended opinion holds that Homo sapiens crossed Siberia no more than 20,000 years ago, yet scientists have discovered numerous pieces of evidence suggesting a much older human presence in the New World. Despite these pieces of evidence being comparable in quality and quantity to those used to support the dominant view, they are rejected by institutional scientists. For example, in 1899, Ernest Volk, a collector for the Peabody Museum of Natural History at Harvard, found a femur of Homo sapiens embedded in glacial layers in Trenton, New

262

Jersey. The layer in which the bone was found has been dated by the New Jersey Geological Survey to about 107,000 years ago. This small statue, found in Nampa, Idaho in 1889, came from a well sunk to a depth of 300 feet. The level at which it was found is now dated by the U.S. Geological Survey between 300,000 and 2 million years ago. The Nampa image is comparable to the famous Venus of Willendorf attributed to Cro-Magnon man in Europe, which was thought not to have created such works of art until 30,000 years ago. By the way, the Venus of Willendorf was found by a road worker. This coin-like object was recovered at a depth of over 100 feet from a well boring in Illinois. The Illinois Geological Survey states that the formation in which it was found dates back from 200,000 to 400,000 years ago. The discovery was initially reported by William E. Dubois of the Smithsonian Institution. In the early 1960s, Louis Leakey identified an anciently inhabited site in Calico, southern California, with stone tools found in layers dated 200,000 years ago. In subsequent years, thousands of tools have been recovered from the Calico site, including a beaked engraver. Scientists are reluctant to change their view of when humans entered the Americas, and they are even more hesitant to change their view that modern man first appeared in the last 40,000 years and evolved from ape-like ancestors originating in Africa. Evolutionists are proud to have eliminated the idea that man was created 10,000 years ago, but not much has changed. The current prevailing opinion is that modern human-like beings can only be dated back a few thousand years. Before that, there was only primitive man who blurred into a life similar to that of monkeys, but this narrative is confronted with abundant evidence that modern human-like beings have existed for tens of millions of years in the past, in geological epochs far removed from our own. It might be objected that this evidence comes from outdated reports, but what about recent discoveries in Africa that seem to clearly establish the evolution of humans from ape-like creatures in the last 3 million years? In 1978, at Laetoli, Kenya, an expedition led by Mary Leakey discovered fossil footprints dated to 3.7 million years ago. Many scientists who studied some of the footprints state that they are indistinguishable from those of modern humans. Could this be possible? For most scientists, the answer is no. Instead, the Laetoli footprints are considered evidence that Australopithecus had feet similar to those of modern humans. Indeed, it is said that Australopithecus was entirely human below its monkey-like head. But some scientists have proposed a completely different picture. The hand bones of the australopithecines suggest to anatomy experts, like C.E. Oxnard, that they were well adapted to tree movement similar to the modern orangutan. Comparing the hand of Australopithecus with that of the orangutan, one notices that the finger bones are strongly curved in both hands. Now, comparing the hand of Australopithecus with that of the chimpanzee, one can see that the finger bones of the chimpanzee are slightly straighter. Finally, when comparing the hand of Australopithecus with that of Homo sapiens, one notes that human finger bones are even straighter. Humans with curved finger bones, like orangutans, are very active in trees, while humans with straight finger bones are not. This suggests that

264

Australopithecus was well adapted to tree life. Lucy's hip bone, the australopithecine now considered at the root of the evolutionary line leading to humans, is often described as almost human in shape. This also applies to the Sterkfontein pelvis, also belonging to an Australopithecus. Here, the similarity of the upper parts, the iliac blades, can be noted, but if these bones are observed in an orientation where the hip cavities are visible, it can be seen that the iliac blades are set at very different angles. Comparing the pelvis bone of Sterkfontein with that of a chimpanzee, one notices in this orientation that both bones appear quite similar and are both different from the human pelvis. In frontal orientation, the pelvises of Australopithecus and that of monkeys appear very dissimilar. The provisional conclusion is that the pelvis of Australopithecus shares characteristics that are both strongly similar to monkeys and strongly similar to humans. By measuring different parts of the bone, its shape can be represented as a point in a multidimensional space. Two measurements of a human femur define a corresponding point in two dimensions. Relationships between the bones of different species can be studied by comparing corresponding points in multidimensional space. Some scientists have claimed that the Australopithecines are intermediate between African monkeys and humans, but this analysis shows them in a separate domain with structural affinities to orangutans. According to the studies we have considered, this is an erroneous representation of the evidence. This is confirmed by a recent discovery in the Olduvai Gorge in Kenya of the first set of skull and limb bones of Homo habilis. In

265

light of this, some humanoid femurs, once attributed to Homo habilis, must now belong to some other creature. They are at least 1.8 million years old. Could they have actually been human? This could also be true for this upper arm bone, very ancient and similar to the human one, found in Kanapoi, Kenya. Given the great difference between Australopithecus and modern man, what kind of being could have possessed this arm bone 4 or 5 million years ago? Could it have been the same creature that left the humanoid footprints at Laetoli? Overall, the evidence does not seem to support the view of Australopithecus as human intermediate ancestors between African monkeys and humans. It is more likely that they were unique creatures, quite different from both monkeys and humans, but with some adaptations for tree climbing similar to orangutans. However, there is much controversy regarding the interpretation of these fragmentary African evidence. The more intensely they are studied, the more it seems like trying to perceive a desired image in a shimmering mirage of possibilities. The origin of human cultural traits is perhaps even more difficult to explain than its physical attributes. This led Alfred Russell Wallace to doubt the standard conception of human evolution. Born in England in 1823, Wallace shared with Darwin the credit for the theory of evolution by natural selection. Wallace failed to explain how, through natural selection, people living in simple tribal societies had acquired intellectual abilities as great as those of educated Englishmen of his time. Wallace came to a heretical conclusion: guided evolution. He postulated the existence of subtle beings capable of intelligently directing the evolutionary

266

process. Darwin was shocked. He wrote to Wallace that by proposing such notions, he had literally killed their common child, the theory of evolution. But years later, in South Africa, a similar heresy was proposed. Dr. Robert Brule, who made many of the most important discoveries on South African australopithecines, also concluded that there was a hierarchy of intelligent subtle beings guiding the evolutionary process. In light of the issues tormenting Wallace, consider the following strange story. According to current thinking, culture remained at a very rudimentary level for two million years. Even with the advent of complete modern man 40,000 years ago, culture remained primitive. Then, about 7,000 years ago, a radical transformation is said to have occurred. Within a few centuries, civilization blossomed with the creation of complex economic and legal systems, architecture, fine arts, and numerous technological innovations. Today, we find that such developments are due to people with strong innate creative talents. The seemingly independent appearance of civilization in many parts of the world suggests that such creative drives are an innate characteristic of Homo sapiens. But how did these talents arise and why did they remain unexpressed for at least 35,000 years after the time of Cro-Magnon man? Surprisingly, we find evidence that civilization may not be so recent. The evidence of human antiquity discussed so far has all been published in scientific journals. But now, we will cross the boundaries of science and enter the realm of general human testimony. According to this newspaper from the 1890s, Mrs. S.W. Culp found a gold chain inside a piece of coal. This coal is dated by the Illinois

267

Geological Survey as dating back to 260-320 million years ago. In 1897, miners at the Lehigh coal mine in Iowa found a stone engraved with identical relief heads. The coal from this mine dates back to the Carboniferous Period, about 280-360 million years ago, when amphibians were thought to be the most advanced vertebrate life form. In 1862, the LaSalle Press reported that in Macoupin County, Illinois, 27 feet underground, under two feet of slate rock, on a bed of coal, the bones of a man were found. The Illinois Geological Survey dated this coal to the Carboniferous Period. The human bones would therefore be about 300 million years old. In 1912, Frank J. Kenwood found an iron pot embedded in a piece of coal at the municipal electric plant in Thomas, Oklahoma. The coal came from the Wilberton mines in Oklahoma and is dated by the Oklahoma Geological Survey to the Carboniferous Period. In June 1852, Scientific American published an article about a exquisitely worked metal vase blasted out of solid rock in Dorchester, Massachusetts. The U.S. Geological Survey reports that this rock is Precambrian, over 600 million years old. Such discoveries continue to be made. In 1968, several metallic tubes were found in a Cretaceous layer in northern France. The discoverers, Drouet and Soltani, thought they were the product of human work. The Cretaceous is in the Mesozoic era and dates back to 65-140 million years ago. These findings so radically violate current scientific conceptions that it is difficult to make sense of them. But we can gain greater understanding by considering another area where human nature violates standard scientific views, the realm of the paranormal. Although most scientists reject paranormal phenomena, others have studied them carefully. One of these was Sir William Crookes, the famous British physicist who invented the cathode ray tube now used in television screens. Crookes became president of the prestigious Royal Society and eventually received the Nobel Prize for his discovery of thallium. Crookes began his investigations to expose fraudulent mediums, but then became convinced of the reality of psychic phenomena. One of the mediums he tested was Daniel Dunglass Holm, a medium famous among European aristocrats and intellectuals for the extraordinary unexplained physical effects that regularly occurred in his presence. With this apparatus, Crookes demonstrated that Holm could, by lightly touching a matchbox placed here with his fingers, cause the scale at the other end of the table to register a pressure of six pounds. With a mechanical disadvantage of about 20, Holm would have had to exert a pressure of about 120 pounds to achieve this result, according to standard physics. And even more extraordinary experiments followed. A concertina would often be observed playing complex melodies while Holm held it with one hand, away from the keyboard. To ensure that Holm was not manipulating the instrument with prestidigitation skills, Crookes constructed a special cage. Positioned under the table, the cage made it impossible for Holm to touch the instrument with his other hand. As a precaution against a possible trick mechanism in the concertina, Crookes provided a brand new concertina never before seen by Holm. Crookes reported that the concertina played as usual. Then Holm withdrew his hand from the cage. Crookes claimed that he and two other present saw the concertina clearly float inside the cage without any visible support. Wallops also reported a similar experience. On several occasions, observers, including Crookes, saw Holm levitate. When Holm levitated, he claimed not to do so by his own force, but to be lifted by invisible, sentient entities. Levitation by professional magicians requires an elaborate apparatus hidden on stage, while Holm's levitations occurred amid crowds of guests in private residences where he was a dinner guest. There are well-documented reports of levitation in various times and places. For example, in 17th-century Italy, St. Joseph of Cupertino often levitated, a phenomenon witnessed by Pope Urban VIII, the Spanish ambassador to the papal court, and the Duke of Brunswick, a Lutheran. Regarding these phenomena, Professor Chalice of Cambridge University said that the testimonies were so abundant that either the facts must be admitted as reported, or the possibility of certifying facts through human testimony must be abandoned. Anomalous facts related to the paranormal and the ancient antiquity of man tend to be rejected by the scientific community. This reveals the operation of a knowledge filter through which people preserve information compatible with their own views and discard those that are in conflict. Science has carefully filtered all information connected with the paranormal, but if we examine human society in general, we find abundant evidence that such phenomena have occurred in almost all times and places. Shamanism is widespread. In trance, shamans contact spirits, allowing them to produce a variety of paranormal phenomena, including psychic healing. A fundamental element of shamanism and many other traditions, ancient and modern, is the existence of a soul distinct from the physical body, capable of traveling outside of it. Some evidence of this comes from modern medical science. Doctors encounter reports of out-of-body experiences, which typically occur during heart attacks and other traumatic experiences. Many people have reported observing their own body from a higher vantage point. Dr. Michael Sabom, initially skeptical of such experiences, sought to confirm them. He asked patients who had experienced heart attacks and reported out-of-body experiences to provide details about their exact medical treatment during the unconscious period. In the group he studied, enough people provided correct details of their treatment to convince Sabom that out-of-body experiences had indeed occurred. Sabom wondered "Could the mind, separated from the physical brain, essentially be the soul, which continues to exist after bodily death, according to some religious doctrines?" This leads to the question of transmigration, the transfer of a conscious entity from one physical body to another at the time of death. Dr. Ian Stevenson, a psychiatrist at the University of Virginia, has extensively compiled reports indicating that people are able to remember past lives. Stevenson studied reports of very young children, not under hypnosis, without the motive or ability to invent elaborate stories of past lives. The reports of past incarnation often included details about the person's habits, possessions, and knowledge. In many cases, Stevenson was able to verify the details and confirm that the previous personality actually existed. Until 1988, Stevenson had cataloged 2,500 cases worldwide.

271

Of these, 881 were investigated thoroughly, and Stevenson was able to verify the reported past incarnation in 546 cases, about 62% of the total cases investigated. These extensive pieces of evidence suggest that human personality may operate outside of the physical body and even migrate from one body to another. This indicates that some elements of human existence are incompatible with physical science and its evolutionary theories. Such elements leave no trace in the Earth's strata. Some insist, however, that all paranormal phenomena are the result of illusions and hoaxes. Yet, spirits, levitations, miraculous healings, out-of-body experiences, and transmigrations have been consistently observed in human societies worldwide for thousands of years. Critics argue that the human mind everywhere generates similar illusions. But if the human mind is universally the same, then the ability to discriminate between reality and illusion should also be widespread. Must we presume that the most intelligent people in nearly every culture have been completely deceived? According to many human traditions, living beings can be organized into a hierarchy. Even in Christianity, during the Middle Ages, paintings were commissioned showing the sensory world below, then the heavenly and intellectual realms inhabited by various types of angels, and finally, the eternal spiritual domain of God. The same idea of a progression of increasingly subtle inhabited realms is also part of Eastern thought. In the esoteric teaching of Jewish Kabbalah, we find a similar idea of a hierarchy of emanations from God. At the lowest levels of such hierarchies are the realms of ghosts and earthbound spirits. Many psychic

272

phenomena are attributed to beings of this kind. Above spectral spirits are various types of more powerful intermediary beings. Beyond these are demigods who have control over the forces of nature. Here are also great souls working for the enlightenment of all living beings. Why have people accepted the existence of beings in this hierarchy such as demigods? One main reason is that people have achieved desired results by venerating such beings. For example, at Lourdes, France, doctors have reported hundreds of miraculous healings of sick and deformed people who immersed themselves in the waters of the spring connected to an apparition of the Virgin Mary. François Massere, a French carpenter, had an extreme case of varicose veins for 30 years and had been declared incurable by three doctors. One evening, he applied compresses with water from Lourdes on his legs. When he woke up the next morning, he found hardly a trace of the varicose veins. In such cases, the restoration of damaged tissues seems to be caused by an intelligent agency operating outside of known physical laws. This is relevant to the question of our origins. If an entity can restructure the human body, it could have built it in the first place at any time in geological history. The ongoing discovery of stone tools and anomalous artifacts, which seem to emerge from periods too remote to be explained by accepted evolutionary theories, might suggest the existence of beings above humans in the universal hierarchy. However, archaeology reveals nothing about living entities superior to humans, and evolutionary theory compels us to consider the idea of such beings as an aberration of the evolving brain. However, this view can only be upheld by ignoring vast areas of

273

human experience, including the perception of a supreme creator at the root of the universal hierarchy of beings. Plato presented the idea of the supreme good, the ultimate absolute cause, which embodies eternal ideal forms. He also hypothesized a demiurge, a subordinate creator who generates the material domain by manifesting copies of these eternal forms. Turning to a completely different culture, we find that almost all Australian Aboriginal tribes believe in a supreme god, sometimes called Baimi or Bunjil, who is absolutely supreme and sole creator and sustainer. The Chinese have traditionally venerated ancestral spirits, as well as a hierarchy of demigods, such as the goddess of mercy. The Chinese believed in a vast array of intermediary beings, including celestial dragons. Even Shang-Ti, the supreme ruler in heaven, was venerated, whose name appears on this tablet in the Imperial Temple complex in Beijing. The Chinese emperor performed sacrifices to Shang-Ti to ensure good harvests. The American chief shaman, Black Elk, became a spiritual leader after experiencing a vision in which he was transported to the presence of guardian ancestors, from whom he received instructions. Black Elk saw all living beings as children of a single supreme spirit. The spiritual tradition of India, embodied in the Vedas, is characterized by many as polytheistic, but in its pure form, it is strongly monotheistic. The supreme lord of the universe, Jagannath, is worshipped in this famous temple in Puri. In addition to this material world, the Vedas teach that there exists the brahmajyoti, the effulgence of the supreme, and even higher, one encounters a variety of spiritual planets. These are presided over by Goloka
274

Vrindavan, the abode of the supreme personality of God, Krishna, and his eternal consort Radha. In the hierarchies described in the world's spiritual traditions, we find a common pattern. This pattern is delineated in detail in the highly developed spiritual philosophy of India. The Vedic scriptures, such as the Bhagavad Gita and the Srimad Bhagavatam, describe the supreme absolute personality. He is the source of an eternal spiritual realm as well as countless temporary material universes inhabited by fallen souls in illusion. Each universe is brought into manifest form by a demiurge lord, Brahma. Brahma generates material bodies for the illusioned souls, starting with great sages and demigods. From demigods and sages, bodies of lower beings, including humans, animals, and plants, are generated by descent with modification. This may be called reverse evolution. Modification occurs rapidly in a manner reminiscent of the rapid tissue reconstruction seen at Lourdes. In reverse evolution, an existing subtle form systematically manifests into a gross physical form. This can be contrasted with the generation by generation accumulation of slight bodily changes postulated by Darwinian evolutionists. The question remains: when did humans arrive on Earth? The ancient Sumerians and Babylonians claimed that their early kings descended to Earth from the heavens and that civilization was given to man by demigods. According to the Bhagavad Gita, about 120 million years ago, Lord Krishna communicated the message of the Gita to the sun god, Vibhishvan, in his abode on the sun. Vibhishvan then repeated these instructions to his son, Manu, the father of mankind. About two million years ago, Manu passed on the same instructions to his

275

son, Ikshvaku, who founded the dynasty of earthly kings. Beings from the sun may have traveled via a vimana, or a Vedic space vehicle, although they were capable of more direct means of travel. These beings were the progenitors of humanity and also the engineers of Earth's natural environment. Given this structure, humans may have been created many times by such demigod progenitors. In fact, the archaeological evidence we have considered suggests that humans may have repeatedly repopulated the Earth and manifested typical cultural traits over tens of millions of years. Furthermore, the psychic and anthropological material examined here suggests that humanity may be part of a much larger interplanetary life system, with its ultimate source in an eternal transcendental dimension. This view allows for the accommodation of all archaeological and anthropological evidence available to science within a systematic framework. On the other hand, Darwinian evolution requires the dismissal of vast amounts of archaeological evidence and the rejection of all paranormal and spiritual phenomena as illusory. Naturally, by its very nature, the evidence available to science does not provide certain knowledge about the remote past and the ultimate origin of man. Therefore, it might be useful to consider higher dimensions of human experience, rather than confining ourselves to seeking answers to these questions in the bones and stones found in the depths of the Earth.

MICHAEL TELLINGER: A LONG JOURNEY IN SEARCH OF TRUTH

THE DRAKONIAN RETAGGING OF THE ANNUNAKI ACCORDING TO MICHAEL TELLINGER

Michael Tellinger has continued, throughout his career as a researcher, to uncover astonishing phenomena that seem endless. As a child, at the age of five, he often found himself looking at the sky wondering when the stars would start speaking to humanity. This childhood curiosity turned into a serious passion for ancient civilizations after reading "Chariots of the Gods" by Erich von Däniken at the age of eighteen. This reading represented a turning point that definitively directed his life towards the study of human origins. Tellinger found himself particularly aligned with the theories of Zecharia Sitchin, the other author we have already discussed, who postulated the existence of ancient extraterrestrial civilizations, the Anunnaki, who allegedly created humanity for their own purposes. Sitchin theorized that these 'gods' came to Earth primarily in search of gold, a fundamental element that, according to him, played a crucial role not only in their technology but also in their survival. During his research, Tellinger found physical evidence supporting Sitchin's claims, especially by exploring specific locations in South Africa that seem to corroborate Sitchin's translations of ancient Sumerian texts regarding the Anunnaki. These discoveries not only validated many of Sitchin's claims but also allowed Tellinger to further expand his research, exploring the vastness and implications of these ancient presences on the southern tip of Africa. The fascination with gold, therefore, is not only a human characteristic but also extends to the Anunnaki, who established a vast mining empire in the area known as Abzu, located at the southern tip of Africa. Gold was not sought for wealth or trade but had more complex and mysterious functions. The Anunnaki, who also introduced the concept of money, did not consider money as part of a barter process for thousands of years. Zechariah Sitchin argued that gold was turned into fine powder and used to create a protective shield around their dying planet, shielding it from universal cosmic rays. This use of gold may have had broader implications, acting as a protective coating that made their planets invisible to the eyes of other conscious beings, thus hiding their activities on them and the abuse of a species created specifically for gold extraction. It is estimated that the Anunnaki extracted gold in massive quantities, which were then camouflaged and made unrecognizable as simple pieces of paper with printed logos, simulating payment for the extracted gold. This method of payment highlights a kind of theft of Earth's resources. Sitchin's studies suggest that the Anunnaki arrived on Earth approximately 435,000 to 450,000 years ago, while more recent research indicates that tools and artifacts related to the origin of humanity date back to approximately 285,000 years ago. This detail opens up intriguing scenarios about the real motivations behind their gold mining and the advanced technologies they possessed, of which we are only now beginning to understand the importance and applications. Investigations into Eve's mitochondria suggest that humanity suddenly appeared about 250,000-300,000 years ago, a fact corroborated by tools and

279

archaeological finds found in places like Adam's Calendar in South Africa, closely related to the Anunnaki and particularly to Enki, dating back approximately 285,000 years ago. According to the aforementioned theories, the Anunnaki came to Earth to mine gold, and when the pre-existing beings on the planet refused to work, the Anunnaki decided to genetically alter these species to create one in their image. This genetic manipulation is not only narrated in Sitchin's translations but is also a common theme in other historical interpretations. Genetic manipulation, aimed at creating workers, demonstrates the advanced mastery of the Anunnaki in technology and genetic manipulation, a mastery that appears to persist to this day. The biblical narrative of Adam and Eve is linked to these practices: the first human beings cloned by the Anunnaki did not possess X or Y sex chromosomes but only 22 pairs of chromosomes. It was only later, when the Anunnaki realized the need for faster reproduction, that they introduced the X and Y chromosomes to allow for procreation. This story intertwines with the biblical narrative when it speaks of Adam, from whom a piece of genetic material was taken—symbolized by the rib—to create a female. This experiment aimed to observe mating and procreation dynamics, a turning point that sheds an entirely new light on the biblical figure of fallen angels and suggests that the Anunnaki are simply a group of entities created by a higher force, indicated as God, the original source of all that is visible and invisible. These revelations not only reinforce the concept of a universal creator but also broaden our understanding of the greatness and extent of such a creative entity.

The narrative of the lost civilizations of southern Africa fascinates and raises fundamental questions about why their existence is little known. This low visibility in mainstream historical discourse can be attributed to the tendency to repeat the same information without exploring older or less documented periods. Michael Tellinger's work has brought to light a much longer history, and the vanished civilizations he has exposed seem to confirm cataclysmic events shared by many ancient cultures, such as the great flood described in Sumerian tablets and the Bible. Such event would have caused massive waves that deposited sediment and sea sand up to the mountain tops, burying the remnants of ancient structures under thick layers of earth. Furthermore, during his research on stone circles in South Africa, Michael also investigated the possible presence of pyramidal structures in the Barbatin Valley, where Adam's Calendar is located. These structures, not yet confirmed as pyramids but suggestive of such form, are connected to Adam's Calendar through a golden spiral and exhibit peculiar phenomena such as loss of GPS signal, production of strange energies and sound and electromagnetic frequencies. These findings suggest that such structures could be energy-generating devices, a key to understanding the advanced technology used by these ancient civilizations. Michael Tellinger has deepened the link between humanity and the Anunnaki, who came from the planet Nibiru. The Anunnaki not only introduced new technologies but also the concept of money, irreversibly changing the course of human history. The concept of "Abzu," mentioned in Zechariah Sitchin's texts, is identified with the ancient gold

281

mining activity in southern Africa, suggesting that these advanced techniques and knowledge could have been disseminated by these extraterrestrial entities. The protective shield they intended to create for their planet through the use of monatomic gold was a technique that may have made their planet invisible. Human diversity is another point of discussion in Tellinger's work, suggesting that the apparent variety of human races may reflect a genetic design influenced by the Anunnaki, each of whom may have contributed to different physical characteristics in human populations. Indeed, Tellinger explores the complexity of the genealogy and power dynamics of the Anunnaki, focusing in particular on key figures such as Enki and Marduk. Enki, often described as a benefactor of humanity, would have played a crucial role in the creation and initial guidance of human beings, not only providing advanced technologies but also directly intervening in their genetic development. Marduk, one of Enki's sons, is described as a central figure in Tellinger's narrative. Marduk would have taken control of certain regions of Earth, particularly Egypt, and his management would have had a lasting and sometimes negative impact on human history. According to Tellinger, Marduk's actions can be linked to a form of authoritarian and oppressive government that influenced human power structures up to the present day. The presence of these two figures at opposite ends of a moral continuum illustrates the internal division among the Anunnaki, which Tellinger suggests is the cause of many conflicts and historical developments on Earth. While some Anunnaki, like Enki, may have sought to promote progress and the well-being of human beings, others, like Marduk, may have pursued more selfish and domineering interests. This dichotomy between "good" and "bad" Anunnaki not only shaped early civilizations but continues to influence global dynamics, with the descendants of the Anunnaki still struggling for influence and control, oscillating between benevolent leadership and oppressive manipulation. The warlike tensions among the Anunnaki were not isolated, as they were not the only extraterrestrial beings active on the planet. Other entities such as the Greys and inhabitants of Zeta Reticuli, among others, interacted with Earth, introducing further complexity to extraterrestrial interactions. The Anunnaki stood out for their power and dominance, stemming primarily from their extensive gold mining operations, which not only exploited Earth's resources but also attracted other alien groups eager to exploit the planet for its mineral wealth. The biblical narrative of the book of Genesis offers striking echoes of these stories, particularly in the way the Elohim (another name used by the Anunnaki according to Tellinger) manifest their obsession with gold, a detail that emerges when speaking of the place called Havilah, where "the gold is good." This obsession extends to the point of transforming gold into a white powder, known as monatomic gold or manna from heaven, attributing to it healing and almost miraculous properties, capable of improving health and potentially prolonging life through ingestion. Research by scholars like David Hudson has explored how this powder could positively influence the human nervous system, facilitating an almost instantaneous transmission of

283

information through the body, and even causing levitation when manipulated under specific experimental conditions. Even more fascinating is the discovery of vast mining tunnels in South Africa, in the Limpopo province, excavated by the Anunnaki, dating back to the 1930s and discovered by modern miners. These tunnels, rich in platinum residues but devoid of gold, indicate that the Anunnaki were solely focused on gold, neglecting other precious metals present. Concurrently, the ruins of circular stone structures, over 10 million, scattered throughout southern Africa, are crucial for understanding the Anunnaki's mining empire. These sites not only served as mines but were also advanced energy devices. The ruins, known for their loss of GPS signal and emission of strange energies, are directly linked to Adam's Calendar through a golden spiral, suggesting a much more advanced and sophisticated energy network than previously imagined.

The ruins of the circular stone structures extend throughout South Africa, Zimbabwe, parts of Botswana, Mozambique, and are believed to cross the Zambezi River into southern Zambia. These structures are best described as the factories and power plants of the Anunnaki's mining empire. Each stone circle has a unique design and serves as an energy-generating device. Detailed studies have revealed that they generate sound frequencies in the gigahertz range, an unprecedented phenomenon. These structures were positioned in specific locations to harness Earth's sound frequencies and energy, making each one a unique energy connection point with the Earth. The stone walls amplify these sound frequencies, turning them into electromagnetic fields. This energy is then shared through channels connecting all the stone circles, creating a vast energy network that supported the extraction and processing of gold and other minerals. The knowledge of these technologies was lost following the great flood, described, as we have seen, in many cultures and scriptures as Noah's flood, which wiped out almost every trace of these ancient civilizations. The flood is believed to have been a catastrophic natural event, rather than a deliberate act as suggested by some biblical interpretations. The Anunnaki, anticipating this calamity, had prepared by hiding the gold in underground tunnels. These tunnels, still rich in gold and human remains, bear witness to the antiquity and catastrophe that befell the Earth about 12,000 years ago. The issue of Atlantis dates back even further than the great flood. The Anunnaki, using sound as an energy source—a method believed to have been known also to Nikola Tesla—developed advanced technologies such as magnetrons, capable of greatly amplifying sound. These devices, similar to those used today in microwave ovens and other secret military projects, could reach sizes of up to 20 meters in diameter. As for their origin, Zachariah Sitchin suggested that the Anunnaki arrived on Earth via spacecraft, using water as a propulsion medium. This hypothesis may not be accurate, as the Anunnaki are described as multidimensional and highly evolved beings, whose existence spans millions, if not billions, of years. Their advanced technological knowledge is intrinsically linked to our DNA. It is now understood that our DNA is connected to a universal morphogenetic field, which contains all accumulated knowledge, allowing us to access this information without the need to reconstruct lost technologies. Furthermore, the genetic manipulation carried out by the Anunnaki has left traces in our genes, demonstrating a direct descent from these beings. The Anunnaki also introduced the concept of money as a tool of control and slavery, establishing the first banking institutions in the temples of Sumer, which served as banks. This monetary system was one of the first means by which the Anunnaki strengthened their control over human populations, laying the groundwork for dynasties and royal bloodlines that have dominated and influenced human civilizations for millennia.

They were, therefore, the pioneers of gold extraction, creating vast mining empires not only in southern Africa but also in other parts of the world, as evidenced by the distinctive African features of the large heads of the Olmecs and the Maya. This connection underscores the global extent of their influence and the adoption of techniques and practices that have deeply marked human history. Near Adam's Calendar, also a site linked to the Anunnaki and specifically to Enki, lies a tomb believed to belong to Dumuzi, Enki's youngest son, who died shortly after the flood. According to Sumerian tablets, Inanna buried Dumuzi near her father's special place, oriented to the east, so that his soul could live forever. The tomb, discovered by Johan Einer and Tellinger himself, was identified using infrared technology that revealed a cavity three meters deep and as long, unusual dimensions for a human burial. This site, known as the Stone Altar, was a place of ancient shamanic rites, confirmed also by Baba Credo Mutwa, an eminent Zulu shaman from South Africa. The Anunnaki may have brought African gold miners to other parts of the world to expand their mining operations, a hypothesis supported by evidence of global mining practices. These beings not only introduced advanced gold extraction techniques but also established monetary and legal systems that persist to this day, perpetuating a form of economic slavery. The observation that systems of power do not want to change is evident, as control, not money, is the true focus of their power. Money primarily serves as a tool to maintain this global control. Recognizing this, the proposed approach involves eliminating dependence on money, promoting a global system that prioritizes people and shared prosperity, freeing us from the chains of the monetary system. The activation of human DNA, which contains traces of Anunnaki DNA, is increasing our awareness and ability to surpass old technologies, suggesting that we can evolve beyond the use of external technologies as the most sophisticated ones are already integrated into our being. This collective awakening could lead us into a new era of cooperation and abundance, where common welfare prevails over individual accumulations.

Regarding the cosmic influence of the Anunnaki, it is hypothesized that they reached hundreds, if not thousands, of planets, spreading their presence and methodologies throughout the universe for millions of years. This raises fundamental questions about their legacy and implications for our understanding of the cosmos and our position within it.

Finally, the revelation that the initial part of the Bible has been misinterpreted for centuries questions many established beliefs. The discovery that the opening phrase of the Bible does not begin with the letter "Aleph," as it should for any sacred text, and that a correct interpretation reveals a different message, aligns biblical narratives with the creation stories of many other ancient cultures. This suggests that the concept of a "father of beginnings" may be a common element in all ancient religious traditions, offering a more integrated and universal view of our spiritual and physical origins. Michael Tellinger suggests a connection between Stonehenge in England and the stone circles of South Africa, explaining that both act as energy-generating devices. Stonehenge, according to him, is an ancient device, likely over a million years old, based on the observed erosion on the stones. This claim is based on direct observations of the site's conditions, suggesting a much older age than conventional estimates. Another theme dear to Tellinger is that of the loss of historical knowledge. Tellinger mentions how, despite the existence of ancient texts such as the Sumerian tablets and Sanskrit texts, much of our past remains a mystery, particularly regarding ancient technologies and their use. He emphasizes the use of quartz and silica in ancient sites, materials that are central to today's most advanced technologies for their conductivity and storage properties. Tellinger criticizes modern capitalism for its approach to the extraction and commercialization of natural resources, including minerals like quartz and medicinal plants. This extraction and sale process, he argues, distracts from the possibility of using these resources in their original, purer, and more potent form. Furthermore, he highlights how the knowledge encapsulated in the minerals of ancient sites is often overlooked or not fully understood in modern society. He argues that the silica contained in ancient stone structures could hold significant historical data on how they were built, by whom, and for what purposes, offering tremendous untapped potential due to current limitations in information extraction technologies.

Tellinger also speaks of a revolutionary development in materials technology: the ability to store digital information in quartz crystals. This progress could open new frontiers in how we store and access information, radically changing traditional methods of data storage and paving the way for future technological discoveries that could revive the use of natural materials in innovative contexts. The technology of Stonehenge and the stone circles in South Africa share similarities, suggesting a possible connection between the two. Such observations raise questions about ancient civilizations and how their knowledge was lost, especially when compared to the persistence of ancient texts like the Sumerian tablets or Sanskrit manuscripts that speak of gods and flying machines. Regarding the introduction of money, Tellinger illustrates how this invention was not part of ancient agrarian societies, where food could have served as a more practical currency than money or gold. He points out how the introduction of money was a tool of control and subjugation, bringing with it the negative aspects of society that still persist today. The solution, for him, lies in transcending the concept of money, promoting a global system that values humanity rather than material wealth. Tellinger proposes rediscovering the use of renewable energies like sound, used by the ancients but now forgotten, to move towards a fuller understanding of free energy. His future work aims to further explore these ancient techniques and promote a philosophy of "contributionism," where each individual contributes to collective well-being, freeing us from the oppression of money-based control and energy. Also interesting is the topic Michael Tellinger speaks of in his new book, "Ubuntu Contributionism," which draws inspiration from the term "Ubuntu," also known for the software created by South African Mark Shuttleworth. The book is a project for human prosperity, focused on social change through generosity and collaboration rather than competition and control. Michael is optimistic about the future, arguing that change is already underway, fueled by programs like the one he is participating in and other similar initiatives that raise awareness and elevate collective consciousness. He invites everyone to become "seeds of consciousness," freely sharing their knowledge to accelerate this global awakening. This approach aims to overcome the principle of "divide and conquer," pushing towards a world of abundance led by the people, for the people, emphasizing that the planet belongs to all who inhabit it. The deep collective amnesia of humanity regarding its origins and purpose is also a condition that Tellinger connects to historical manipulation and the loss of ancient knowledge. Through DNA activation and the rediscovery of ancient wisdom, he suggests that humanity is gradually awakening, reaching levels of enlightenment that will allow us to break free from the chains of global oppression. With confidence, he states that the process of liberation is already underway, with growing consciousness movements spreading globally, akin to those of the 1960s, promoting a new renaissance of awareness and unity. Michael Tellinger discusses the importance of bringing together current research, writers, and musicians to amplify the impact of their discoveries and collective awareness. He emphasizes how this synergy could further strengthen the message of global awakening. Responding to a question about what he would like to know immediately, Tellinger expresses the desire to have visible confirmation of the assistance we are receiving from beings of higher consciousness. This, he says, could offer comfort and reinforce the belief that we are not alone in the endeavor to save the planet and free humanity from slavery. In his books, he also touches on the topic of karma, suggesting that, unlike the common interpretation, karma on Earth could be a trap created by the Anunnaki to keep humanity in a state of submission. He contrasts this view with that of other cosmic civilizations, where souls can reincarnate freely, aware of their past lives, suggesting that on Earth reincarnation occurs without memory, keeping souls in a cycle of ignorance and subjugation.

MICHAEL TELLINGER AND THE HIDDEN WISDOM OF THE ANCIENTS: EXPLORING THE FORGOTTEN ORIGINS OF HUMANITY

Michael Tellinger, known for his commitment to elucidating humanity's origins, has been traveling the world giving lectures since 2006. Through these engagements, Tellinger has noted a widespread sense of dissatisfaction: none of the audience members seem pleased with the direction the world is taking or convinced that governments are effectively fulfilling their roles. This realization has prompted Tellinger to seek solutions through the wisdom of ancient civilizations. He delves into humanity's ancient past, discussing vanished civilizations and their advanced technologies that today seem almost incomprehensible. He explores the role of gold in human history, a fascination inherited from the gods according to ancient narratives, and touches on themes such as astronomy, geology, archaeology, physics, and mathematics. Tellinger urges us to consider this ancient knowledge not as obscure or threatening curiosities but as keys to unlocking and enlightening our understanding of the world, providing a solid foundation for building new social structures. He emphasizes the importance of using this ancient information to address contemporary challenges and build a better future. The series aims to connect historical dots, looking at the statues of Easter Island that symbolize a gaze both into the past and into the future, to gather essential information capable of supporting this new vision. In exploring ancient civilizations, it emerges that they possessed profound knowledge about our species, our dark ancient history, and the origins of humanity. A recurring belief among these cultures is that we come from the stars, an idea that contrasts with the vehement denials of our modern history books. Faced with these discoveries, it becomes essential to learn from the ancients, assimilate their knowledge, and acknowledge their contribution. Modern humanity seems afflicted by a sort of collective amnesia, ignoring its origins, identity, and purpose. This "species amnesia" appears widespread globally. It could be hypothesized that the final assault on this knowledge began about 500 years ago, when Europeans began invading and dominating territories outside Europe, imposing Eurocentric belief systems and history books and erasing indigenous knowledge. This process of cultural amnesia leads us to ask ourselves: who are we, where do we come from, and why are we here? These fundamental questions are often obscured by the narrative of the victors in our school and university textbooks, which do not convey true knowledge but reflect an agenda set by the winners of wars and conflicts, who have taken control of governments and lands. An illuminating example is the Gospel of Thomas, where it is recounted that the disciples ask Jesus to reveal how their end will be. Jesus' response highlights a profound principle: "If you understand the beginning, you will know the end and not experience death." This suggests that a complete understanding of our origins is fundamental to understanding our destiny and that much of our history has been written by those who triumphed in conflicts, filtering and shaping knowledge to their

293

advantage. When discussing with someone who asserts the certainties derived from history books, it is worth asking: how much do we really know about our human history? Tellinger asserts that our understanding of human origins is lower than the laws of physics would allow us to suppose. This claim is surprising. How can we prove it? Through a simple mathematical equation. If we consider that history is written by the victors, how much can we really know about historical events involving Alexander the Great? Who was he really? What did he actually do? We mainly know about him that he conquered the world, invading countries, looting, and usurping lands and houses, and yet we call him "the Great," a title he perhaps does not deserve. Take, for example, the story of the Tower of Babel, a famous but deeply enigmatic historical event. The biblical narrative places this event at a time when Babylon was already an empire and many languages were already spoken worldwide. The concept of "confusing their languages" to prevent them from "becoming like us" therefore appears nonsensical. This demonstrates that deep deceptions are encoded in such historical events. Continuing with this critical examination of history, we note that the further we go back into the past, the more blurred the line between history and mythology becomes. Who decides when history becomes mythology? We discover that ancient cultures revered gods and feared entities that were very real to them, as for the Romans and Greeks, who did not consider their gods at all as mythical or imaginary beings. Going back about 6,000 years, to the time of the Sumerians and that murky period of human history, we can hypothesize that we originally had
294

complete knowledge of who we are, where we come from, and why we are here. If we assume that every year there is a war, causing the loss of 50% of information and knowledge each time, we see how this knowledge degrades rapidly. Starting from 100% knowledge, after one year there would be only 50% left, and so on, until it is reduced to less than 1% in just 7 or 8 years. In just 124 years, the remaining knowledge would be less than 10^{-34} of the original knowledge, an extremely small number, close to the value of Planck's constant. This illustrates how little we know about our origins, well below what is allowed by the laws of physics. When someone claims to know history because they have read textbooks, they are probably following the wrong track. The truth is that we have all been told a distorted version of reality. Everything we have been taught is fundamentally wrong. We need to start over, adopting a new set of knowledge and information that allow us to build a better future for humanity and our planet. Human and planetary history is much older, stranger, and more fascinating than most of us can imagine, akin to living in a science fiction or horror movie. Taking ancient sites like Stonehenge, the evidence of their antiquity is evident from the erosion of the stones. Despite the fact that Stonehenge was reconstructed in 1954, a thorough analysis suggests that the stones are much older than generally accepted. This restructuring may have been a malicious attempt to make the site appear more recent than it actually is. The erosion on one of the stones, which broke at a certain point, shows about 50 centimeters of erosion, an amount that cannot be achieved in just a few millennia, indicating that

Stonehenge could be much older than a million years. The Bible itself speaks of giants on the Earth in ancient times, a topic that often elicits laughter when mentioned in casual conversations, as if discussing a sports team. However, texts like the book of Numbers describe these giants in a way that humans seem like "grasshoppers" in comparison to them. This echoes rabbinic traditions that speak of titanic races like the Anakim, the Nephilim, and others, presented as historical realities rather than myths. This view suggests a very blurred line between recorded history and mythology, prompting a reconsideration of what we truly know about our history and the historical figures that populate it. The presence of giants in human history dates back thousands of years and is mentioned by all ancient cultures. Near where I live in South Africa, on the border with Swaziland, there is a giant footprint left on raw granite, a deep mystery that raises doubts about our understanding of geology and material formation on this planet. Klaus Donner, an expert in ancient artifacts and mysterious objects from Austria, discovered in Ecuador the remains of a giant about 7.5 meters tall. Among the findings are a nasal bone, a heel bone, and a fragment of a skull, analyzed and genetically confirmed to belong to a humanoid of that stature. This find underscores how little we know about our human history. At the University of Witwatersrand in Johannesburg, where Tellinger graduated in pharmaceuticals in 1983, there is a bone fragment of a giant found in an ancient mine in Namibia in 1960. This artifact is kept away from public view, as is the famous Boskop skull, housed at the museum in Port Elizabeth, which shows that these individuals were 25 to 30% larger than modern humans. Elongated skulls, found not only in South America or Mexico but also in Europe and the East, continue to emerge, suggesting a much more mysterious history of our planet than commonly accepted. The discussion about Akhenaten and Nefertiti, and speculations about their possible connection to the Nephilim, along with other strange creatures that defy our current understanding of history, add further doubts. Photographs of giants found recently, such as in Ohio mounds or Irish bogs, are quickly removed from public view. At the center of these mysterious cover-ups seems to be the Smithsonian, accused of systematically removing this evidence. Thus, while giants have been an integral part of human history for millennia, their study remains a taboo topic in mainstream history and archaeology. There is a truly exceptional find: a giant bone, probably about 5 meters tall. It was discovered by an American archaeologist in the 1930s in the Middle East and subsequently brought to the United States. Another testimony is the mummified finger of a giant, photographed by a tourist named George Sporey in 1988, who paid $300 to see this artifact. Egyptian paintings show very large beings next to much smaller figures. Some argue that it is just a matter of perspective, others do not. However, it is evident that there were beings of gigantic proportions next to people of normal stature in Egypt and that region of the world. Moreover, small humanoid beings have been discovered around the world, emphasizing how mysterious the history of our planet is. One of the greatest mysteries lies in ancient texts, which are crucial to understanding who we are, where we come from, and why we are here as a species. However, many of these texts contain deceptions. One of the greatest deceptions imposed on humanity is found in the planet's most popular book: the Bible. The opening phrase has been clearly manipulated. It is commonly believed to begin with "In the beginning God created the heavens and the earth," but that is no longer the case. Michal Ledwitz, who was an advisor to the popes at the Vatican for 17 years, is a scholar of the Bible and the Hebrew language. He discovered that the Hebrew text of the Bible does not begin with the first letter of the Hebrew alphabet, Aleph. Currently, the reading begins with the letter B, which makes no grammatical sense. By inserting Aleph, the phrase begins with "Abba," which means "father," completely changing the opening statement and aligning Judeo-Christianity with ancient cultures and civilizations, where sound and resonance are seen as the origin of everything. This discovery confirms that everything was created through sound and resonance, a concept shared by all ancient civilizations. This brings us to the common denominator between humanity and ancient cultures: the obsession with gold that accompanies us to this day and which, as we saw in the previous chapter, is a legacy left to men by the Annunaki.

ANOMALIES AND OUT-OF-PLACE ARTIFACTS: THE REVELATION OF MICHAEL TELLINGER

We continue our exploration of ancient civilizations with Tellinger, seeking to discover what we can learn from ancient times that could benefit our future. Among these mysterious discoveries are tools and artifacts, these strange utensils collected in South Africa. To understand these tools, we must accept that we are dealing with an advanced and now vanished civilization. Unfortunately, this reality has been completely misunderstood by historians and archaeologists, who tend to ignore these findings, as repeatedly emphasized in this book. Our history books and archaeologists make us believe that the ancients were primitive, that we come from caves, and that these peoples could not have had advanced knowledge and technologies like those today. At the same time, we are told that these people with their sticks and long hair are the same ones who built ancient sites like Stonehenge. In reality, when we visit Stonehenge, we realize that they continue to deceive us, trying to make us swallow the lie of loincloth-clad men with long hair dragging giant blocks to erect Stonehenge. They continue to propose and promote this falsehood from antiquity to keep our species in a state of amnesia. And so, we are told, it was these cave people who built such sites, apparently, and similar places. The more one thinks about it, the more one realizes how absurd it is that cave people and primitive men and women of ancient times could have built even a fraction of what we find in ancient civilizations. What we discover is that the technology used by ancient civilizations until today has undergone a kind of regression, and that is why we can truly define ourselves as a species with amnesia. Clearly, when they built these ancient sites, they did so because it was easy for them, not difficult. If we still had this ability today, we would continue to build similar sites, but clearly we are not doing so. This brings us to the three sacred pillars of our educational system. We must first overcome our conceptual error about who the ancients were, what they did, and what knowledge they possessed, to address the discovery of some of these ancient technologies and civilizations. These three sacred pillars of our education are the three foundations of our science and physics, and we repeat them continuously in class. In fact, if you answer this incorrectly, you will fail in school and feel very bad. These three points are: humans evolved from monkeys, nothing can travel faster than light, and energy cannot be created or destroyed, but only transformed from one form to another. Well, these, according to Tellinger, are all three lies. They are lies that have been imposed on us for so long that now we all believe them and continue to regurgitate these lies over and over again because we believe that those who provide us with this information are of higher authority, that they know what they are talking about. But soon we will find out that they are just perpetuated lies that are repeated endlessly to keep our species in a state of amnesia. The theory of evolution has been repeatedly refuted, but we must come to refute the alleged truth that nothing can move faster than light. In 2005, at Middle Tennessee State University, three university students and two high school students apparently succeeded in making sound travel faster than light. This was well documented by the American Institute of Physics in 2007 and quickly buried under a heap of misinformation, because it is not convenient for people to know that sound can travel faster than light. Many may be confused by this information. How can sound travel faster than light? This is where we really need to reevaluate what we have learned about sound, resonance, and their true nature, and about how sound and resonance have led to the creation of everything. Let us remember that if sound and resonance are the source of all things in creation, surely we should be able to do everything through sound and resonance. And let us remember that the Bible tells us that God said, "Let there be light," and light is a consequence of sound. For example, in the current reality, in this density, on Earth where we are today, we all know that when light passes through a specific, denser medium, the denser the medium, the slower the light. In fact, when light passes through a Bose-Einstein concentrate, which is a very dense substance, the speed of light slows down to what is called bicycle speed. So, we know that light slows down the denser the medium. Conversely, for sound, the denser the medium, the faster the speed of sound. For example, sound moves much faster in water because water is much denser than air. So, if you have an infinitely dense medium, sound will move infinitely fast. This is a very simple explanation of how sound, even in this reality, in this density, can potentially move faster, and infinitely faster, than light. But the true understanding of how sound moves faster than light, and permeates

301

everything in creation instantaneously through the resonance of sound, comes from understanding the so-called vacuum, or ether, or the other side of this reality in which we find ourselves. It has been shown, through various formulas and studies on the density of the vacuum, that the density of the vacuum, as Nassim Haramein would define it, is infinite.

Let's see what the void is, as Tellinger understands it. It represents a gateway to other dimensions, present at the core of every cell in our bodies. This portal, imagined as a tiny black hole, connects us to the ether or morphogenetic field, through which every thought, word, or action is instantly transmitted throughout the fabric of creation. This conception explains how sound can travel faster than light. For example, when light passes through a dense medium, it slows down, while sound accelerates in a denser medium, such as water. Theoretically, in an infinitely dense medium, sound could travel infinitely fast. Such understanding expands our perception of reality and challenges traditionally accepted physical laws, underscoring how our ancient ancestors might have understood and utilized these sound properties for purposes we are only beginning to rediscover. The implications of this sound dynamics lead us to reconsider the concept of energy as well. Contrary to the assertion that energy cannot be created but only transformed, astronomical observations suggest that galaxies continue to emerge from black holes, challenging the idea that energy and matter emerged only once during the Big Bang. Instead, it seems that creation is a continuous process, occurring on a cosmic scale as well as at the quantum level, reflecting the Hermetic principle "as above, so below." This revelation urges us to reassess our understanding of human history and ancient technologies, which may have harnessed principles now considered revolutionary or even impossible by modern standards. The instruments and artifacts we are discovering in ancient African ruins may not be simple everyday objects, but advanced devices linked to resonance and sound, capable of influencing reality in ways we are only beginning to understand. Over the past eight years, photographs of anomalous and unusual instruments have been collected, emerging as a new class of tools. Particular interest is focused on the conical instruments discovered around stone circles, but also found globally. These conical instruments are just one part of a broader variety, which also includes the famous sacred donut-shaped stones, scattered throughout southern Africa. Despite their abundance, these stones are not easily accessible. Other curious shapes include elongated stones resembling French bread loaves, which, when struck, emit a bell-like sound, introducing a new perspective on what these objects might represent in antiquity. There are also phallic stones scattered near the ruins, varying greatly in size and seemingly having had significant symbolic meaning for ancient civilizations. Additionally, extraordinary bird-shaped stones and birds on pedestals are found, particularly in the vicinity of the ruins of Great Zimbabwe and other areas of southern Africa. These bird-shaped stones could be prototypes of the Zimbabwe birds, famous since the mid-1800s when they were discovered in the ruins of Great Zimbabwe. These instruments and artifacts mainly come from the vicinity of stone circles and stone ruins in southern Africa, often mistakenly described as livestock enclosures by academics. This misinterpretation denotes the ignorance of historians and archaeologists exploring these ancient sites, who rarely conduct new research or excavations, merely repeating old theories without fully understanding the meaning and importance of what they actually discover.

About five hundred years ago, the first references to these ancient structures in southern Africa were recorded by Portuguese explorers such as João de Barros and Antonio Fernandcz, who sailed around the Cape of Good Hope and landed, encountering the Karanga and Makalanga peoples. These explorers discovered numerous circular stone structures, but when they asked the indigenous people who built such sites, the answer was that they did not know. However, modern historians seem to have precise ideas about who built these structures, ignoring the testimonies of local peoples, which contributes to creating a sort of amnesia, manipulating facts and historical events. These stone ruins, scattered over vast territories including South Africa, Zimbabwe, Botswana, Mozambique, and beyond the Zambezi River in Zambia, are impressive and numerous. Already documented from the Portuguese era, they were also studied by German and British archaeologists from the mid-19th century until the early 20th century. It is interesting to note that the last true explorations at Great Zimbabwe, located in present-day Zimbabwe, took place in 1930. This demonstrates how knowledge of these civilizations has been suppressed, similar to what happens with the Egyptian pyramids, where further excavations could reveal advanced knowledge uncomfortable for conventional historical narrative. Johan Heine, over fifteen years, has collected a spectacular series of aerial photographs demonstrating intense ancient human activity at the southern end of Africa. These structures are all circular, but each one is unique; there are no two identical ones. Some of these circles have unusual shapes, such as horseshoes or ohm-shaped atoms, which become crucial in understanding their function. Additionally, flower-shaped patterns have been discovered, visible only from an aerial perspective. The ruins have been mainly studied by Heine since the 1990s. It has been found that they are aligned with the movements of the sun, such as solstices and equinoxes, and incorporated into them are sacred geometry patterns. This demonstrates careful planning and a deep understanding of solar systems, stars, and natural laws, suggesting that those who built these structures had advanced knowledge of reality and natural laws. It is fascinating to discover that the stone circles in southern Africa are connected by channels which, seen from aerial photographs, might appear as roads, but they are not. Modern historians and archaeologists persist in the mistake of defining them as such, arguing that they served to create a cohesive community. However, it is important to clarify that these are not roads. They are channels that connect all these stone structures for hundreds of miles, and no stone circle is found isolated; all are part of a large and original group of ruins covering vast areas of southern Africa. Aerial photos clearly show

305

that these channels are a main feature of these structures. Additionally, the stone circles are found within much larger grids, similar to giant spider webs connecting them. It is a vast network of stone circles, connected by channels and this immense network of agricultural terraces and other activities that unite them. It is estimated that there are over 450,000 square kilometers of agricultural terraces covering South Africa and Great Zimbabwe, indicating a populous ancient population, in stark contrast to what is reported in history books describing southern Africa as sparsely populated. These terraces are spectacular: driving around southern Africa, for example in the town of Vatafalbuifun, one can see mountains literally covered with these structures. Aerial photographs, including those from Google, reveal extensive areas of southern Africa dominated by these ancient terraces. In Botswana, known as the mountainous kingdom, it is almost impossible to find areas without agricultural terraces on Google Earth. It is unthinkable that such extensive constructions could be made by a population as small as described in historical texts. A photograph taken shows stone circles and agricultural terraces forming a network similar to a spider's web, with channels connecting the circles to this large grid that extends over large areas of southern Africa. From the top of a nearby mountain, it can be observed that the ancient structures cover an area with a radius of about 50-60 miles. Another mysterious anomaly dates back to 1939 when archaeological drawings made by the University of Bloemfontein revealed that these stone circles or ancient ruins had no doors or entrances and were all connected to each other by these particular

306

channels. Some of these circles were formed by concentric circles, without doors or entrances, increasing the mystery of their purpose and function.

Exploring the ancient stone ruins in southern Africa reveals a very different story from the commonly accepted one. The earliest estimates of these structures date back to 1891 when Theodore Bent, crossing Mashonaland and other areas of southern Africa on horseback, documented about 4,000 of these ruins. His observations were later expanded upon by Roger Summers in 1974, who raised the number to about 20,000. However, it was only with further investigations by Rebel Mason, former head of archaeology at the University of Wits, that the estimate reached and exceeded 100,000 sites, suggesting a much higher population density than previously thought. This revelation challenges the traditional narrative that describes southern Africa as sparsely populated. Research has shown that the stone ruins, often mistakenly interpreted as simple dwellings or livestock enclosures, are actually remnants of advanced and complex civilizations, with structures connected by channels stretching for hundreds of miles, forming an intricate network of connections. Evidence of a vast network of agricultural terraces, spanning over 450,000 square kilometers, further supports the hypothesis of a populous and technologically advanced population. Despite this, the exploration and documentation work of these ruins is often overlooked by the academic community, which tends to repeat old theories rather than further investigate. Even the ruins of Great Zimbabwe, one of the most emblematic sites, have not been subjected to significant excavations since 1930. This lack of recognition and the consequent lack of further archaeological investigations keep much of this ancient history in the shadows, perpetuating what seems to be a collective amnesia about the true origins and capabilities of the ancient civilizations of southern Africa.

This chapter on Michael Tellinger draws extensively from the inspirations gleaned from his numerous books and lectures over the years. The ideas and theories expressed here reflect the innovative approach and depth of study that characterize Tellinger's work, who has dedicated his life to exploring the connections between ancient spiritual traditions and new insights into human and universal consciousness. The information presented pays homage to his career and significant contributions, which continue to influence and stimulate debate on these fascinating topics.

DRUNVALO MELCHIZEDEK: JOURNEY THROUGH SPIRITUALITY AND SACRED GEOMETRY

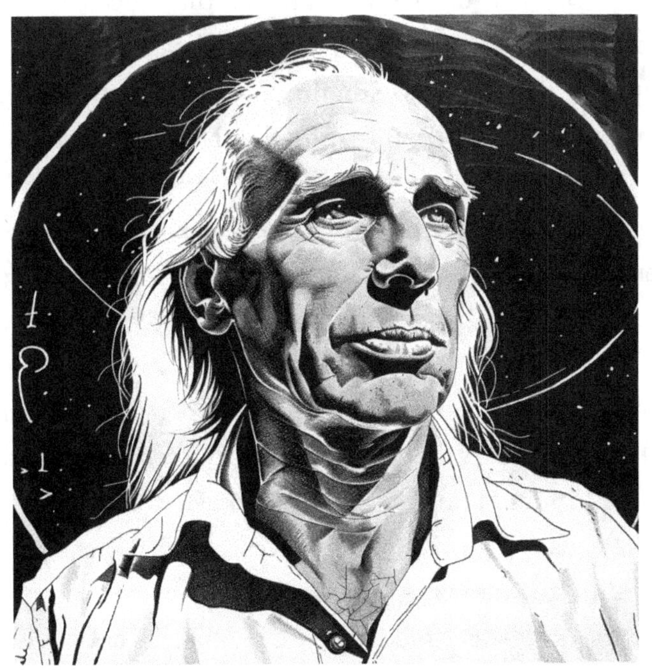

ROOTS AND REVOLUTIONS: FIRST PART OF THE HIDDEN HISTORY OF HUMANITY'S ORIGINS

Drunvalo Melchizedek has always addressed the importance of understanding our history to fully grasp our current situation in the world. He emphasizes that, despite some considering it unnecessary to know the past, it is fundamental to understand the very nature of life. A key aspect of this understanding, according to him, is represented by the Fibonacci series, a numerical sequence that influences multiple aspects of the organic world, including plant growth. This series, which proceeds by adding the two preceding numbers to obtain the next one (1, 1, 2, 3, 5, 8, 13, etc.), demonstrates how plants follow a predetermined growth pattern, developing leaves sequentially that reflect this series. Melchizedek extends this logic to the concept of time, explaining that our perception of the present is inherently linked to our understanding of the past. Without knowledge of the past, the individual lacks a basis to orient themselves towards the future. He criticizes the conception of consciousness based on duality such as good and evil, black and white, highlighting how each polarity includes a third element that creates balance. Examples of this principle include the relationship between earth and sun, where the moon plays an essential role, or the dichotomy of male and female, which includes the child. For Melchizedek, understanding these trinities is crucial for understanding reality. He emphasizes that the entire fabric of the universe is built on tripartite components like protons, electrons, and neutrons, and that our experience of time and space is similarly structured. This three-dimensional approach is fundamental to interpreting and navigating our reality. Drunvalo Melchizedek presents an innovative approach to understanding history, suggesting that to properly interpret our present and predict our future, it is essential to know two of the three components of a mathematical sequence, a concept he calls the "tri-world" or "trinity of the world". According to him, all mathematical sequences, except for the golden section that underlies the others, can be understood by knowing only three components. This principle is applied to our temporal perception: by knowing the past and present, one can deduce the future, and vice versa. Melchizedek, who has long studied and taught these theories, explains how he initially taught history lessons based solely on Thoth's point of view, a historical figure whom he believes lived for a long time. However, the introduction to the works of Zecharia Sitchin, a scholar he has never personally met, has expanded and corroborated his teachings. Sitchin's texts, which analyze ancient clay tablets, align surprisingly with Thoth's narrations, so much so that Melchizedek decided to integrate both viewpoints into his teachings. Through the exploration of Sitchin's texts, he offers a narrative that speaks of giants on Earth, a theme that Thoth had already introduced without providing details about their origin or identity. This narrative also finds echoes in the Bible, in the Book of Genesis, where it speaks of the "sons of God" joining with the daughters of men, producing a race of giants and famous men. These ancient accounts,

311

interpreted by Melchizedek and corroborated by Sitchin, suggest a much more complex human history intertwined with the divine than commonly accepted. Melchizedek's encouragement to study these sources is not only academic but part of a broader attempt to awaken a deeper understanding of our history and our place in the universe. He emphasizes the importance of a critical and open approach, inviting people not to passively accept information but to actively explore and question traditional narratives. In this way, Melchizedek not only educates but seeks to inspire a change in how we perceive and interact with our historical and mythological past. Drunvalo Melchizedek, addressing the theme of ancient history, underscores the importance of knowing events narrated in Sumerian texts, which occurred long before the writing of Genesis by Moses around 1250 BCE. These ancient Sumerian documents, dating back to about 2300 years before Moses' time, describe in detail stories remarkably similar to those of Genesis, including the tale of Adam and Eve and their descendants. According to Sumerian texts, there was another planet in our solar system that orbited in a retrograde direction compared to the other planets. This celestial body, which according to the tablets returns approximately every 3600 years, had a catastrophic impact with another large planet called Tiamat. In a catastrophic encounter, one of Nibiru's satellites (so named by the Babylonians and identified by various names in different ancient cultures) struck Tiamat, dividing the giant planet into two parts: the larger part became Earth and the smaller part shattered, forming what we now know as the asteroid belt. The narratives, also reported by Zacharia Sitchin, also speak of advanced extraterrestrial civilizations living on Nibiru, which about 450,000 years ago decided to visit Earth to solve an atmospheric problem on their planet, caused by heat loss in space. The solution found was to disperse gold dust into the atmosphere of Nibiru to reflect heat back to the planet, a method that could stabilize their environment. The tablets narrate that a small group of leaders and hundreds of extraterrestrial workers arrived on Earth with the goal of extracting gold. Using not particularly advanced technologies, similar to those of rockets, these Anunnaki, as they are commonly called, had to wait for the close passage of Mars to transfer the accumulated gold and replenish their planet. These individuals had very long lifespans, making our temporal standards seem insignificant. Over time, however, the workers rebelled, tired of the harsh working conditions in the gold mines. In response, the leaders decided to create a subspecies to continue the work in their place. This new race, according to Sumerian chronicles, was created by combining clay with the blood and sperm of young Anunnaki, through techniques that today we recognize as advanced biotechnologies, including genetic manipulation and cloning.

These stories, which once may have seemed pure science fiction, are now within the reach of modern science, demonstrating how ancient narratives may have a basis in today's technological reality. Drunvalo Melchizedek has explored multiple times, in his works, the promising frontier of genetics, highlighting the progress that has led the scientific world towards complete DNA mapping, aiming to identify the function of each of the approximately 100,000 genes. This knowledge could allow scientists today to design any type of human being, including a superior race, according to desired specifications. Melchizedek suggests that, considering a hypothetical future 400,000 or even 10 million years from now, the possibilities of genetic manipulation would be extraordinarily advanced. And he arrives at the obvious conclusion that an advanced alien race may have influenced human evolution in the past, causing a significant evolutionary leap between archaic Homo sapiens and modern Homo sapiens, a change that current science cannot explain through normal evolutionary processes. According to Melchizedek's most well-known theory, there were seven giant entities who, on a higher dimensional level, transformed their physical forms into spheres of light, creating a pattern known as the "flower of life". This event would have generated a high blue-white flame about one meter and twenty high, described as pure life energy or "prana", which would have been used as a female ovum. This ovum, according to the narratives, was placed in the "Rooms of Lament", a dimensional fold associated with Egyptian mythology and located beyond an unknown membrane that surrounds the Earth at 440,000 miles away. This place, not visible from Earth but accessible on a slightly higher dimensional level, is described as structured in the shape of a uterus. In this mythological scenario, a family of 32 individuals from the star Sirius - 16 males and 16 females - would have interacted with this flame in a conception ritual. These beings, ranging

314

from 3 to 5 meters tall, would have participated in a fusion process with the ovum placed in the flame. Melchizedek's narratives prompt reflection on the influence of external civilizations on human evolution and the future potential of genetics. Such discussions open the door to new interpretations of ancient human stories, suggesting a complex interaction between science, mythology, and the origins of life on Earth. For two thousand years, these entities thus joined in a conception process that, on a planetary scale, far exceeds human times. While human gestation lasts nine months, here we are talking about a much greater time span. In this period, they conceived until they achieved the birth of the first being. At the same time, on a three-dimensional terrestrial level, Sumerian accounts tell of experiments conducted in laboratories, using test tubes and other instruments, to create the perfect being. The next step was the selection of seven women, as attested by ancient chronicles. These women were implanted with the previously created ova, giving birth to seven children, both male and female. However, these newborns were sterile and unable to procreate. Images of these imposing Anunnaki, ranging from 3 to 5 meters tall, holding fragile naked humans in their arms, are visible in many artifacts. These accounts are not just words on paper, but they are accompanied by drawings, engravings, bas-reliefs, and illustrations. According to the Sumerians, we were created for the primary purpose of gold extraction. Returning to concrete archaeological records, Melchizedek examines the theory of Mitochondrial Eve, a theory that examines DNA and has identified an overlapping process that allows us to trace all world human races back to a single woman, originating from a specific valley in southeastern Africa. Although currently this theory is the subject of debate, the collected data remains impressive. It is interesting to note how this valley is the same one mentioned in Sumerian records as the place of origin. In this valley, extremely ancient gold mines have been discovered, dating back to 100,000 years ago, with human bones of Homo sapiens scattered around the extraction sites. So, one wonders, why did our ancestors, devoid of advanced technologies, engage in gold extraction? This metal apparently had no practical utility for them as a tool or usable resource. These findings suggest that gold extraction continued for thousands of years, even just 20,000 years ago, during recurring glacial periods. The planet was not completely frozen, but the polar caps extended farther down than during interglacial periods. Our survival through these glacial eras shows extraordinary resilience and adaptability. Drunvalo does not speak of just a few isolated documents, but of a hundred thousand documents that are coming to light. All the ancient cities mentioned in the Bible, once considered mythological, have now been discovered. Archaeologists have located all the ancient Sumerian cities, which stretch across southern Iraq, including the historic Babylon. These cities, once lost to time, have been revealed, and excavations continue to unearth new artifacts. What was long considered only myth now takes on the concrete forms of history. According to Sumerian accounts, two Anunnaki brothers, one known as the Serpent, played a crucial role in these cities that once stretched across the Middle East, an

316

area that was not a desert but a dense jungle, testifying to how radically different the climate was in those ancient times. These metropolises were surrounded by vast and laborious gardens. Many of the gold mine workers were transferred to these gardens to care for and maintain them. It is in this lush scenario that, according to Sumerian tablets, one of the Anunnaki incited Adam and Eve to eat from the so-called tree of knowledge of good and evil. Eating its fruits would grant them the ability to procreate. Following this advice, the two ate the fruit and, as ancient inscriptions narrate, began to procreate. Shortly thereafter, Anil's brother, another key figure in the narrative, crossed the garden, as also described in the Bible, where he is seen as a divine figure strolling among the plants. Upon his arrival, he found Adam and Eve hiding, covered only by their shame. Without showing any supernatural power, he called them to him. He thus discovered their sin, but instead of punishing them with death, he exiled them mercifully from the garden.

This benevolent being continued to monitor them from afar, recording their names and their descendants, guarding a long register of their lives and future generations. These details, carefully annotated, have been preserved for millennia in Sumerian inscriptions, offering us a unique and profound insight into the beliefs and narratives of one of the most enigmatic civilizations in human history. These facts lead to deep and sometimes uncomfortable reflections: were we truly destined to be mere slaves of gold? This interpretation of ancient texts challenges us to consider our history in an entirely new light, rich in mysteries yet to be deciphered. In the narrative of our so intricate and mystical past, we find ourselves exploring two distinct human lineages that took different paths in their evolution. On one hand, we have a race of mine workers, artificially created and incapable of reproducing autonomously. These beings, called female eunuchs, could only procreate through external intervention, where the created ova were implanted and brought to term by them. This process was repeated whenever it was necessary to replace or increase their number. In parallel, there existed another race capable of reproducing naturally, which was carefully observed by their creators. These primeval human beings undertook extraordinary journeys, moving across vast territories and tides of time. Melchizedek recounts how he became aware of a human species living on an island west of Africa, in the south of the continent. Initially, this revelation seemed strange and incompatible with Sumerian accounts and conventional theories that locate the Garden of Eden in the Middle East. However, he argues that the true point of origin of humanity was precisely this vast island, called Gondwanaland, a designation recurring in African legends. Creation stories from various cultures along the western coasts of Africa agree on the common origin from Gondwanaland, despite varying narratives in detail. According to Melchizedek, Gondwanaland could have been almost as large as a continent, and it was located in a position that is difficult to specify today; it could have been partially connected or completely separated from present-day Africa. This is the part of the story that he himself admits to never having fully clarified. After a long isolation, which allowed humans to develop and mature culturally and socially, their creators transferred them to southeastern Africa to work in the mines. Later, they moved to the area we now know as Iraq, and it is believed that Cain, one of the first men according to the Bible, migrated to what is now South America. The story of the original Adam and Eve, those who were authorized to continue and multiply, tells of a prolonged era of stability, interrupted only by a dramatic shift in the Earth's poles. This catastrophic event caused their land to sink and forced them to migrate to new lands in the Pacific. Melchizedek suggests that this cataclysm may have been a controlled event, or at least foreseen by the Anunnaki, although there are no certain details about this process. The consequences of these ancient events have been profound and have shaped not only the geological history of our planet but also the cultural and spiritual strands that have influenced subsequent human civilizations. However, many of these narratives remain shrouded in mystery, awaiting new discoveries that may provide further insights into a past as remote as it is fascinating. The history of Lemuria is also shrouded in a veil of mystery and fascination, almost relegated to the realm of myth in modern minds. However, there was a period, precisely in the early 1900s, notably between 1910 and 1915, during which interest in Lemuria reached its peak, fueled by discoveries and research that seemed to confirm its historical existence. This fascination was abruptly interrupted by the outbreak of the First World War in 1914, which diverted global attention from such esoteric research, causing Lemuria to fall back into

319

oblivion until the 1960s, when interest in similar topics was revived. During that fervent period of research, figures like James Churchworth and the French Laplosian became known for their studies on Lemuria and Atlantis, widely discussed in the newspapers of the time. Churchworth, in particular, wrote several books exploring these ancient civilizations, contributing to keeping public interest alive in these subjects. One of these books, titled "Atlantis, the Mother of Empires," published around 1913, contained extraordinary information regarding the area of the Pacific Ocean, particularly an area near Easter Island. The research revealed the existence of extensive coral rings in the Pacific Ocean, which were unusually deep. These rings, found at 1800 feet below the water's surface, suggested that the island had been above water and had sunk very slowly, allowing the corals to continue growing without dying. Such slowness in the sinking process highlighted a geological stability that only a large landmass could provide. In parallel, remarkable similarities were discovered in the fauna and flora along a chain of islands extending from Easter Island to the Tahitian islands and then to Hawaii. The consistency of plants, trees, insects, and bacteria along this chain clearly indicated that there was once a much larger landmass, perhaps a lost continent, connecting these islands. This theory was further bolstered by the discovery of the aforementioned deep coral rings, which could not have formed without the presence of emerged land gradually sinking. These discoveries offered tangible support to theories of Lemuria as a concrete geographical reality rather than a mere legend.

320

Scholars of that time, armed with this evidence, postulated that Lemuria, similar to Atlantis, was an advanced civilization, perhaps even culturally and historically connected to the civilizations of the Pacific Ocean. The persistent ecological uniformity among the islands indicated not only a biological sharing but also a possible cultural exchange supported by a more accessible and vast landmass in ancient times. The reconstruction of this historical narrative, although interrupted by the global tragedies of the twentieth century, leaves a legacy of curiosity and speculation that continues to influence scholars and enthusiasts of ancient mysteries. The research of Churchworth, Laplosian, and others laid the groundwork for a deeper understanding of how human civilizations might have been much more interconnected than traditional history has long supposed, prompting ongoing research and inquiry in future generations.

According to the theories expressed by Thoth, the continent of Lemuria was not a continuous physical entity but rather a vast series of dispersed islands forming a sort of landmass. This archipelago extended from Kauai to Easter Island, representing the western shores of Lemuria before much of it disappeared beneath the sea. In this isolated place, Lemurian civilization reached surprisingly advanced technological levels, developing right-brain type technologies focused on psychotronics and other capabilities that we are just beginning to understand today. This technology, very different from the logical and rational one we are accustomed to, allowed achievements that challenge our current scientific understanding. Lemurian society, during this period of great advancement, began to develop eminently feminine characteristics, symbolized by the transition to a model of thought and creativity typically associated with the right hemisphere of the brain. Before the catastrophe that marked the end of Lemuria, this civilization had reached a stage of development comparable to that of a preadolescent. Throughout this time, the immortal Sirians observed and supervised the development of Lemuria without ever intervening directly, ensuring that everything proceeded smoothly. Even the Anunnaki, the other influential entities of that time, decided not to interfere with Lemurian affairs, allowing society to evolve freely. However, the unexpected arrival of a visitor from the tenth planet, known as the eagle, marked a turning point. This being, emerging from the waters as a hybrid between a fish and a man, introduced a completely new dynamic in Earth's history. Its presence was one of the countless mysteries that Sitchin failed to explain. The eagle's entrance from the vast ocean represented a direct connection with the race of cetaceans, specifically dolphins and whales, which possess a consciousness and historical memory much older and more evolved than humans or even the Anunnaki themselves. Dolphins, closely linked to the Sirius B planet, a mass of water with limited emerged land, represented not only a bridge between our world and the stars but were seen as keepers of deep and ancestral wisdom. These aquatic creatures, which some believe to be transformations of Sirian beings, were an integral part of the creation and development process of the human race on Earth. With such an interconnection of stellar and terrestrial civilizations, the narrative about our origin and evolution becomes even more complicated. The Sirians themselves, some still present on our planet incognito, perhaps live in the ocean depths, sustained not by oxygen but by prana, the life energy that permeates everything. This revelation not only expands our understanding of the possible but also prepares us for a future where the veil between human and extraterrestrial could be definitively lifted. According to ancient records, the Anunnaki had devised a plan for the survival of their race that might seem like a massive transgression of cosmic laws: the use of genetically modified slave labor. This practice, evidently in violation of free will, raised profound moral and ethical questions. However, it was clear that these beings were not advanced enough to directly manifest what they needed; they still relied on rudimentary technologies like propulsion spacecraft. This placed them only a step above the current human technological level, despite their apparent superiority in terms of awareness. However, the true complexity of the situation emerged from their deep involvement in the so-called Lucifer Rebellion, a mythological event that would have seen these races openly disobey universal laws. The question of whether they had obtained permission to begin their experiment on Earth remained unresolved, as the higher records that could have provided such information were inaccessible or not disclosed. This historical context led to a broader reflection on the kind of soul that would choose to incarnate into a body designed for forced labor. The surprising answer was that many of us had chosen that path. According to Drunvalo, this reality suggested that, beyond appearances and superficial judgments, there might be a deeper and more complex reason behind this choice, a reason that might even transcend our current understandings of justice and morality. The story of the Anunnaki was also a story of redemption and change. They had foreseen a global flood that could have annihilated humanity, and initially, they had planned to leave humans to perish. However, when confronted with the reality of the impending disaster, feelings of empathy overcame their original plans. Their change of heart was witnessed by the survival of Noah, an event they had not intended to allow but ended up being celebrated as a sign of hope. The continued interest and involvement of the Anunnaki in human life underscored an unexpected complexity in their interactions with us. They were still present, albeit in reduced numbers — no more than 612 — and lived in specific, secretive locations within the Earth. Their hidden presence continued to influence earthly events in ways that only the future could reveal. Ultimately, the story of the Anunnaki and their interaction with humanity was a vivid reminder that the history we know might be just the tip of the iceberg. The implications of these interstellar interactions were vast, offering a glimpse into how little we still know about the universe and its ancient civilizations.

Within the mystical school of McCall, which housed approximately a thousand people, including 330 families, advanced techniques aimed at immortality research were taught. This institute had the potential to transform the entire human race if given enough time. However, about a thousand years after its founding, a natural cataclysm radically changed the course of events: a shift in the Earth's axis caused the unexpected submergence of Lemuria. The island's inhabitants, endowed with feminine and psychic intuition, were aware of the impending disaster and managed to rescue many of their sacred objects, significantly reducing the loss of human lives. Before their final disappearance, they managed to transfer many of these sacred artifacts to various locations around the world, primarily to Lake Titicaca in Peru, a place that became a new base for the survivors. From there, many migrated along the western coasts of North and South America, reaching places like California and Mount Shasta. McCall's school relocated by air to an island that would later be identified with Atlantis, a place composed of ten main islands, one of which served as a connection between a continent and an island. In Atlantis, the Masters of McCall undertook a bold architectural and conceptual experiment: they built a dividing wall that separated the island into two halves, with further divisions creating four distinct quadrants. This structure was a metaphor for the human brain, with its left and right hemispheres and frontal and posterior divisions, reflecting the duality of logic and experience. The left, masculine side, was governed by the geometric logic of triangles and squares, while the right, feminine side, favored a lived experience, less bound to conventional logic and more influenced by pentagonal geometry. This complex arrangement symbolized not only the human brain structure but also the integration of different experiences and perceptions of reality, suggesting that each element of sacred geometry corresponds to a specific human experience. This advanced idea proposed that even concepts like love could be interpreted through geometric forms, a revolutionary concept that our scientists are only now beginning to understand and accept. In summary, McCall's school sought not only physical immortality but also a profound spiritual and intellectual transformation of humanity, using the islands of Atlantis as a living laboratory to explore and achieve the fusion of intellectual logic and experiential intuition. This fusion, according to Drunvalo Melchizedek's visions, represents a crucial step in the human evolutionary path, a transition from a polarized understanding of the world to a more holistic and integrated one. Dan Winter, a researcher from Eden, New York, was one of the first to explore correlations between the bioelectrical signals of the human body and emotions. Using biofeedback systems connected to monitors, Winter was able to visualize specific sine wave signatures corresponding to precise emotional responses. This method allowed observers to identify people's emotions in separate rooms simply by analyzing these signatures on a screen. Continuing his research, Winter discovered how sacred geometries could be reduced to angles and how these angles could in turn be transformed into geometric patterns, thus demonstrating a direct relationship between geometric shapes and wave signatures. In parallel, Michael Helius distinguished himself for his ability to convert shapes into sounds, further exploring the link between geometry and sensory perception. Another researcher, Manford Clines, independently and following a different approach, arrived at similar conclusions regarding the correlation between emotions and geometry, as reported in a Wall Street Journal article. These findings underline a revolutionary concept: emotions not only have a shape but can also be described through geometry.

This concept fits perfectly into the philosophy that guided the island of Atlantis, where the immortals of Lemuria were divided into two groups: one representing the feminine psychic aspect and the other the masculine logical aspect. The two groups, living in separate areas of the island divided by a wall, reflected and amplified their own qualities, creating a dynamic of mirroring similar to the functioning of the human brain hemispheres. This structure not only symbolized the duality of the human psyche but also the integration between logic and experience, essential for a profound understanding of reality. The physical layout of the island, with its divisions, was a tangible representation of how different human experiences were interconnected and necessary to form a complete consciousness. This configuration was supposed to facilitate an evolutionary leap, but the process was interrupted by a cataclysm that changed the course of Atlantis' history. The concept that love and other emotions can be reduced to geometric forms underscores a deeper understanding of our inner world and its connections to the physical universe, a truth that the ancients sought to codify and that we are only beginning to grasp today. Life has an innate tendency to fill empty spaces, just as it happens on highways, where every small gap between cars is inevitably filled. This phenomenon also manifests in human history with the arrival of extraterrestrial races.

According to the revelations of Thoth, the first of these were the Jews, who, coming from another world, did not create problems at the time of their arrival. They asked for and obtained permission to integrate, in a process that could have been obstacle-free if it hadn't been for the arrival of another race. This latter race, according to Melchizedek, the tenth group to arrive, has represented a continuous challenge from its appearance to the present day. This conflict has ancient roots and still persists. The story of this race, first told by Drunvalo Melchizedek, has particular and incredible origins that initially seemed strange even to him. According to reports, these beings came from Mars, a planet that a million years ago was flourishing and lush, very similar to Earth, complete with oceans and forests. The Martian civilization, however, was trapped in continuous internal conflicts. At one point, realizing that their destruction was inevitable, a small group decided to seek an escape route. They focused on experiments in various locations on Mars, mainly in Cydonia, where they built enormous pyramidal structures, towering up to fifty thousand feet, a size difficult to imagine by today's Earth standards. These gigantic monuments were not just buildings but part of a desperate escape attempt that reflected their advanced technological level. The Martians knew that the end was near and, like the current terrestrial superpowers foreseeing global catastrophes, sought extreme solutions to survive. This story of survival and advanced technology underscores a recurring theme: no matter how advanced a civilization may be, challenges to its existence can drive it to extreme and often desperate solutions. So, on the planet Mars, in a distant era (about a million years ago), there were immense structures that no earthly mountain can match in height. These constructions, as will be described later, embodied a particular geometric shape called a stellated tetrahedron, inserted in a sphere. This figure is the basis of the Merkaba, a concept that will be further explored later on. The Merkaba is not simply a means of transportation but a vehicle capable of traversing dimensional levels, spanning through time and space. Time, conceived as a function of dimension and a golden spiral, takes on a spherical form, allowing for temporal movements forward and backward. The Martians used their Merkabas to explore and discovered Earth, a planet that intersected their future by a million years and our past by about 65,000 or 70,000 years, an epoch that coincides with the dawn of Atlantis. They were not billions, but probably only thousands, between a few thousand and a maximum of 150,000 individuals, who were transferred from Mars to Earth without any permission, an act of rebellion within a broader context known as the Lucifer Rebellion. These Martians, according to Melchizedek's account, intellectually advanced but devoid of empathy or emotional understanding, clashed with the inhabitants of Earth in an immediate conflict. Despite their technological advantage, their number was insufficient to dominate, and they soon realized they could not win. They decided to try to understand and integrate rather than continue the conflict. This period of self-imposed isolation and integration attempts lasted for thousands of years, during which Atlantis underwent a profound Martian influence. Their advanced science, particularly that related to crystallography, had a decisive impact on Atlantean technology. Over time, Martian influence profoundly altered Atlantean society, leading to a radical change: from a predominantly feminine society, it became markedly masculine. This transformation was so profound that the previous dominance of feminine thought and capabilities gave way to a more masculine and rational approach, a reversal that marked the end of Lemuria and the rise of a new era dominated by logical and scientific thinking. About 16,000 years ago, as Melchizedek recounts, during an unusual period in the precession cycle of the equinoxes, a significant event occurred on Earth. At that time, Earth was in a position very close to the center of the galaxy, a position that corresponds exactly to where we are today. It was then that the Earth's poles underwent a slight variation, a change confirmed by our current scientific knowledge. This slight shift caused a portion of Atlantis to sink into the ocean, triggering a wave of fear among the inhabitants who feared losing everything they had built. This terror lasted for about 200 years, during which the Atlanteans lived in fear of another imminent catastrophe. However, over time, the fear subsided as they moved away from the critical moment, gradually returning to tranquility and allowing the evolutionary cycle to resume its usual course. The climax of this series of events occurred precisely 16,000 years ago when an asteroid or comet threatened to strike directly at Earth. Faced with this threat, there emerged a division of opinions between the two dominant cultural factions on the planet: the Lemurians, who followed a Taoist approach preferring to let nature take its course, and the Martians, who favored direct intervention to deflect or destroy the celestial threat. After lengthy discussions, the Lemurians prevailed, deciding not to intervene. The celestial object passed close to Earth and struck an area not far from Atlantis, now known as Charleston, South Carolina. The impact, which could have leveled it to the ground, only grazed the city but still caused significant damage, catapulting a huge portion of Atlantis into the ocean and devastating many of the sectors controlled by the Martians, who understandably reacted with great anger. These events deeply marked the planet's history, highlighting the profound divisions between the two cultures and their different philosophies of interaction with the forces of nature and the cosmos.

ROOTS AND REVOLUTIONS: THE SECOND PART OF THE HIDDEN HISTORY OF HUMANITY'S ORIGINS

So Drunvalo Melchizedek tells a complex and vast story that intertwines cosmic struggles and earthly consequences, tracing the secret origins of Atlantis to its catastrophic experiments that altered Earth's dimensional stability. The narrative connects a range of elements including ancient technologies, interdimensional impacts, and mythical narratives of conflicts and cooperation among different cultural aspects of a lost civilization. This rich tapestry of mythological, historical, and cosmic threads raises philosophical and metaphysical questions about the nature of reality and our place within it. Such stories offer a deep well of material for exploration in various forms of media, from books to films to games, each providing a unique lens on the underlying themes of power, responsibility, and transformation. Melchizedek explains that, looking back through all the other things we have seen, all the unusual events that have happened, one can easily understand the nature of what a Merkaba is. Furthermore, he details how the ancients knew that humanity would fall and hoped that it would not descend lower than the current level. They knew that once they got here, if all went well, they could help us ascend once we reached another critical point, which is where we are now. To prevent a prolonged fall into darkness, they decided to intervene synthetically, or alchemically, to recreate the grid of Christ consciousness that was destroyed when we fell. This operation was initiated 200 years before the actual fall. They moved to an area we now know as the Giza Desert in Egypt, then a lush rainforest, where they accessed a vital energy point. In these "Halls of Amenti," a place where the flame of consciousness that the Anunnaki and Assyrians created a long time ago for us, there are poles emanating various levels of consciousness that humanity is destined to reach, including the Christ consciousness. This pole emerges from the Earth at an incredibly precise point, similar to the size of an atom. Once reaching this place, Ra, Aragat, and Thoth, three members of Nicole's Mystery School, created a deep hole about a mile into the ground, surrounded by bricks, representing a direct connection to these higher energies. This hole not only served as an anchor point for the Christ consciousness grid but also as a channel for the masculine and feminine energies emanating from two opposite poles, one located on the island of Morea in the Pacific. These actions, Drunvalo explains, were not simply physical gestures but were steeped in deep spiritual and cosmic implications, designed to directly influence humanity's evolutionary path towards higher levels of awareness and harmony.

According to him, a group of individuals of high intellectual and spiritual level had deeply understood the potential of ancestral construction techniques. These individuals did not need to physically dig to create structures; rather, they were capable of materializing with thought what they desired. Melchizedek believes they opted to use natural materials like stone, instead of advanced metals or other high-tech materials, for a specific reason, perhaps related to greater harmony with the environment and the earth's energies. From an aerial viewpoint, the result of these constructions appeared as a vortex extending into space, casting a circular shadow on the earth's surface. Of all the emerging vortices, the builders selected a specific one, although the reasons for the choice remain unknown. On a four-dimensional level, they built three pyramids with apexes aligned along a precise spiral. The most famous among these is the Great Pyramid, created from top to bottom through the power of thought. When modern science dated the carbon of the construction materials, it discovered that the oldest stones were at the top and the youngest at the base, a discovery that baffled scholars to the point of being almost ignored due to its incompatibility with commonly accepted theories. Additionally, a building discovered only recently, after decades of obscurity, stood not far from the pyramids. This building, visible only in small part, followed the proportions of the golden rectangle. Aerial surveys showed that the center of the building, the south facade of the building, and the north facade of the Great Pyramid were precisely aligned over a distance of over a mile, an alignment so accurate as to seem impossible for the Egyptian capabilities of the time. This extraordinary precision marked the center of a deep hole in the ground, part of an elaborate network that included Fibonacci spirals and golden spirals, crucial distinctions for Egyptian resurrection philosophy, according to which knowledge of the differences between these spirals was essential. This particular point and the alignment system constituted the key to the beginning of a global grid of sacred places, also known as power sites, estimated to be about 83,000 worldwide. This network of sites is not only a legacy of ancient knowledge but continues to be a focus of study and spiritual interest, testifying to the deep connection between ancient civilizations and the universal laws governing consciousness and physical reality. Drunvalo Melchizedek has hypothesized that geomantic locations along Earth's ley lines and grids influence the electromagnetic field that shapes the planet. Through the laying of sticks in the ground and the construction of pyramids, as well as the insertion of crystals at specific points, it is possible to shape a geometrically perfect, albeit weak, electromagnetic field around the Earth. This field was initially created on a four-dimensional level by three men. Over 13,000 years, people around the world were drawn to these places, such as Machu Picchu and Taxiwomba, and built structures following an inner guidance and higher intention. According to Melchizedek, this vast network of 83,000 sacred sites was not completed until 1989. He suggested that all these sacred sites are arranged following logarithmic or golden spirals, mathematically connected to a common point of origin. The structures along the Nile, for example, follow this pattern, as do other sites worldwide, indicating a higher mind coordinating these global efforts. Drunvalo mentioned that this system is holographic: knowing one structure, it is possible to predict the next, showing an intertemporal and intercultural connection between different civilizations. Evidence of this global synchronization continues to accumulate. The starting point of these constructions was a pyramid, located above a huge subterranean temple city, beneath the

335

Great Pyramid of Giza. This city, part of a massive structure of solid rock, was designed to accommodate about 10,000 people, although the maximum number of individuals who achieved immortality did not exceed 8,000.

Additionally, Drunvalo corrected some misconceptions about the Emerald Tablets made by Doreal, specifying that some details, such as the "atomic engines," were inaccurate. In reality, he explained that there are no engines in the described ship, as it operates through a Merkaba resonance field, not requiring physical engines. According to Drunvalo Melchizedek, the Merkaba field is activated and maintained through thought and emotion, without the need for conventional engines. The Sphinx, for its part, represents an ancient marker whose origin dates back over 5.5 million years, a much older period than the usual 10,000 years considered by scholars. Although buried in sand up to its neck when discovered by Napoleon, the age of the Sphinx remains uncertain, but it is suspected to have been partially buried for a long time. Under the Sphinx, a mile deep, lies what Drunvalo describes as the world's oldest synthetic object: a circular vehicle, resembling a disc, two city blocks wide and about 22 feet tall. This vehicle, according to the dimensions of the Great Pyramid of Giza, has a direct relationship with the structure of the pyramid itself, which lacks its upper apex, a five-and-a-half-inch tall golden capstone, representing a holographic image of the pyramid. Drunvalo recounts that the last flight of this vehicle was commanded by himself, in a past life of which he remembers perfectly.

The ship was activated using Thoth's spinal column and lifted to an octave higher than the Earth's level, allowing the vehicle to pass through the Earth's surface and reach the atmosphere. From there, it flew to Atlantis to gather the last immortals, about 1,600 people, just as the last part of Atlantis sank into the waters. The vehicle subsequently landed in Egypt, on the perfectly smooth platform of the Great Pyramid. The circumference of the ship exactly matched that of the pyramid's base, a detail Drunvalo emphasizes to be significant in sacred geometry and the dimension of life itself. With the imminent shift of the Earth's poles, Drunvalo explains the importance of the Merkaba field in maintaining stable electromagnetic and magnetic fields. He describes how, in the years preceding a pole shift, the Earth's magnetic field progressively weakens, influencing the behavior of migratory animals and heralding significant changes. He also reveals that human brain cells contain magnets that contribute to memory, dependent on a weak but geometrically specific external magnetic field. The loss of this field, he says, could lead to memory loss, as happened during the Atlantean cataclysm, leaving the highly evolved inhabitants without memories and consciousness in a short period of time. Imagine the sudden consequence of being deprived of one's memory: it would be impossible even just to leave a building or open a door. People, suddenly reduced to basic survival, would have to start again from the most elementary actions, like making a fire or keeping warm. However, some, thanks to the creation of their own Merkaba field, retained their memories intact. This field, as Drunvalo defines it, allows memory to be preserved regardless of

circumstances, even the most extreme, such as the explosion of an atomic bomb or exposure to the solar core. This creation pattern, which Drunvalo identifies as a way out of any cosmic experiment, ensured that the memories of these individuals remained protected while others were erased. A notable exception to this general memory loss was the Maya people. According to Drunvalo, the Maya retained the memory of Atlantis, as evidenced by the Troano Document, currently at the British Museum, which recounts the destruction of Atlantis and the escape of the Maya. Despite the widespread destruction, it is believed that the survivors of Atlantis dispersed into what is now Europe, starting practically from scratch. This period would correspond to the biblical account of Noah's Ark and the Great Flood. Drunvalo questions the narrative that sees Noah and his family as the only survivors, citing over 118 global flood stories, suggesting a broader survival. According to Peruvian legends, after the flood, Thoth descended and handed a golden rod to Mancos, who became the first king of the Inca empire, marking the beginning of the reconstruction of civilization with the founding of Cusco. The story goes that, despite the loss of advanced knowledge and technologies, the survivors still possessed 'high-tech bodies,' lacking only the 'software' needed to fully operate them. Drunvalo highlights how, despite adversity, humanity managed to persevere and rebuild, albeit starting from very primitive bases. After the flood, which saw the complete melting of the poles to where the Hawaiian Islands are today, the Earth was overwhelmed by a huge amount of water from its interior, as suggested by recent scientific discoveries
338

that corroborate ancient tales of suddenly emerging water sources. The Great Pyramids were also submerged to two-thirds of their height for a long period, evidence that their construction preceded by far the fourth Egyptian dynasty, despite the resistance of experts to recognize this evidence. The water level left a clear mark on the structures, and the interior of the pyramids was found covered with a layer of sea salt, evidence of ancient immersion under the waters. In Melchizedek's account, the term "ship" is also mentioned, referring to an ancient vehicle of mystical and technological origin described as part of the narrative linked to Thoth and the Ascended Masters of the Mystery School of Nicole. According to the story, this ship was not a simple means of transportation but possessed exceptional capabilities, such as flying and traversing great geographical and dimensional distances. In the context of the narrative, the ship serves as a connection between various significant points in human and mythological history, linking ancient civilizations through the advanced abilities of its occupants. It begins its journey from the Great Pyramids of Egypt, considered the geometric center of all the Earth's land masses, and serves as a means to physically and spiritually move some chosen individuals among the Ascended Masters. Ra, a key figure, uses this ship to initiate Egyptian civilization, bringing with him a group of Masters. After Egypt, the ship heads to Peru, where Thoth, one of the most enigmatic and powerful figures of Egyptian mythology, interacts with local populations and influences the formation of the Inca Empire. The story continues with the ship's journey to other significant destinations, such as the Himalayan mountains, before returning to the Sphinx, where it is hidden or kept until recent times. This element of the "ship" symbolizes the transmission of knowledge and advanced capabilities between different cultures and epochs, playing a crucial role in the preservation and evolution of ancient knowledge through the ages. These narratives are closely linked to the geomantic and geographical energies of the Earth, with Egypt representing the male aspect of the grid of Christ consciousness, while Yucatan and Peru embody the feminine aspect, and Tibet the neutral or childlike energy. Drunvalo anticipates that the next focus will be on Egypt, where the survivors of Atlantis and members of the Mystery School of Nicole gathered, unlike other places influenced by different races like the Incas. Subsequent discussions will focus on these cultural and energetic dynamics, particularly exploring the role of Egypt in post-Atlantean history.

The perception that many Christians and Catholics have of Egypt is often shrouded in a veneer of mystery and mistrust, seeing it more as a cult than a valid repository of historical or spiritual wisdom. However, there is a period in Egypt's long history, lasting 17 and a half years during a particular dynasty, that represents a remarkable exception. During that time span, there was an intense "explosion of illuminating light," marked by the assertion of belief in a single God. This era was not only crucial for Egypt's internal development but, according to revelations received by Drunvalo Melchizedek from Thoth, in one of his past lives in Egypt, laid the spiritual and philosophical foundations from which the Christian religion later developed. The Egyptian mystery schools, particularly during this period, exerted a profound influence on the Copts and the Essenes. The latter, known for their ascetic lifestyle and spiritual practices, were directly inspired by the teachings of this Egyptian school, demonstrating how resonances from a brief period of enlightenment can propagate through centuries and cultures. In his reflections, Drunvalo Melchizedek grapples with the paradox of ascended masters, such as Thoth, Ra, and Akhenaten, capable of extraordinary earthly manifestations — such as the construction of pyramids and the creation of deep underground cavities — that nevertheless required vehicles for their movements. This need seems to contradict their high ability to manipulate reality and raises significant questions regarding interference in natural human evolution. The use of these vehicles, described as warships in the Emerald Tablets and employed during periods of cosmic transition, underscores a period when the dark aspect of human nature attempts to prevail, a cyclical struggle that has perpetuated for millions of years. These vehicles, activated by universal and unconditional love and guided by Christ consciousness, symbolize a synthesis between technological advancement and spiritual elevation. Drunvalo illustrates how even a single individual, seemingly weak, can utilize such means to effect significant planetary changes. This emphasizes the power of the individual in wielding tools of great potency when driven by pure intentions. Drunvalo's dialogue with the concepts of non-interference and divine assistance opens up broader issues, including the role of extraterrestrials like the Grays and their interaction with humanity. Their presence and influence, sometimes considered manipulative, highlight a complex interweaving of interstellar relationships reflected in ongoing efforts to understand and navigate the challenges posed by cosmic and earthly evolution. In this vast scenario, Drunvalo's narratives prompt us to reflect on our position in the universe, the teachings we can glean from ancient civilizations, and the responsibilities that accompany the use of technology and spiritual power, revealing a constantly evolving history that continually challenges our perception of reality.

This chapter dedicated to Drunvalo Melchizedek has been drafted extensively drawing inspiration from his numerous books and lectures held over the years. The reflections and theories presented reflect the innovative spirit and depth of research that characterize Melchizedek's work, who has dedicated his life to studying the connections between ancient spiritual traditions and new perspectives on human and universal consciousness. The information presented here is a tribute to his career and contributions, which continue to influence and stimulate debate on these fascinating topics.

BIBLIOGRAPHY

Here is a bibliography listing some of the main works of each of the mentioned individuals, useful for delving into their contributions in their respective fields of study or interest:

Erich von Däniken:

1. "Chariots of the Gods" (1968)

2. "Return to the Stars" (1970)

3. "Gods from Outer Space" (1970)

4. "The Gold of the Gods" (1972)

Graham Hancock:

1. "Fingerprints of the Gods" (1995)

2. "The Sign and the Seal" (1992)

3. "Magicians of the Gods" (2015)

4. "America Before: The Key to Earth's Lost Civilization" (2019)

Michael Tellinger:

1. "Slave Species of the Gods: The Secret History of the Anunnaki and Their Mission on Earth" (2005)

2. "Adam's Calendar: Discovering the Oldest Man-made Structure on Earth" (2008)

3. "Ubuntu Contributionism: A Blueprint for Human

Prosperity" (2013)

Billy Carson:

1. "The Compendium of the Emerald Tablets" (2018)

2. "Woke Doesn't Mean Broke" (2021)

Drunvalo Melchizedek:

1. "The Ancient Secret of the Flower of Life, Vol. 1" (1999)

2. "The Ancient Secret of the Flower of Life, Vol. 2" (2000)

3. "Living in the Heart: How to Enter into the Sacred Space within the Heart" (2003)

Greg Braden:

1. "The Divine Matrix: Bridging Time, Space, Miracles, and Belief" (2007)

2. "Fractal Time: The Secret of 2012 and a New World Age" (2009)

3. "The God Code:The Secret of Our Past, the Promise of Our Future" (2004)

Mathias de Stefano:

1. "Initiation" (2021) - Serie di video didattici

2. "Reintegration" (2021) - Serie di seminari

Tim Tactical:

Since he hasn't authored any books, it's recommended to search for his interviews online or consult video streaming platforms where his sessions are available.

This bibliography provides an essential overview of publications and primary resources related to these authors and thinkers, useful for those wishing to further explore their works and theories.

Dear reader,

I hope you found the journey through the pages of this book stimulating and enriching. If the ideas and stories we've explored together have inspired you or brought new awareness, I would be immensely grateful if you could take a moment to leave a positive review on Amazon.

Your impressions not only help other readers discover this book but also support the spread of its vital message. Every review counts enormously and contributes significantly to bringing these important conversations to a wider audience.

Thank you for your time and support. Your voice can truly make a difference!

With gratitude,

Francesca Ferrari

Discover a World of Knowledge and Inspiration

Visit **www.libriutili.it**

Dear reader,

We hope you have found inspiration and utility within the pages of this book. If your thirst for knowledge and personal growth is not yet satisfied, we have a special surprise for you!

We invite you to explore the world of LuminaLibria at www.libriutili.it, where a universe of books awaits you. LuminaLibria is an oasis for every type of reader, offering a wide range of genres that will enrich your reading experience.

For Young Explorers: Browse our collection of Children's Books and Stories for Kids, perfect for sparking the imagination and curiosity of the youngest readers.

For Art and Relaxation: Let yourself be captivated by our Adult and Children's Coloring Books, a creative way to relax and express yourself.

For Personal Growth: Explore our Self-Help, Personal Growth, and Biographies, to inspire and motivate you on your life journey.

For Curious Spirits: Deepen your spiritual journey with our Books on Spiritual Themes.

This is just a small part of what LuminaLibria has to offer. We believe that every book is a window to new worlds, ideas, and possibilities. Whether you are seeking adventure, knowledge, or inspiration, you will find a book that speaks to your heart on www.libriutili.it. And remember, on the website you will find books in Italian, English, German, and Spanish.

Scan the QR Code below to begin your journey into the world of LuminaLibria books.

Thank you for joining us on this journey of discovery and growth. We're excited to see you explore even more with LuminaLibria.

Happy reading and continued exploration!

The LuminaLibria Team